UNBOWED

UNBOWED

A SOLDIER'S JOURNEY
BACK FROM PARALYSIS

BILLY HEDDERMAN

MERCIER PRESS

MERCIER PRESS

Cork

www.mercierpress.ie

© Billy Hedderman, 2018

ISBN: 978 1 78117 593 4

10 9 8 7 6 5 4 3 2 1

A CIP record for this title is available from the British Library

Printed and bound in the EU.

CONTENTS

ABBREVIATIONS

2IC	Second-in-Command
6 RAR	6th Battalion, Royal Australian Regiment
ADF	Australian Defence Force
APC	Armoured Personnel Carrier
ARW	Army Ranger Wing
Bn	Battalion
CAO	Central Applications Office
CCS	Central Cord Syndrome
CO	Commanding Officer
CP	Command Post
DF	Defence Forces
DS	Directing Staff
HQ	Headquarters
HVT	High Value Target
LFTT	Live Fire Tactical Training course
MTC	Multi-Training Centre
NCO	Non-Commissioned Officer
NGO	Non-Governmental Organisation
OC	Officer Commanding
OIC	Officer in Charge

OT	Occupational Therapy
P&O	Prosthetics and Orthotics
PA	Princess Alexandra Hospital, Brisbane
PESA	Physical Employment Standard Assessment
PT	Physical Training
QRF	Quick Reaction Force
Reo	Reinforcement cycle
RSM	Regimental Sergeant Major
RTU	Return to Unit
RV	Rendezvous
SCI	Spinal Cord Injury
SERE	Survival, Escape and evasion, Resistance to interrogation and Extraction
SF	Special Forces
SIU	Spinal Injury Unit
SOTU-M	Special Operations Task Unit – Maritime
UL	University of Limerick

Prologue

'YOU WROTE A BOOK?'

I woke to the sight of a hospital ceiling. For that first blissful second, I forgot that I was paralysed. While attempting to distract my brain from the ever-present pain, I concentrated on each item I could see within my motionless field of view, staring intensely at each minor stain on every grey ceiling square. I was then brought to life as my wife, Rita, pressed down on the bed remote control to lift the top half of the bed, raising me semi-upright, Frankenstein-style. I fixed my gaze on the printed poem hanging from the bottom of the TV screen and read it again.

Invictus – William Ernest Henley

Out of the night that covers me,
Black as the pit from pole to pole,
I thank whatever gods may be,
For my unconquerable soul.

In the fell clutch of circumstance,
I have not winced nor cried aloud,
Under the bludgeonings of chance,
My head is bloody, but unbowed.

Beyond this place of wrath and tears,
Looms but the Horror of the shade,
And yet the menace of the years,
Finds, and shall find me, unafraid.

It matters not how strait the gate,
How charged with punishments the scroll,
I am the master of my fate:
I am the captain of my soul.

I reminded myself of this message every day. I may not have been able to move but I was still in control of my thoughts. I read it when in pain. I read it when I felt low. I read it when I was bored.

***

Throughout the four months I spent in hospital after my accident, I received numerous good wishes in the form of letters from extended family, gifts from friends and texts from many connections of all types. I was also sent video messages by Irish Army mates, pictures from friends all over the world and drawings from young relations. It was humbling to feel so cared for and to know that people were wishing the best for me. It was also incredibly motivating.

On top of this I was contacted by a number of people I didn't even know. I received an email from Nathan Kirwan, a fellow Corkman, who described his own fight against paralysis and wished me well. Afterwards, I followed his progress in his robotic exoskeleton, and his determination and positive attitude were fantastic to see. I also received a video message from Mark

Pollock wishing me well for my recovery. I had heard of Mark, racing blind across the Pole, then tragically becoming paraplegic through an accident, yet still managing to maintain an incredible outlook on life. I had heard of his organisation, the Mark Pollock Trust, and his charity run called Run in the Dark. In fact, my mother had participated in one of these runs, although I have to admit that I didn't know exactly what the Trust did at the time. It was quite exciting and humbling to watch his video message, where he spoke directly to me. Overall, I was really taken aback by the number of good wishes I received.

As I started to recover I decided that I wanted to return some form of thank you to everyone that I could. I apologise now to anyone I didn't get back to! I really wanted to try to explain to everybody how much their support helped. 'If there's one person that I know can pull through this, it's you Bill', was the type of message I received. It probably only took a few minutes for people to write these messages, but every one of them gave me that extra tiny piece of affirmation not to give in. I needed to let people know that their kind words really helped.

When in hospital, I had required a splint to even hold a pencil. However, as my condition slightly improved, I eventually reached a stage where I was able to hold one without a splint and I began to attend writing classes as part of my occupational therapy (OT). It was incredibly tedious and, for some reason, much more depressing than most of my other therapies. I think it was probably because the page didn't lie: I could see how poor my writing was. If I could not even write, how would I ever get back to work?

Patience and persistence pay off, though, and in the end, I improvised in order to overcome this difficulty. This involved routing my pencil through my index and middle finger – rather than between my thumb and forefinger – as

I didn't (and still don't) have the pincer dexterity to write shapes accurately through the traditional holding position. A few weeks post-discharge from hospital, I sat down in my office at home and pulled out an A4 notebook. I wedged the pencil in, held the page as steadily as I could, and leant my head down close to my hand. The first letter I replied to had been sent by a large group of Rita's friends who had been superb to us both. They even pooled money together to buy me an iPad loaded with applications on which to conduct hand and finger therapy. I thought it would be best to write my reply by hand to those who had done so much for me. It was excellent practice for me, while also showing the recipients how well I was recovering. I wrote a three-page letter of thanks and praise to all those wonderful and thoughtful people. Following this, I wrote back to many more well-wishers. I actually enjoyed reflecting on how each one had assisted me and, honestly, I just wanted them to know that it had helped.

As well as learning to write again, I also had to relearn typing. After my release from hospital, I began intensive therapies at home. Physio and OT became the daily grind. In one of my first home sessions, the occupational therapist asked me to select a book from my collection and bring it to the laptop. We opened Brian O'Driscoll's autobiography together and read the first paragraph. She asked me to type it out in a Word document, so I did, as she stared at her watch. Again. And again. And again. With my fingers hovering in place over the keyboard, I had to concentrate on selecting the appropriate finger for the correct letter, and then focus on pushing downward with the finger, as opposed to the hand. A word was annoying, a sentence was frustrating and a paragraph was hell. That evening I was given 'lines' to type as part of my 'homework'. It was exceptionally boring.

After only a few days of typing practice I had had enough of lines. *Maybe*

I can incorporate the typing practice, my story of resilience and my thanks into something else, I thought. Quite soon after my accident, my brother and I had decided to start a daily log. Every night before my family left me motionless in my darkened hospital room, I asked whoever was present to log all the visitors and to transcribe the positive and negative feelings I'd had that day into a little notebook. Sometimes I felt terrible all day, but I always had to find a positive to add to our notebook before another quadriplegic day came to a close. *Always find the good in any day*. It was an excellent tool that we employed throughout my time in hospital. I kept the notebook and still like to read over it from time to time. When I got bored with typing lines it became a good place to start from. *Hey, instead of just writing lines from someone else's story, why don't I start writing my own, adding to the notebook we wrote in hospital?* I asked myself.

I had been told that writing and logging events throughout my recovery would be good for my mental state, so, at first, I justified my self-indulgence of writing what soon developed into this autobiographical book by convincing myself that it was a form of hand therapy and mental well-being. But then I realised that rather than just writing for myself, I wanted to spread my story in order to let others know that, in certain cases, it is possible to recover some way from paralysis.

Although the first drafts were not particularly eloquent, I persevered. Parts of this book were originally typed with single-finger punches from partially paralysed hands, as I furiously concentrated on spelling out each word. But in the end I had a complete manuscript and that is what you are reading now. The aim of this book is to outline to the reader that high levels of resilience and self-belief helped me through difficult times, and that they can do the same for you.

1

RELAX, BILL

BRISBANE, AUSTRALIA – DECEMBER 2014

It was late December 2014, and Rita and I had been living in Australia for almost three months. What family and friends back in Ireland had touted as being the biggest move of our lives seemed to be working out quite well. The weather and lifestyle were fantastic. We were living in a beautiful house on the northwest side of Brisbane, only a two-minute drive to the army base where I worked. Our estate was filled with other Australian Defence Force (ADF) families, each with a house as fine as ours. It was a clichéd existence, with everyone barbecuing and walking their dogs around the nearby pond, their kids playing outside in what seemed like eternal sunshine.

Rita and I tried to get out as much as possible in Oz, to embrace the new country. After all, having moved to the far side of the world, we had to live our lives fully; otherwise what was the point in moving? Naturally, part of this lifestyle was going to the beach, which we did regularly. After spending our first Christmas away from home with some of our newly acquired Oz-based friends, we decided to travel up the coast to Caloundra on New Years' Eve for a beach day. Just Rita, our dog, Ozzie, and me.

When I'm on leave I tend to move slowly at times, and this was the case as we prepared for the trip to Caloundra. In contrast, Rita rushed around the house, getting ready, packing towels, slicing and dicing lunch for us, and, of course, continuously interrupting the dog and me from our TV viewing – the events of *Mythbusters* were not high on her list of priorities. I was ordered a number of times to get out of my pyjama pants and assist with the preparations. I looked to Ozzie for some sympathy but he glanced away, leaving me on my own. He is clever, in that he never takes sides. I eventually pulled myself away from the couch and began the process of packing for the beach. I was in slow motion while Rita was in fast forward.

As soon as we stepped outside to pack up our newly purchased Toyota Yaris my mood changed. *Just another absolutely amazing day in Brisbane.* I truly believe that weather can affect your mood. In this case it undoubtedly had a positive effect, as I loaded an Esky (cooler box), a blanket and, of course, our little VIP, Ozzie, the Scottie from Ireland, into the back seat. *Oh, almost forgot the body board and rash vest,* I thought; they had been staring at me from the garage.

Shades on, GPS on, Classic 90s dance tunes on; we were good to go. Soon we were backing out of the driveway and on our way. We weren't long into the drive when Rita reached over and turned the music down, much to my dismay. I worried about what was coming. We had been a little off with each other over the previous few days, as we had been arguing over our finances and how we were managing our accounts. So it was to my surprise that we ended up having a long, lovely discussion en route to Caloundra, agreeing not to worry about the small things and to just enjoy ourselves. We decided that the New Year was going to bring us happiness, and that while saving was important, living for now was more so. I glanced back at

Ozzie, but he just raised his eyebrows. I have to say, I felt good after our family team talk.

On our arrival at Kings Beach I conducted my usual army-style unloading drills. Eventually, we found a spot that satisfied Rita's requirement to be close to the water and the dog's requirement for constant supervision – territorial Scotties can be quite the handful when other dogs decide to invade. We laid out our blanket on a grass patch just off the beach and plonked ourselves down.

Man, this is awesome, I thought. I am one of those people who has to get into the sea as soon as possible upon arrival at the beach, so I grabbed my vest and board and shuffled towards the water. Stopping short, I gazed across the surf. I picked a spot that had a few, but not too many, boarders around. I was nervous about potentially running over some child in the water, so I didn't want to squeeze in where most of the other boarders were located. As I waded in, I found that the waves were stronger than they looked. I noted the rocky wall 100m to my right as I leaned my shoulder into crashing and quite fast waves. Once beyond the break, I set up in an area where other body-boarders were riding the waves. After a while, I caught a few waves, riding them all the way to the shoreline. Each time I caught one I felt a little more confident. I started adding turns into my glides.

I had notions of starting surfing, but for now I was stuck with the smaller board. It was good, easy fun. As I zipped along the crest of the wave, the spray kicked up into my eyes and stung. On reaching the shoreline, I would stand up, wipe my face, fix my shorts and then traipse back out again. It was a nice activity but not something I was overly fond of. There was a small buzz in riding the wave, but it took a lot of work to get back out through the waves to go again. After thirty minutes, I stumbled from the water as waves struck my back, pushing me out, telling me I wasn't wanted there any more.

As part of our 'embracing life' policy, Rita had come up with a rule that we had to say yes to anything we were invited to. I liked it. It forced us to get to know people and make new friends. We were to meet some of our new friends that evening in Brisbane to ring in the New Year, so after lunch and a dog walk, we began to plan the journey home. Before we left, however, I told Rita that I wanted to go in for one more dip. I was so genuinely happy with life that I felt I had to share it with my family in Ireland, and maybe rub it in a little! So I made a quick video, showing off how great life was at the beach, and posted it off to my family on our WhatsApp group before heading down to the water.

Due to the beach-loving culture, many people jump into the Australian surf with no prior exposure to or knowledge of what they are doing. However, I'd been body-boarding plenty of times before and surfing a few times in Ireland; in fact, I'd had a surfing lesson only six months earlier. Worse still, I had YouTubed 'body-boarding techniques' to ensure I was doing it correctly. I've always been that way. I like doing exciting or 'extreme' things but I never take safety for granted. It's like risk mitigation. Yes, do something extreme, but do it the correct way. I'm not sure from where I picked up this value. Maybe it's a military thing. Rita calls it my 'inner old man'.

Anyway, this time I would take the board out to about four or five feet of water and turn it inwards. I would watch over my shoulder, waiting for a wave to crest and then extend the board out. Then I would paddle and kick until the point where I could feel the wave lift both the board and me, speeding me towards the beach and flattening out as I neared the shoreline. A few times as I waited for it, the wave would turn a little too early and either I'd get the white horses running towards me, or worse, it would turn just on top of me, in which case I would get a little bit of a trashing. Not ideal, but I'd give myself a quick little debrief then try again.

I contemplated heading back in after about ten minutes, but I couldn't leave on anything other than a good surf. My last one couldn't be a wipe-out. So, I set up for a wave. As it came closer, I could feel that it was going to be bigger and stronger than those that had preceded it. The waves on Kings Beach can be powerful and have a very strong pull back as they gather volume. I turned and faced inwards towards the shore as this one came close. The wave crested just behind me and I could feel it pulling me up and backwards. My hips raised up higher than my core and I knew then that I was going to get wiped out. The initial pull back seemed to take an eternity, as if the wave itself was suspending time, but after that everything else happened so quickly, the speed and power catching me unawares. The top of the board caught in the water below and the board flipped out from under me so that I was propelled, forward and downward, through the violent momentum of the wave. I felt a strong and hard thud as I hit the top of my head off the sand, while my torso was being pushed forward over my head. Basically my body was caught in something like a very ungraceful and powerful forward roll with a sharp neck inversion. I immediately felt heavily dazed.

I have been concussed a number of times, but an underwater concussion is a surreal experience. I can vividly recall what I could see and how the sand was moving forward and back below me, while waves continued to ride over my head. Although my mind was hazy, I knew I needed to stand. When nothing happened, I didn't panic straightaway. Even in my haze, I thought I would shake it off within a few seconds and stand up. I continued staring at the movement of the sand. In and out. In and out. Still dazed, I was beginning to grow confused as to why I wasn't standing up. My chest quickly began to remind me that I was underwater. It started sucking in and out. I began panicking. I was drowning.

Stand up, Billy. Roll over, Bill. Do something!

From time to time, I replay these seconds in my mind. In fact, writing about it now brings it close. After what seemed like a long time, I heard a faint murmuring voice: 'You okay … hey, you all right?'

I could tell someone was nearby. I was finding it difficult to control my chest. Suddenly my head was slightly out of the water. I spluttered and took in a shallow and broken breath. Water came in over my face. I was disorientated and in complete shock. My breathing was extremely shallow and my chest, which felt incredibly tight, was exploding in and out. *What the hell is going on?*

One of the young guys who had been body-boarding around me earlier was talking to me. He was around fifteen or so. He wasn't very strong as he was holding me funny and the shallow waves kept coming over my face. I was struggling to breathe with water rushing over my mouth. I heard other voices and suddenly I realised I was moving out of the water. I remember thinking: *Hey guys, if you're going to carry me out of the water organise yourselves a bit more, you're not holding me properly, who owns this arm hanging down here … wait, what the hell … that's my arm! Oh my God, what's going on?*

They laid me down on my side and I heard someone say something about 'C spine'. I tried whispering it in a weak attempt to agree with them. I recalled my army medical training, which stated that if there is any chance of a spinal injury, during the immediate actions one should fix the head and neck in a neutral position. I was still attempting to catch my breath, desperately searching for a moment's relief.

I felt so messed up that I thought I might be dying. I was genuinely worried I was going to drift off. Thankfully, after a few seconds I was able to collect my thoughts. I gave myself a little talking to and started going through my A, B, Cs. *Okay, airway: well, I can whisper. Breathing: shallow but okay. Circulation: no cuts that I know of and the heart is still just about pumping. Hey, I'm okay. Now relax, Bill, settle down, you're not going to die.*

2

LEADERSHIP 101

Unlike in many of the classic rags-to-riches biographies that I have enjoyed reading, there is no tale of woe from my upbringing. My parents made sure we were never deprived. We were not well-off, but we were also not poor. I am the second eldest of four children, two girls and two boys. We kids fought a lot growing up, as tends to be the case when siblings are close in age. My mam stayed at home while my dad worked as a car salesman. We lived in a housing estate in Glanmire, County Cork, until I was eight years old, and then moved to a detached bungalow in the country, 3 miles from the village of Watergrasshill.

My mam is extremely knowledgeable, caring and very passionate, which is where I get my argumentative streak, I think. Both she and my dad were very involved in sport, which was bred into their children. My mam used to drive us to training or matches all over Cork, always supporting us in any endeavour and telling us that we had done well. She also pretty much ran the household, was an amazing cook and kept us from killing each other. We were exceptionally lucky to have been raised by her; however, I probably didn't appreciate it enough during my immature teenage years.

My younger brother, Simon, and I looked up to my father so much growing up. Any praise or criticism from him was taken very seriously. We had heard so many stories about his skill and speed as a Gaelic footballer, how he captained the Cork minor team, and played senior football from the age of sixteen. As our parents were relatively young when we were growing up, we watched my dad in action many times playing soccer and Gaelic football with local teams. He was super aggressive, strong and skilful. This was most likely one of the main reasons why we were both so competitive and tenacious.

My parents always prioritised their children, never once showing any favouritism, and they backed us all, no matter what. They challenged us hard and always seemed to be in agreement when it came to us. They made us study, they encouraged us in everything, from art, sport and drama to part-time jobs, and were there to watch, critique and praise after each activity.

However, I still went through a classic case of teenage identity crisis. I was a very different person depending on the group I was with. At home, I could be belligerent to my mother and on occasions actively sought out fights with my siblings. In school I clowned around a bit in my own class, letting people know that I wasn't a 'swot', but with those outside of my direct peer group (and in particular with any girls on a higher coolness rating) I would be extremely quiet. In fact, I used to regularly blush when talking or awkwardly hanging out with girlfriends and their friends. But even just a few hours after my shy interactions, I would go out to play rugby with Sundays Well, a team I started playing with when I was nine years old, where I was cocky, bossy and thought I was the best out-half in Cork for my age.

I was always extremely competitive. No matter what the activity, I had to try as hard as possible to win. I was particularly focused when playing organised sport. I just hated losing at anything. I would spend hours on end outside practising a certain aspect of a skill: smashing a football off the garage door over and over, curling it around the exterior corner of our house as I concentrated on hitting the top corner lip as often as possible. We regularly organised mammoth games of football/soccer/rugby/hurling in the back garden with the entire family and neighbours that would last for hours as my brother and I dreamt of scoring the last-minute goal for our team. Simon and I loved beating each other in any challenge, although I had an unfair advantage of four years over him. We competed in literally everything. We would devise silly games to see who could win. 'Right, you have to hit the wall below the kitchen window without the sliothar hitting the ground first.' Not surprisingly, this led to a substantial number of broken windows. One window was broken so many times that my parents decided to change it to Perspex!

***

What type of career suits a super competitive, team sports-playing teenager? The army, of course. It came as no surprise that both my parents backed me when I chose to conduct an army officer cadetship straight out of school. They may even have been more confident about my ability to adapt to the military than I was. They were proud of me, if maybe a little nervous, which in turn gave me confidence.

After saying my goodbyes to my mam and siblings very early on 1 October 2001, I hopped into the car with my dad, wearing my finest Dunnes Stores suit (my only suit) and off we headed to the Curragh Camp in County Kildare, where I was to begin my officer training with the Irish

Army. About thirty minutes into the journey, the talk died down and I fell asleep. Without the motorways in those days, the trip took approximately three hours. The 9/11 attacks just weeks previously had left a lot of people profoundly worried, even in Ireland, and lots of friends and family thought it was not a good time to join the military. But it didn't affect my thinking in any way. To this day my dad still can't fathom how I could sleep. He tells me of how he looked over at me snoozing and said to himself, 'Does this young fella have any clue what he's getting himself into?'

Honestly, I didn't really. Although I had been a team captain or group leader on many occasions throughout my adolescence, this was something vastly different. I liked the idea of being in charge and making decisions, but I had little experience in true leadership and was probably lucky to have been selected to undergo army officer training. I may have had some of the raw materials (I felt I had plenty of exposure to leading teams in competitive environments), but I had a very limited understanding of the military and I had never been overly interested in becoming a soldier. While the army seemed kind of interesting, initially it was the prestige of being offered a cadetship that I liked the sound of. But once I was offered that cadetship, which was seen as an honour, that triggered my interest further, although I was quite nervous at the thought of leading soldiers. How was I going to do that when I couldn't tell one end of a rifle from the other?

We exited towards the Curragh Camp. For anyone who has not experienced coming off the dual carriageway and heading towards the camp, it is quite the movie scene. The distinct rattle from vehicles shooting over a cattle grid signifies the start of a single straight road with nothing but vast open green plains either side that leads to the camp hidden in a mass of large trees almost a kilometre ahead. A water tower peers over the treeline in front, greeting all approaching from the civilian world beyond. A mini Mordor, if you will.

Since the foundation of the Irish Defence Forces, each cadet class has been numbered accordingly. Mine was the 78th Cadet Class. My dad left me at the cadets' mess where we were told to fall in (whatever that was). I thought he was a bit emotional when I left him but he was trying hard not to show it, so I ignored it. We were marched to our lines (rooms) and I met the lads with whom I would be sharing a passage – a dorm-like area with individual rooms off a communal hallway and wash area. There were eight passages, each filled with eight young nervous wrecks. One naval service cadet in our passage would leave at Christmas to conduct his specific training, then our two air corps cadets would leave after seven months to learn how to fly. The other army guys in the passage were all from Dublin or Kildare. The 'Rebel' in me didn't like this set-up at all! I felt like the country mouse, just turned eighteen years old and stuck in with all these 'Jackeens'.

I hated the first two days. I contemplated going home. It wasn't anything in particular that triggered the thought, I just felt as if the hype of joining the army was now gone and had been replaced with a lonely existence in a dorm of strangers, a myriad of cleaning tasks and a realisation that this was actually what I had applied for. But I had never really given up on something just like that before. Even from an early age, I never quit anything easily. If I didn't correctly execute whatever skill I was practising, I would continue until I got it right. I would stay long after everyone else had finished rugby training until I got my penalty kicking more accurate. No matter how badly any team I played with was being beaten, I absolutely refused to give up before the very final whistle and was furious with those who did.

I wasn't keen to start giving up now, just because I was feeling sorry for myself. I rang home on my new mobile phone (I had refused to get one until then) and had a chat with my dad. He said that the family would totally support me no matter what I chose to do. Then, on day three, I got up and thought to myself, *Right, stop your whinging and let's do this*. I have no idea why it clicked, but I never thought about quitting again, not once.

I buddied off with Cahill B, the guy in the room opposite me (there were two other Cahills, J and E). He had a broad Dublin accent, and was tall and jovial. He was a comic genius and kept passage morale high with his hilarious quips and impersonations. I started to get over the stupid issue I had that all these guys were from Dublin and soon we really began to enjoy each other's company.

We were in a section together with a few other characters from the passage alongside us. A section is the smallest sub-unit grouping in the army, usually consisting of nine soldiers. We had an excellent mix of personalities and I thoroughly enjoyed it, probably due to my prior love of team environments growing up. We had an absolute 'animal' from Galway; in fact that became his nickname. John was our weapon in Section 1. We had two guys from Tipperary, both incredible rugby players. Denis was a prop forward who had previously served as a private in the 4th Infantry Battalion in Cork, and Colin was a stocky, Neil Back-type back row with a reputation of being one of the finest young rugby players in Munster. They were both super strong, which was of great assistance during our vast array of team physical activities.

Helen was a local army brat (military slang for someone who had a parent high up in the army and therefore got teased for perceived favouritism towards them), and although she was small and struggled at physical training

(PT), she was quick-witted and well able to join in with the fun and the banter. Dave from Naas was in a room next to Cahill B and he was a dark horse. He was good at most things and cool as a breeze. He was passionate about only one thing: horses.

Mike from Finglas was in the room alongside me. I didn't know what to make of him. He was quiet and had a thick Dublin accent. He was a little older than us and already had his master's degree, never mind a bachelor's, in economics! I thought this guy was in the wrong game, that he was too smart to be polishing taps and waxing floors with us idiots, as we were still working out right from left while marching.

After a short stint, we were told to change buddies and I ended up with Finglas Mike, while Dave took Cahill B. Mike and I got on quite well. He looked out for me and vice versa. I recall after one Battle PT session he couldn't open his laces as his fingers were too cold, so I dived down and opened them up while under time pressure myself. On countless other occasions he looked after me. That was the nature of the buddy system. Simple. You were not joined at the hip, but assistance was there when you needed it. The buddy system was one of the first lessons we learned in the cadet school. Suddenly you were responsible for someone else. Before every inspection (of which there were many every day), a good buddy checked you. If your buddy had a pocket open during an inspection, it was your fault, and both would get punished. The technique was so simple but almost immediately taught us that selflessness was a key part of leadership.

The last member of our section, Mac, was to us what Murdock is to the A-team. Mac had accidentally blown himself up in a petrol fire about two months prior to enlistment, so his face, hands and hair were still a bit raw. The guy just loved everything exciting about the army. He hated running but he just couldn't get enough of the shooting, blowing stuff up and generally playing soldier. The class voted him in charge of the cadet school air-rifle association, which was designed to assist those in need of further marksmanship training to practice in a simple shooting gallery downstairs in the mess. Mac used to load up on a Sunday morning prior to mass parade, in his number one inspection uniform, and patrol the verandas, scaring crows brazen enough to trespass and drop presents on our passageways.

Dave once regaled us with a tale of an occasion where he awoke on a fresh bright Sunday morning and gazed outside his window over the first-floor walkway onto the inner square as a happy little crow gracefully hopped up onto the bannister next to his window, almost throwing him a good-morning wink. Suddenly the perfect morning scene was interrupted as a swift crack was heard and the crow looked as if it had seen the commanding officer (CO) of the cadet school, before tipping over the edge, one storey below, to its doom. About five seconds later, Mac patrolled past with an air rifle at the ready position and gave a slight nod into the room as if to say, 'You're welcome.' In fact, there are unconfirmed reports that an air rifle was used in taking down a crazed member of a rival passage during a 'passage war'.

That's the kind of stuff we got up to when we weren't cleaning, marching, drilling, cleaning, running, doing stupid tasks for the senior cadets, cleaning, being given lessons and, of course, more cleaning. All these tasks are not designed to make you the biggest neat-freak in the country (just a potentially helpful by-product), but in fact to create a sense of team, discipline and work ethic. Again, it is simple, it is crude, but it works.

They say you make friends for life in the cadet school, and they are right. Mac was my groomsman and Mike was in command of my guard of honour for my wedding. John flew from Sydney to Brisbane specifically to visit me during the time when I was still badly injured. Sully, my roommate from my second year in the cadet school, is now my brother-in-law. He, Mac and other classmates all became part of our skydiving crew years later. They are my friends for life. An NCO (non-commissioned officer, i.e. sergeant or corporal) once said to me, 'There's only three ways you can get guys to bond together: booze, women and grief' (a local term for pain, or something that causes immense discomfort). In this case it was the shared experience of going through that initial 'grief' together.

Each character added to the dynamic of the group. Each was expected to grow a thicker skin as we began to develop our cruel military sense of humour. Each was expected to change from civilian to soldier and from soldier to leader.

The officer cadet school wasn't just about the boring leadership lessons we were given by staff. It was also about the life lessons we took away from the experience of the combined hardship or sense of unfairness. I conducted all of my initial exercises with these people. All of our initial exposure was shared. We lost our military virginity together. We dug and lived in trenches together. We carried backpacks over the various mountain ranges of Ireland together. We delivered our first set of tactical orders to each other. We failed in front of each other. We made asses of ourselves in each other's company regularly. We, in turn, would have to lead groups of our peers for whatever task or exercise we were carrying out. It was true experiential learning as we didn't have rank to hide behind. If your peers respected you, they would do what they were told in order to help. This was 'Learning to Lead 101'. The best lessons were not those taught directly but in fact those learned by osmosis.

Over the course of our twenty-one-month cadetship we were exposed to some really positive examples of leaders. Two of the senior NCOs and one of the officers in particular were superb. They displayed high standards in everything they did, from delivering engaging lessons, to personal examples of dress and bearing. They consistently demonstrated exceptional professionalism in every interaction with us. They expected high standards from us but also displayed exemplary standards in return. The NCOs conducted drill to an immaculate standard at all times and had a biting sense of humour, used to defuse what they must have noticed as nervous new situations for the young cadets.

I immediately took note of this approach. The officer in particular rarely raised his voice or used typical instructor bravado, but instead delivered creative lessons, showed us what a good set of orders was, and regularly led us through difficult physical training. He encouraged the weak and pushed the strong. During tactics training, he challenged us to be better at our skills and awareness, and would often take extra time to coach and mentor young cadets. He was my first role model in the army. I felt he understood how to be a leader and I watched his interactions intently.

One Saturday morning, a number of my classmates were removed from parade following a uniform inspection. The usual protocol was to withdraw the offenders' weekend pass, a fate almost worse than death. The officer stated to the group that effort was mostly in the mind. He said he didn't want to take time from them, so if they showed increased effort and each performed fifty push-ups on the spot, he would not report anyone removed from parade.

During our training, there was also a member of staff who was quite unfair on the class and was hypercritical of our performances. For example, on the rare occasions when this staff member conducted physical training with us, they mostly stood and shouted abuse at us, as opposed to actually doing the exercises. This person placed emphasis on the wrong things during our training and although they fought very hard not to show it, the rest of the staff, officers and NCOs seemed displeased by this person's actions.

This leadership style led to poor class morale. Their interaction with cadets was rude, aggressive and usually led to some sort of punishment. When they delivered lessons, everyone was afraid to ask questions. If anyone had an issue, the last person in the world they would turn to was this person. This staff member was clearly not a positive example of leadership. Even close to the completion of our training, they maintained their harsh persona, including issuing punishments to certain cadets (me included) right up to our commissioning as officers of the Defence Forces (DF).

In some ways, this was the opposite of the sort of leader I wanted to be. However, in hindsight, this also served as an excellent leadership lesson for me. What did it teach me? It taught me the best lesson I learned during my time in the cadet school – never ever be *that* sort of leader. Rule number one in my book of how to be an officer is to lead by example. I'm not saying I always do that myself, but I try as best I can and I think people can understand and relate to that.

On a beautiful Tuesday in July 2003, I was handed my commissioning certificate by the Minister for Defence at a large ceremony. I was delighted that my parents, siblings and grandparents were there to witness my commissioning, as my rank was pinned to my jacket epaulettes and I became an Irish Army officer, as decreed by the President of Ireland herself. The sun's reflection bounced off my immaculate Sam Browne belt as I spoke gleefully with my parents after the ceremony. *The hard part is over*, I thought, as I regaled them with 'crazy' stories from the cadet school. My training was complete and I was clearly now 'an awesome officer'. *Watch out 3rd Infantry Battalion in Kilkenny, because I am ready to lead.*

3

REALISATION

KINGS BEACH, AUSTRALIA – NEW YEAR'S EVE 2014

I was quite disorientated, but I remained calm and was fully lucid. A lady outside of my field of view began talking to me. She was firing questions my way as I suddenly started to notice lifeguards rushing around me. I was struggling to respond to her but she kept asking all the basics. 'What's your name? Where are you from? What age are you? Who are you here with? Do you know where you are? What day is it today?' Typical questions used to keep a conscious injured party engaged while monitoring vitals.

I knew what she was doing. I was barely able to muster low-toned responses. I asked her to get someone to fetch my wife. I described how she was up on the grass area at the back of the beach and that she would be sitting with a black Scottish terrier. Not a common sight at Kings Beach one would guess. I asked whoever was listening to be gentle when telling her as I didn't want her to freak out or get upset. The sun was in my eyes and all I could see in my field of vision were black silhouettes. I had no idea whether there were twenty people around me or just two or three. I wanted to close my eyes but knew I had to stay awake and keep telling the same story over and over, every time someone new came on the scene.

The initial adrenaline must have worn off, as I felt weary. I asked a life-guard to stand over my legs to block the sun. It all felt very uncomfortable and awkward. Not painful, but very strange. No one had given me any indication as to what was *actually* going on. I wasn't sure myself. In fact, the idea of being paralysed hadn't even crossed my mind.

Then I heard Rita's voice. She was standing somewhere to my left. I called her to me and she briefly stood in my eyeline. I told her I was okay, that I had had a bit of an accident and it looked bad but I would be fine. I didn't even know what was going on, but my initial assessment was that because I was able to chat and had a clear thought process, it couldn't be too serious. I guessed it may be some sort of 'stinger', where I was stunned for a little while.

I asked the kind lady I had been speaking with if the young boy who noticed me in the water was around so I could thank him. He was gone. I wish I could thank him. He saved my life, no doubt about it. Those that took me out of the water and their immediate actions definitely made a huge difference to my subsequent recovery, but had that boy not noticed me or alerted anybody, I would have drowned.

Paramedics eventually arrived, rolled me onto a spinal board and lifted me off the beach and into an ambulance. I felt as if there were a lot of people gathered watching the paramedics stabilise my neck and slide the board under me. I felt pain now. The initial shock was subsiding. The realisation that this wasn't just a stinger or something I would shake off in a few hours had started to dawn on me.

After the paramedics placed me into the ambulance, they tested me for movement and sensation. I felt nothing. 'Are you sure you're touching me?' It was all so surreal, like an out-of-body experience. I had no perspective of whether my legs were even attached to my body. I didn't know where my arms were. 'Okay, Billy, wiggle your fingers for me … good.' I had no idea if I was moving anything. No clue. After some focused concentration and lots of encouragement, I was told I made the slightest of movements in one big toe and one thumb. That was all I could muster.

It was all beginning to sink in. This was serious. *Very serious.*

Rita sat into the front of the ambulance as one of the paramedics rigged up some morphine. I didn't feel a pinch but I suddenly noticed the cold rush around my body as the strong numbness kicked in and the pain subsided slightly. They were trying to organise a chopper immediately from the beach back to Brisbane, but eventually elected to drive to the town of Nambour, where the nearest hospital was, as my condition was stable and the availability of the chopper was continuously changing.

As the paramedics stepped outside to make another phone call, I got the opportunity to speak one-on-one with Rita. We were both calm but I stated that I was really lucky to be alive after being pulled from the water, so anything else after that was a bonus. I still hadn't gone near the thought that I might be paralysed. Whenever I feel sorry for myself, I remind myself of this conversation. It's important to put things into perspective. It's a really big message for me to stay grounded, particularly when I'm getting caught up in something, usually at work. Anything else after being alive is a bonus. Lots of people much better than me have not been so fortunate.

In Nambour the emergency doctors met me in the hallway and briefed me on the next steps. It was difficult to orientate myself while laid out with a spinal collar locking my face skyward. My perspective was limited to ceilings and various medical staff leaning into the corner of my field of vision.

No one wanted to discuss the obvious. You don't want to be the doctor who tells someone that they are paralysed, particularly if you are not 100 per cent sure. Everyone was very non-committal when talking to us. 'Too early to tell' or 'there's too much swelling around the spinal cord right now, we can't be certain' was the general response from staff. We both maintained our calm exterior, although it must have been very disconcerting for Rita.

The hospital staff began with a few tests for sensation and fitted a new collar on my neck. They then sent me for an MRI and a CT scan. The MRI machine broke down halfway through and we had to start again. I still had the tight neck collar on, was dosed up on high levels of morphine and was unable to move a muscle.

They rolled my stretcher bed into a room where there was a clock just within my field of vision. It was coming close to midnight on New Year's Eve 2014. Over the screams of a nearby patient, the doctors gave me the first indication of my diagnosis. One of them said they believed that I had damaged my spinal cord, which had led to paralysis, but they were still unsure how serious it was. They then told me that the best course of action would be for me to be moved to Brisbane and that I would be flown down there to the Princess Alexandra (PA) Hospital, which had a dedicated spinal injuries unit, that night. Once there, I would be seen by the best consultant in Queensland, and it would then be decided whether I would be immediately operated on or not.

With the knowledge of probable paralysis and neck surgery in my immediate future I knew what I had to do. I had held out on letting my family know what had happened until I had a better understanding of my diagnosis. Now I asked Rita to hold the phone up to my ear. This wasn't going to be easy. I broke the news to my mother, and I have to say her initial reaction was better than I thought. She was calm and collected. I found it difficult to actually say the words 'I'm paralysed' to her, and it upset me actually saying it aloud for the first time. But it was good that I was able to speak to her personally. I think it gave her, and my siblings, whom I also called, a huge sense of relief that I could actually talk over the phone.

It was just an unbelievable position to suddenly be in. Only a few hours ago I had been chilling on the beach, eating my lunch. Now I was calling my family, high on drugs, letting them know I couldn't move from the neck down. I attempted to make some really bad neck-related jokes but, in truth, these were horrible conversations.

Rita stayed with me for a while longer, until we had confirmation that the chopper had arrived. Even at this early stage, friends of ours were already assisting us greatly. My mate Joe had gotten a lift up to the Sunshine Coast to collect our car and our dog. Our friends, Andy, Jen, Simon and Priscilla still met us on New Year's Eve, except in the ER in Nambour Hospital and not in the fancy restaurant in Brisbane as we had planned. They were kind enough to drive Rita back to Brisbane as the paramedics prepared me for the chopper ride.

Rita didn't want to leave me. She was very afraid about how fragile I appeared. I got the impression that she felt as though she wouldn't see me again. I attempted to reassure her, but I could tell she still left in a very worried state. We agreed to rendezvous in Brisbane after she had gotten a shower and I had enjoyed the spin in the chopper. She wanted to get to Brisbane and get back to my side as soon as possible.

Before she left I called after her: 'Oh hey, Rit, Happy New Year.'

***

I was high as a kite in the helicopter. In fact, it was a bit of a thrill to get back into a 'heli' flying at night. The only difference was that the last time it happened I had been in the Special Forces (SF), fast roping from it.

By the time I was wheeled into the intensive care unit in the PA, it all seemed so crazy, so fake, like some sort of bad dream. You don't see much when you are only able to stare up at the ceiling, so it gives you little perspective of where you are and what is going on around you. I knew people were coming in and out of the room they had put me in, but it seemed like it was a big wide room with various tables and contraptions by the walls.

By the time Rita arrived, three hours later, the pain cycle had become very noticeable. I would chat jovially with the staff at first, before getting gradually quieter as I noticed discomfort, and then quite soon afterwards came the onset of immense pain. Cue relief via morphine, which brought me back to my chatty self again. By late that night in the intensive care unit I was maxing out my pain-relief allowance.

It was after 4 a.m. in the morning of New Year's Day when the emergency doctors reviewed some tests and began discussions with me. A finger up the bum would tell a lot, they said. Awkward to say but, when they inserted it, I was glad to feel it! That I could meant they believed my spinal cord injury (SCI) was incomplete.

'Okay, that sounds good, what does that mean?' I asked.

We had a ten-minute conversation with the orthopaedic doctor on call, as he gave us his diagnosis. It would change everything for me. Paraphrased it went something like: 'Billy, you have fractured your neck (C3/4) and back (T5) and you have incomplete tetraplegia due to spinal cord damage from the trauma received to your neck during the accident. Essentially you are paralysed from the neck down, but you have some very slight movement in your toe and thumb. I believe you have Central Cord Syndrome (CCS). This is not a bad thing. CCS sufferers have the best chance of recovery from an SCI. However, if you do get recovery your legs will come back stronger than your arms, and we have no way of telling how much movement and feeling, if any, will come back.'

I asked the questions that I imagine most SCI sufferers throw out: 'Doc, will I ever walk again; am I going to be able to get back to normal?'

In my experience to date, doctors will very rarely commit to answering straight but he gave an excellent answer: 'I dunno ... maybe.'

That's all I needed to hear. It wasn't a 'No.'

From that moment on, I knew I had a job to do. From then on, there was hope.

A nurse appeared in my field of vision. 'Hi, Billy, I'm the on-call nurse. Has anyone spoken to you yet about a catheter?'

Eh, what?

4

SELECTION

KILDARE, IRELAND – MAY 2004

I first heard of the Army Ranger Wing (ARW) when I was in the officer cadet school and knew it to be Ireland's elite SF unit. On rare occasions we saw men in dark-green berets with beards or long hair around the Curragh Camp. Their uniforms were worn differently: sleeves were half rolled down, shirts with nametags were tucked in with a black harness belt, and trousers were left untied around the ankles. As officer cadets still in training, we were in awe of these men.

The ARW was based in the Curragh and would run a course once a year to select candidates for potential future service in the unit. It was open to all ranks and all services. During the course, the staff would regularly run the candidates up the camp to the cookhouse next to the cadet school lines. They looked dishevelled and tired, like they were constantly being 'beasted' – common military slang for being absolutely destroyed by staff through physical and mental pressure. They wore helmets with the covers removed and a number drawn onto the front and back. As they ran in formation to the side of the cookhouse, the staff would halt and then order the candidates into the hall. On the order to fall out, the candidates would turn and shout 'RANGER' before running into the cookhouse to queue for their meal. They had to run everywhere, at all times. Two candidates would guard the weapons while the others ate. We snuck Mars bars for them to eat into the toilets that they used. They were not allowed to speak to each other at any stage when eating.

These were my first impressions of 'selection', the toughest course in the DF. The ARW accounts for around 1 per cent of the membership of the Irish Defence Forces. Selection courses have begun with as many as seventy candidates, with the pass rate somewhere between 5 and 20 per cent; however, there have been courses where no one has passed. (And even passing selection didn't guarantee a place in the ARW.) But these courses are not run for statistics or pass-rate percentages. If you make the standards required you will pass; if everyone makes that standard, then everyone will pass. Well, this was the general spiel delivered by ARW members to potential candidates during their annual roadshows advertising for the course.

Some guys in cadet school talked about it constantly, guessing who in our class would potentially pass the course. People didn't consider me too much and that was okay. I kept any thoughts I had about attempting the course to myself; but I did have thoughts about it. Why would any officer not want to serve in the best there was on offer? Why wouldn't you want to be the best?

After commissioning, I was posted to the 3rd Infantry Battalion in Kilkenny and, despite the fact that work was busy and interesting, I had this mad notion in the back of my mind. Over Christmas 2003 I thought about putting my name forward and committed to it fully from 1 January 2004. ARW selection course 'KILO ONE', as it was called, started on 9 May, so the countdown had begun. As soon as an officer puts his name in, word gets around quickly. Within the battalion all the other officers and men know that you're in training for it, so any group PT session is like a little challenge to test your fitness. Talk in officers' messes around the country will always include young officers discussing who in their cohort is going for selection this year.

Quite soon after I submitted my application, paranoia set in. I could picture guys in Dublin, Cork or Athlone saying how I'd never have a chance, that I was good but not good enough. It really motivated me throughout my training. I regularly pictured different people not giving me a chance – too weak, too slow and not very strong tactically. A lot of my motivation to complete the course was to show people that I was good enough, which, in hindsight, I see was a perfect example of extrinsic motivation (i.e. to be motivated by external factors such as recognition from others, whereas those intrinsically motivated are driven by factors such as a sense of self-achievement). I hadn't really ever thought about what would happen afterwards, should I pass the course, and hadn't considered the potential of actually working in the ARW. I was fixated only on the task at hand. I had, in the words of the officer in charge (OIC) of the selection course, 'put my cock on the block'. If nothing else, I had shown the courage to attempt it. I was a twenty-year-old 2nd lieutenant at the time, as green as St Patrick's Day. Was I making a massive mistake? For an officer, failing the course was always looked upon in a dim light. Personally, I felt it would be embarrassing for an officer to come back to a unit and attempt to lead men who knew he was 'not good enough'. Or, much worse, that he had given up. But for now, I had to focus on my training programme.

So how does one train for an SF selection course? Lots of books have been written on the subject, but there are some very obvious principles to adhere to. First, find out what physical tests are on the course. You must train for these. If you don't pass them, it's all over. You must start with the knowns. Go out at the start of your training cycle, run through all the known physical tests and see where you stand. It sounds very obvious to give this advice, but a large number of people continue to show up on courses knowing various physical tests are required and yet they have not conducted them to exact test conditions prior to the course. Even from a psychological perspective, knowing that one has already been able to successfully pass a required physical test before they begin is of massive benefit. Also, remember that fatigue will be a factor when you attempt these tests during the course, so the aim prior to finishing your training cycle is that you should be able to comfortably pass all these tests.

I had a simple enough training plan based around the physical tests. The course had a number of 'Ranger tests', as they were called. They included the following:

1) Table Walk: This was a speed hike test in the Glen of Imaal, County Wicklow, from Knickeen Ford to 100m beyond the elbow on Table Mountain. 45lbs had to be carried before adding water and weapon. This was to be completed in one hour. Height climbed was approximately 400m over the 6km distance.

2) 10km Road Run in under forty-five minutes.

3) 8km Speed March: This was conducted around the boundary of the Curragh plains. 35lbs was to be carried before water and weapon. This was to be completed in under one hour.

4) 12-mile Route March: This was conducted from Coolmoney Military Camp in the Glen of Imaal to Dunlavin village via road. 45lbs was carried before water and weapon and the march was to be completed at course pace. (That was to say the staff would set the pace and those that dropped out immediately failed.)

5) Hill Circuit: This was a well-known and feared test, consisting of conducting three laps of a route marked through the 'tank tracks' on the Curragh plains, close to Athgarvan village. The route took candidates up and down very steep tracks purposely designed for testing off-road driving. Each lap consisted of four relatively short but very steep hills to summit. 35lbs was to be carried before water and weapon and the circuit had to be completed in under forty-five minutes.

6) Fore Man/Aft Man: This was also a classic and renowned test. It consisted of a 16km speed hike following a route above the famous Glendalough in Wicklow. The route started at Glenmacnass Waterfall, immediately climbing to the peaks of Brown Mountain and Kanturk Mountain, then descending almost into the village of Laragh, climbing again up the side of Brochagh Mountain, before finally assaulting the steep face of Tonelagee Mountain (the Irish, *Tóin Le Gaoith*, directly translates to 'Ass of the Wind'!) to the finish at the summit. 55lbs was carried in the main pack before adding water and weapon. A staff member stays in front to set the pace and is known as the 'Fore Man'. A staff member at the rear stays 50m from him and is known as the 'Aft Man'.

Candidates dropping back from the Aft Man at the rear meet a third staff member who delivers a warning to them. After one warning, should the candidate drop back again, they fail the test. Courses would take approximately four to four-and-a-half hours to complete. This was usually one of the most difficult tests, with a high number of failures.

7) Gym Test: This test consisted of push-ups, sit-ups, pull-ups, hand-claps, burpees and a 3.2km run. It was a simple, best effort within one minute test and graded within a scoring system. For instance, sixteen pull-ups were worth 100 points, whereas four pull-ups were worth 20 points. A pass was 400 points.

Also, there were three 'life' tests. These were confidence tests to determine fears or phobias and consisted of:

1) Water Tower Test: One was required to abseil backwards twice from the top of the water tower in the Curragh Camp which is approximately 80ft high. A stall or resistance to go would result in a warning, then a fail.

2) Bridge Jump: One was required to jump off Blessington Bridge into Blessington Lake twice; this was an approximate forty-foot drop. A stall or resistance would again result in a warning, then a fail.

3) Claustrophobia Test: This was different each year and hard to

train for. It would be uncomfortable but I didn't know much else about it.

All these tests would be coupled with the infamous 'Scratch' exercise usually held on the first night, which was a type of 'hell night' of insane physical and mental pressure placed on candidates, designed to get rid of the pretenders. Scratch had a fearsome reputation as an extremely tough exercise. I had heard many horror stories, which I hoped had grown arms and legs over time. It was the ultimate 'beasting' session from what I was told, with screaming Rangers abusing candidates through hours of physical activities in particularly uncomfortable terrain (consisting mostly of waist-deep, ice-cold mud and steep inclines).

A candidate was required to pass all tests with no retests; a fail meant an immediate return to unit (RTU). Candidates could request to RTU of their own accord at any stage throughout the course. The majority of course failures came via RTU, followed by test failure and injury. Should a candidate be successful in surviving Scratch and passing all the tests, they could look forward to a ten-day tactical exercise and assessment, followed by a route march in full kit from the Wicklow Mountains back to ARW headquarters in the Curragh, which is just a touch longer than an official marathon. If you were still standing at the very end of selection, at ARW headquarters you would receive your official ARW tab to wear on the left shoulder of your uniform.

The tab reads 'FIANÓGLACH'. There is no direct English translation of this word, but the principle of the tab was stolen from the American Ranger battalions. In fact, the colour and shape are very similar, even though the units' respective roles are not. 'FIANÓGLACH', however, can be broken down into two parts. The first half of the name, Fian, is derived from 'Na Fianna', in ancient mythology a group of Ireland's best warriors led by Fionn Mac Cumhaill. The second part of the name, Óglach, comes from Óglaigh na hÉireann which is the official name of the Irish Defence Forces. To wear the 'FIANÓGLACH' tab was an honour given only to those who successfully completed the selection course, and it immediately distinguishes those wearing it on their formal uniform. However, only members who went on to successfully complete the basic skills course or what is commonly called the 'reinforcement cycle' (the follow-on intensive SF skills suite of courses conducted over approximately seven months) would actually become a qualified Ranger, receive the coveted green beret and get an extra red band around the tab to signify that they served in the unit. To wear the green beret was the ultimate goal for anyone attempting selection.

My weekly training looked something like this:

2 x 10km runs in PT gear.

2 x weighted runs in PT gear – 45lbs in a day sack.

1 x Battle PT in battle order (webbing, day sack, helmet and weapon, when I was allowed to take one to train with). I would usually carry 45lbs. I had a number of zip-lock bags filled with wet sand that I then taped up heavily and used as weights. A 'Battle PT' was any high-intensity PT session used to simulate battlefield conditions. This could take the form of a circuit, including crawling on my belly, running 10-yard shuttles then down into firing position, sprints, tyre flipping and carrying heavy loads over distance as quick as possible. It

could also just be a long run with full patrol kit on, going as fast as I could. A Battle PT is always seen as a challenging PT session within army circles.

5 x gym sessions a week, focusing on push-ups, pull-ups and body resistance.

Weekends usually consisted of some sort of cross-country hill walk with heavy weight.

I mostly trained either in Wicklow, practising the tests, or in the Galtee Mountains, since they were en route from Cork to Kilkenny. I also drove to the Curragh on a number of occasions to conduct trial runs on some of the actual tests, such as the Hill Circuit and Speed March.

I started preparing my personal kit in my room in Kilkenny. First, my 'admin in the field' had to be 'squared away'. Administration in the field is a common military term for everything you carry during tactics. To have good admin was to be 'squared away', which meant to have everything in neat order and the correct location. To have poor admin meant it looked like a bomb went off inside your pack as you were looking for your camouflage cream. To help with this, we were given a list of exactly what to carry, which brings me to another basic tip if you are ever involved in this: pack exactly what it says! I was meticulous about it: I had a big table in my room in officers' lines on which I laid out all my admin. I got a second set of belt webbing and kitted it out exactly as the first one, including personal preferences such as hip pads, an extra pouch for my bivouac bag and bungee cord threaded around the outside of the pouches. I trained using both, so if we were given a twenty-four-hour break during the course (which was common during the longer courses, and this course was to be five weeks in duration) I could swap kits completely instead of attempting to clean my only webbing during our rest period. I also had two day sacks with the exact same kit. I spent money on extra kit and the smaller items that one would never think of as being important. I sealed everything in waterproof bags.

As an officer I would be expected to plan missions during the course, deliver orders to my subordinates and lead during the execution of the mission. In order to be confident in my order-briefing ability, I read various order formats over and over. I had two sets of tactical aides-memoire (booklets to assist in the writing of orders, providing templates for reporting to higher headquarters and reminders on considerations for planning various types of missions). It was an absolute full-time investment in the process. Once committed to passing the course I became obsessed. I even bought two watches and planned to wear them both during the field phase in case one stopped.

I was also incredibly anxious. Instrumental in helping with my nerves was a diary I kept of all the training I was conducting. I would regularly flick back through it to see my progress. This actually acted as a great confidence booster towards the end of my training cycle. Whenever I questioned whether I had prepared myself physically, my diary always told me that I had done enough.

The main reason for my nerves was the mental beasting that I knew would come. All the preparations in the world wouldn't matter when *that* moment arrived. *That* moment could occur at any one stage, or at multiple times during the course. That was when all other things had been stripped away and only you could answer the question of 'How badly do you want this?' The message from speaking to those who had attempted the course was always the same: no matter how physically strong you are, success was ultimately gained above all through mental strength. I hoped that when the moment arrived I would have that mental strength. During training sessions, I would often question myself: have I grossly overestimated my abilities? I'm a brand-new officer, only twenty years old. Are they going to destroy me?

But my greatest fear was not any one particular physical test or challenge. It was, instead, the unavoidable and honest judgement from the SF soldiers – that they wouldn't think I was good enough.

***

Doug and J Bag, two friends of mine and classmates from the cadet school, were also attempting selection that year. Doug was a red-haired, wild man from Thurles, while J Bag was a guy from Salthill with a Fonzi-like coolness and a fondness for crazy stunts. Doug was the fittest of the three of us and J Bag had a mad toughness in him, so I felt they both had a good chance of passing the course. They trained a bit together, whereas I mostly preferred training alone. I felt it prepared me mentally, leaving me with my thoughts, chasing my own doubts, with no one telling me to push on, because, in my opinion, I needed to be able to tell myself that. J Bag trained with a slab of beer as part of his pack weight. He kept saying that after he finished the course, he was going to drink every last can in his buddy's camper van in Salthill. I think both Doug and I hoped to join him. They were (and remain) very good friends of mine, and it was nice to have people I knew with me when going through something so challenging. But I also knew that you can't let friendships get in the way when you're on selection. If even one of them decided to RTU, there was no way I would follow. In fact, very early on I decided that I would never RTU myself, no matter what. Even though I was nervous and worried, I was certain about that.

A few weeks prior to the commencement of the course, Doug called me while I was on call in Gormanstown Camp due to the G8 Summit riots. He had messed up. He had been on a course in the Curragh and gotten drunk on the last night. Walking back from the mess, he started banging on a door to some accommodation, when a man appeared. Doug had a quick verbal exchange with the man and then left with assistance from others on the course. Not a major story, it seemed. A few days later, he rang the ARW to gain some last-minute information on the administrative details of the course. The course OIC was a big rugby type, with a fierce presence. He stated that he would transfer Doug to the operations officer. A familiar voice came on the line. Doug got an awful realisation that this was the same man he had encountered a few days earlier. He was the infamous 'MOB', a man noted for his short temper and crazy stares. He reminded Doug that they had met recently late at night and that he was looking forward to reacquainting himself with Doug on the first night of the course.

With only a few days to go, Doug was now very nervous about attending the course. I told him the same thing J Bag had – that it was a test to see if he would crumble. Doug knew that too, and never thought about pulling out; he just needed affirmation. That's not to say that he wasn't going to get beasted on the first night – he was absolutely going to get destroyed – but at this stage, if he backed out he'd never be looked at for potential in the unit, ever. We all knew that. In fact, it would show immense bravery and courage to present himself on the first night knowing his card was already marked. So he accepted his impending fate and hung up. I went back to watching the news while bathing my feet in iodine: fail to prepare, prepare to fail.

On the first day of the course I showed up to the officers' mess in the Curragh and left my spare gear in a room. I met the other two guys and we wished each other luck. I drove my car down to the square outside the ARW headquarters compound, and fell in with about fifty other hopefuls. About twenty minutes later a group of four Green Berets walked around the steel fence and towards us. I was petrified. The smallest of them introduced himself as the course sergeant. He had a horrible Louth accent. The other staff spoke briefly. I guessed that these NCOs were from the Midlands and Dublin respectively. Off we went into the compound and into the Multi-Training Centre (MTC), a big hall with high ceilings. As I walked in I noticed the wall to our immediate right had a climbing wall built into it. The opposite end of the hall dropped down one storey with a stairway to toilets and a steel ladder leading from the dropped floor high up to a platform 25m above. There were pull-up bars along the side, benches underneath and a massive stack of filthy-looking, thin sponge mattresses in the corner.

We all received a mattress and had a number written onto our helmets. My number was twenty-two. From then on I was addressed as Ranger Twenty-Two. I was one of only three officers who showed up on the course. Doug, J Bag and I were all brand-new 2nd lieutenants, a.k.a. 'red-arses' (military slang for a new guy). I was sweating bucket-loads, nervous every time a member of staff walked near or addressed me, afraid that they would zone in on me at any second.

They began simply, with a kit inspection. However, punishments started kicking in slowly, and before long it was mayhem. Candidates were leopard crawling around the hall, swinging from the pull-up bars in webbing and helmet, while staff amused themselves by ordering others to wrestle each other. *It was on, now.* I really wanted to get out of the compound and go get beasted outside. I don't know why, I just felt trapped in there.

Ever more crazy physical tasks were thrust upon us, with kit flung everywhere, as all the while more and more Green Berets came into the hall from everywhere. Finally, after a quick briefing from the OIC, we were ordered outside. We had walked into the MTC at 5 p.m. and by now it was almost dark, nearing 10 p.m. After quickly being broken into small teams, we ran out to the plains and began small team battle drills. Then, just as I thought we would be making our way towards the tank tracks to be destroyed in waist-deep sludge, we turned around and headed back into camp – the first of the constant mind games. We ran down to the swimming pool, where a number of zodiac inflatable dinghies awaited us in the adjacent car park. We were absolutely flogged with physical tasks in and out of the pool, out around the car park and back again. We did a number of high practice jumps into the dive pool, to simulate the bridge jump later in the course. We conducted what seemed like hundreds of in/outs at the poolside, coupled with horrible body resistance work in the car park. At one point Doug was pulled aside and brought outside to where MOB was waiting for him alone. Doug was directed to conduct continuous exercises for about thirty minutes before he rejoined us. The air was now cleared, it seemed. Big boys' rules: 'You mess up, you pay for it, then we get on with life.'

The beasting continued with absolutely no let-up. We kept going until the early hours, then eventually got brought back to the compound. Those still present appeared to still be alive, just. I had noticed a few guys giving up during the night, but didn't focus too much on it, as I was a little busy, to say the least. We got a few hours' sleep before a large speaker blasted out an Islamic morning prayer. I didn't sleep much regardless, as I thought that any second the staff would storm back in to continue the beasting. Also, as a means of sleep deprivation, we had to rotate a guard on the front door to the hall every night, so I volunteered for the graveyard shift, and would continue to do so as often as possible.

In the morning we were made run to breakfast. As with the previous courses I had seen, we were going to have to run everywhere. When running you were dressed in combat clothing, carrying webbing, day sack and weapon. If we weren't ordered to run, then we were ordered to leopard crawl across the tarmac, which seemed a personal favourite of the staff. I hated it. Leopard crawling is an official method of movement as defined in military doctrine. It's down on your belly, crawling using elbows and knees to slide over the ground with the weapon out in front of the face. This was the preferred method of beasting of one particularly sadistic staff member with a Cork accent and Yoda-like presence.

We got back from breakfast on that first morning and got a better idea of the course outline. We had already been briefed in a pre-course package. The course would be broken into two phases: the preparation phase and the test phase. The preparation phase would be the first three weeks, where we could conduct all the Ranger tests as a trial with no repercussions for failure, coupled with other PT and lessons. The test phase would be the real deal: a full Scratch on Sunday, two Ranger tests each on Monday, Tuesday and Wednesday, with Fore Man/Aft Man on Thursday, then orders and straight out onto the full mission exercise phase for ten days, finishing with the walk back. Absolutely insane. *Don't focus on that just yet, worry about today!*

During the preparation weeks, we usually had a PT session, a Ranger test (another PT session) and then lessons into the wee hours. We would conduct a life test either on Friday or Saturday morning. That was the general structure, but there was much more thrown in. For example, we conducted a number of patrols up to the grenade range in the Curragh one night, with a follow-on action of a raid the following night. I was the patrol commander for the raid and the CO of the unit sat in on my orders. Both the orders and the direct action went well, and we got some praise from staff afterwards. Of course, that fades in a few hours during your next PT session or Ranger test.

The idea behind the preparation phase was sound, but the application didn't seem to be achieving the desired outcome. The OIC maintained that the idea of the phase was to assist in readying us for the later pass-or-fail tests. But any candidate who failed any of the Ranger tests within the preparation phase would request an RTU immediately thereafter. Most were of the opinion that if they couldn't pass when we only had one test a day (and since bodies would get more fatigued as the course went on), then they definitely wouldn't pass during the test phase. It was a point well made, I suppose. Physically, I was relatively comfortable in all tests, neither the fastest nor slowest in any of them. Doug had a massive engine and was in the top few, along with two privates from Cork who were incredible athletes, one having run competitively as a national-level athlete. J Bag was maybe around the middle but never near the back.

Some of the other ranks were excellent soldiers with great attitudes, but others were questionable. As with my original training in the army, the 'buddy' system was employed on this course. My course 'buddy' was a private from the 1st Air Defence Regiment in the Curragh. He had an alternative outlook, which he articulated to me one night while we were cleaning weapons: 'Every day longer I stay here I'm more of a legend in my unit, but unless you pass you're a failure. And they give you so much more shit as an officer, fuck that!'

I think he may have picked up some of the bad thinking I've seen seeping into soldiers in some of the units across the country. The 'I'll just do enough to get by' mentality. It is disappointing to see soldiers with that lack of motivation. But, at the same time, I liked him. His attitude was almost a breath of fresh air, although probably not right for the ARW, but who was I to say? I looked after him, and vice versa, on a number of occasions for small things – like minutes after he had expressed his views, when he almost sliced his finger off. Ah, the age-old army buddy system working its magic.

Although Doug was doing well physically, a couple of small things started to create an atmosphere where he began being zoned in on by staff. One day, directly after a weapons inspection, we were told to fall in outside and run to our next lesson. My bed was over by the far wall so I made it a point to assist anyone lagging behind as I made my way out. Anyone over by my side did the same. Doug looked panicked as I ran over to him and knelt alongside him. 'All okay?' 'No, I can't find my firing pin.' Staff started hovering over us. The rest of the students outside could be heard shouting 'I'm waiting on my buddy, I'm waiting on my buddy', probably doing burpees or push-ups. Doug thought it may have slipped into the slit in the mattress lining and was in the sponge somewhere. He frantically searched in the mattress, while I assisted, noting the staff were like vultures, staring at us but saying nothing. I had a thought. 'Doug, check your cleaning kit.' He reached around into his webbing, pulled out his cleaning kit and out popped the pin. The silence was deafening. He put his weapon together and we ran outside. The staff followed us out and one NCO took a notebook from his pocket and began writing while looking at Doug. I had never seen staff do that before.

One morning the staff came in and ordered us to pull out our warm skip hats, black tape and ear muffs. They stretched the hats down fully over our heads and faces, put on the ear muffs and then wrapped the black tape across our eyes to keep it all in place. They bound our hands in front. Then came the good stuff. A few slaps and punches while they shuffled us around and then they bailed us onto a truck face down and power-hosed us. We were all shivering vigorously. Off the truck went. Anyone moving got a kick.

We eventually got out somewhere and they started putting us into a series of horrible 'stress' positions. A stress position is an awkward body position to hold. Arms straight out to the side – our hands were untied for the duration of this task – or kneeling or fingertips leaning against a wall. A lot of mocking and jeering, grabbing and dragging – it was very disorientating. I was cold and extremely uncomfortable with the situation. In fact, it was the most uncomfortable thing I had ever experienced. Suddenly, I was manhandled up onto a platform and someone asked questions about the unit, who I was, where I was last night, etc. He said that if I didn't tell him he'd throw me in the river. I gave him nothing and he pushed me. I got that horrible realisation that I actually was falling from a height. I thought it may have been a trick and it was only a step down. No such luck!

Splash. *Holy fucking shit, I'm drowning. This is insane.*

Despite my enormous panic, fear and shock, I managed to bring my feet around below me and suddenly I felt the soft bottom. I stood up, still blindfolded, freezing, in shock, sucking for air whilst still bound. The man began questioning again from what I thought was the riverbank above me. I refused to answer his questions. Two men grabbed me from either side and shoved me under the water. They were strong and aggressive. *Okay, I need to breathe.* They pulled me by the back of the neck up out of the water. Huuuuh … air! But it was all messed up; as soon as I tried breathing in, the water from the hat would suck inwards and start choking me. It was my first (but

57

not last) experience of dry-drowning or waterboarding. They did it a few times then let me go. There is nothing as disturbing as not having personal control of your breathing. At any stage, they could take it away from me, and take away my recovery breaths just as quickly. Although I wasn't panicking overtly, it was very upsetting. I did my best to keep my mind relaxed. *It will stop. It has to, they can't kill me.*

I was suddenly handed over to another staff member, the man with the Cork accent. He said there was a tunnel in front of me and I had to dive down and swim through it, otherwise I'd get stuck. *Okay, let me at it.* Down I went and wriggled as hard as I could being blindfolded and ear-muffed.

I need air. Up, up, up.

Then I came to the surface. Another man grabbed me and whispered at me to stay quiet. He removed my blindfold and muffs, and motioned at me to stay quiet. I looked across and saw most of the course alongside me, having just experienced the same fate. I looked around. It was actually more controlled than we thought. We were in a four-foot small canal, with the truck tail backed off the side of it. There were a number of safety staff in the water and no tunnel, just the staff pretending by sticking out their arms! The senior staff were on the bank assessing our reactions, as we watched the last few candidates running through the torture. *Thank God, the claustrophobia test is over,* I thought, as we clambered back onto the truck.

The last Friday of the prep phase dawned. We knew we would be getting off on the Friday but would have to be back on Sunday evening for the test phase. Or so we thought. Staff bombed into the hall early in the morning. It's always worse when you have a good idea of what's coming. We got the same deprivation drills up to the point where we were tied, blindfolded and beat on. We had dropped from forty-five starting the course to approximately fifteen at this stage, but what happened next, I can only describe as pure and utter agony.

I had thought that the previous stress tests were the most uncomfortable experiences I had ever felt. And they were, until now. What followed was non-stop anguish, through a mixture of evil stress positions and insane mind games that were nothing short of torturous. Examples included, but were by no means limited to, leaning forward with fingers only on a wall with thistles under your palms, which inflicted pain when you gave the position up; kneeling with bricks in either hand while in a crucifix position; star-jumping with a thistle bush down your shirt. The stress positions in particular seemed endless, as we were forced to hold various body positions while being sensory-deprived and in receipt of a torrent of abuse.

I was bundled into a small steel locker, which was then beaten with sticks. They laid us down and pressed the front wheel of an Army four-wheel drive in between our legs, bouncing the clutch. (They actually used the spare tyre but we didn't know that!) We also received a number of power hosings for good measure in what was hours and hours of grief.

I kept talking to myself. Even after what we had experienced only a few days earlier, this was incredibly challenging. I wanted so badly for it to be over. Although I knew it had to stop some time, it just seemed to continue without end, and with constant pain and discomfort. We weren't given a moment of respite. I simply tried to remain calm while doing exactly what they forced me to do as best I could. My body would crumble from various positions after only seconds. I could hear others wailing or groaning as staff jeered. *Stay Zen, Billy. Don't let it get to you.* 'Pain is temporary, it will end sometime,' an amazing instructor of mine used to say. *Just hang in there. They want you to give up. They want you to RTU. Never. Never ever.*

All of a sudden, it stopped. They dragged us around to the front of the MTC as a group. We were unbound, and the muffs and blindfolds came off. As they removed our blindfolds and my eyes adjusted, I breathed a massive sigh of relief and looked at the others, who were similarly shaken by the experience. The course sergeant said we were kicking straight into the test phase now and asked if anyone wanted to leave. It was another mind game, a trap to see if anyone would give up. Surprisingly no one did.

Instead, we were released for a thirty-six-hour break and I got out of there as quickly as I could. That had been the single most difficult experience of my life. Unfortunately, the actual test phase was still to come.

5

MY FIRST WEEK
AS A QUADRIPLEGIC

PRINCESS ALEXANDRA HOSPITAL, BRISBANE, AUSTRALIA – JANUARY 2015

How do I accurately describe what happened after I was told that I was paralysed? I can list the series of events that occurred post-trauma, but how can I depict the internal turmoil that someone goes through when they're beginning to come to terms with the fact that they're paralysed? I'm not sure I can, as it is difficult to describe the feeling of not moving. Many people asked if I was scared. No, I wasn't. I was very much in the lucky-to-be-alive-and-I'm-going-to-get-better camp.

Of course, I had awful thoughts. Immediate things like: *Will I ever walk again? Will I ever use my hands again? Will my penis ever work again? Will I lose my job? Am I going to be a burden to my wife and family from now on?* But I have always had an almost callous, objective mindset. I knew that I could think about these things but not let them fill my mind.

I try not to deal in hypotheticals. *Look down the road, sure, but there's no need to walk that way; you know there's nothing good down there.* But I felt like my life goals, like potential service in the Australian Special Forces, were now out the window and it is nothing short of heartbreaking to have deep life ambitions ripped from you and destroyed in an instant.

Shut up. Stop that self-pity, Bill; think about those things some other time. For now, focus on today. The best thing you can do for you and those around you is to remain focused, determined and positive. That's the correct road to take, no matter where it leads you. And hey, don't just talk the talk, walk the walk.

Dr Kate Campbell spoke with us on the afternoon of 1 January 2015. I had been in ICU all night and was moved to an acute orthopaedic ward in the morning. She had looked at my MRI and CT results and concurred with Dr Bala's initial assessment. She was quite personable, which can be rare in consultants. I listened closely to what she had to say. She was clearly an expert, asked lots of questions about how the accident happened and how I now felt. I tried describing it as best I could but it was difficult to illustrate. It's very hard to explain how you feel. You concentrate really hard to move something but there's nothing. You even doubt that your brain is sending the message down. Not even a flicker from a strand of muscle anywhere, no matter how hard you focus. It was very weird and very disconcerting.

I was also hugely uncomfortable. I was on a lot of pain medication and a pain cycle was apparent. Dr Campbell said I had two options:

1) Elect to get surgery on my spine to fuse the C3 and C4 (neck) bones together to ensure there would be no further spinal cord damage while the fractures were healing.

2) Elect to wear a halo brace and chest vest to lock the neck in place

to ensure there would be no further spinal cord damage while the fractures were healing.

She said the T5 (mid-back) fracture wasn't of much importance as it was minute and would most likely heal in a few weeks. These measures were to treat the vertebral fractures only. But either way, I was still paralysed from the spinal cord damage.

'Which would you recommend?' I asked.

She replied, 'Well, even though I'm the surgeon that would be doing it, I would advise against invasive means when possible. The halo is uncomfortable, but where there is an option not to conduct surgery on your neck, I would suggest taking it.' She then proceeded to try to convince me that wearing a halo wasn't actually *so* bad and people gain an affinity to it over time. I did not believe that for a second. But I asked Rita if she was okay with it, and when she said that she was, I elected to have the halo fitted and resigned myself to the fact that this was going to be *extremely* unpleasant.

I started mentally preparing myself for it, drawing on my previous life experiences, and kept telling myself that I was tougher than this. The more crap life throws at you, the more confident you get at being able to deal with it. I'm not saying I've had much crap to deal with in comparison to others in much more dire circumstances, but thus far I had been able to harness and control whatever I'd come up against, turning it into positive mental strength when required. It's just something that I don't question. Maybe I overestimate my mental strength, but it's worked so far. Even while motionless on that hospital bed, I had derived a high level of self-confidence from my mental toughness in past performances.

On 2 January I got fitted for my halo. I didn't sleep much the night before. Pain and discomfort are difficult to ignore when you cannot move. It was sometimes hard to distinguish exactly where they were coming from. So many times, I wanted to wipe my eye or scratch my nose. I had been cut out of my rash vest and shorts but still had sand over my body and in my hair. It was a real trial of patience.

A team from prosthetics and orthotics (P&O) arrived at my bedside and briefed me on the process. John was the senior member and gave a good description of what was going to happen. They would size me up for a chest brace and then place the crown on, screwing four pins into my head, two in the forehead, and one behind each ear. The crown would then be staked into the chest brace using four upright bars.

They put it on in the ward, at my bed space, but it felt like I was elsewhere. John was supervising the young woman putting the halo on. She seemed a little bit nervous. It was quite uncomfortable but not as bad as I had expected. They would be back in forty-eight hours to tighten it to the required 8lbs pressure through each pin. In the meantime, that was it. The hospital staff dissipated from around my bed and I was left there, staring at the ceiling once again, contemplating my circumstances. I was now a tetraplegic (a.k.a. quadriplegic) laid on a bed, with a black metal frame around my head bracketed to a chest brace under my purple hospital gown. At least that's what I was told I was wearing. Medical staff regularly checked in.

Even at this early stage the catheter was very uncomfortable. I was in less pain when on my side, but actually moving me was a large-scale effort. In order to do so, we would buzz for two wardies. It might take up to thirty minutes for their arrival. It was very busy in there. They would slip a silk-like sheet under my body, then slide me to the side of the bed. They would then hitch up my knee and pull it across the bed whilst simultaneously rolling my back. I would lie there for some respite until it again became completely untenable, and the process was repeated.

I found it difficult to talk much and swallowing was a real struggle due to the halo completely locking my head, neck and shoulders in place. Until then, I hadn't considered the slight neck movements that are required when swallowing. They gave me soft foods only, mostly soups, but I didn't eat much, as it was very awkward. Even drinking water was uncomfortable. Of course, all these tasks were being completed by nurses, Rita or friends. How insane is it to think that two days after lying on the beach with your partner you were now accepting soup and water from them through a straw?

In trying situations, you see traits in people that you don't normally notice. Recent friends of ours in Brisbane became our saviours. Army friends of mine kicked into military mode and couldn't have done more for us. Our dog was well cared for and they ensured that my chain of command was fully informed as to what had happened. It's something that I'll never forget and I now have a bond with these people that will never be broken.

During the day, Rita and others would keep me company. Every few hours I'd get my visitors to raise the bed to a seated position where I could see people – it was nice to actually be able to see people – then back down after it became too painful.

One of my most frequent visitors in those early days was Joe. I'd met him at Australia House in London the day we signed our contracts with the ADF, which was shortly after I'd resigned from the Irish Defence Forces. We flew onwards separately, then met again during our induction briefings in Gallipoli Barracks in Brisbane. An ex-Royal Marine Commando captain, he was cool, laid back and good with the banter. Sometimes you just know when you meet someone that they are a good officer. The two of us probably differ a little in style, but we got on well, had comparable notions about ourselves, were of a similar age and had similar family situations.

We became close friends quite quickly in Brisbane, working in sister units in the same base. On the day of the accident Joe got his fiancée's sister to drive him up to the accident site from Brisbane to collect our car and babysit our dog. He did it without question or hesitation. He pretty much lived in the hospital over the first few days, helping Rita and keeping me company, talking about everything and anything, which was much appreciated. It was during this period that I saw the true meaning of 'mateship'.

The ADF, and Australians in general, place a big emphasis on 'mateship', which, as you might have guessed, means to help out your mates in times of need. How ironic it was then that an ex-Paddy and a Brit officer were exemplifying it in a hospital ward in the heart of Queensland.

In that initial period I found that the nights were the most difficult time. I was woken every few hours to get my next hit of pain and nerve relief (they gave me a mix of relievers both intravenously and in the belly), but in truth, I found it very difficult to sleep anyway, especially with the halo on. It didn't help that being in the one position for hours without being able to move was intensely frustrating. The wardies would visit every few hours throughout the day and night and roll me, but once they left you in position that was it. If I was in pain an hour later, the process of calling them had to start all over again. A tube had been positioned near my mouth and attached to the bed for me to blow on to call for assistance, but sometimes it might slightly move away from my mouth and I couldn't reach it. As it got bright in the morning, my eyes would water and begin to sting badly. I needed to be 'squared away' first thing in the morning: my eyes wiped, my nose cleared, or whatever immense frustration that I had been stuck with all night fixed, such as an itch, an awkward pillow position or the bed sheet having slipped off my chest.

After two nights in the ward, with very little sleep due to discomfort and noise, I confided in Rita that the early mornings were particularly difficult for me, as after I called staff it would take quite a while for them to come around and I was in a lot of distress with the pain relief wearing off. The next morning, at 5.30 a.m., I noticed a shadowed figure sitting in the chair alongside me. A worried night nurse came over quite quickly, asking what the hell this person thought they were doing. I could tell it was Joe. I guessed Rita had mentioned to him how uncomfortable the morning was for me and he had offered to do the early morning shift to give her a little time to relax. He was kicked out by the nurse but returned at 7 a.m. on the dot with a coffee and newspaper in hand. He proceeded to clean me up, and stayed talking and helping all day. I joked with him about his being a night-stalker; in reality, it was an amazing and kind gesture.

I was completely unable to fend for myself – a fact I was not comfortable with – and a person I had only known for a little over three months was showing me what true mateship was all about. Also, I think he immediately understood my mindset, and therefore was able to relate to and talk with me at length. He didn't ask how terrible this all was but instead asked about the training I had been doing the previous week and told me that I'd be back to it soon. He said what a great challenge it would be to get out of all this, knowing that was exactly how I was viewing it. Any time I mention to him and Sarah (Joe's then fiancée and now wife, who was away during the first few days but who, along with her family, also showed us immense kindness and support) how grateful I was and still am, it's as if he just took out my bins or walked the dog. 'No big deal, sure what would you expect someone to do?'

In the initial days, during a phone call with my dad, something he said really stuck with me. He cited a conversation he and I had had over a few drinks prior to my emigration. I had asked him if there were any goals he really wanted to achieve now that he was finished working. He smiled and said no, that he was very happy. He asked me the same question. 'I have done a lot of challenging activities throughout my life to date but I would like to try one of the ultra-endurance races as a test of character,' I said.

He reminded me of this conversation during our phone call. 'You wanted a really tough challenge; well here it is: the challenge of your life. So it's up to you now to conquer this. It's your biggest challenge yet.'

Joe had also been hammering this same point home. It really resonated with me.

Joe wasn't the only person providing me with support during these initial stages. Rita was bombarded with messages on both her and my phone. Emails, texts and WhatsApp messages flooded in. Friends of ours had gathered in the hospital and were really helping out.

I wasn't aware of it at the time, but my family back in Ireland were finding it difficult to cope. A fundraising-type Facebook page had been created by army friends of mine, knowledge of which was kept from me, as my family were angered by its existence because it assumed we would need financial assistance. My father made a number of unfriendly phone calls in order to have the page deleted. Months later, when I was told about this, I was annoyed at my family, first for not telling me, but also for the way they treated people who were clearly attempting to assist, even if the application was a little misplaced. I never saw the page. I was told it had over 1,600 likes within two days. I hope the pictures were kind!

The Facebook page also clearly illustrates how quickly word moves in today's world. People in our local village, Watergrasshill, were commiserating with my mother, 'Sorry for your troubles', as if I were dead! It was obviously a distressing time for my family and friends in Ireland as they were only receiving information second-hand, like everyone else. I understood that all the messages, no matter how ill-informed or inaccurate, showed that people cared. 'Heart in the right place' sentiments, which I greatly appreciated. Rita would read out the texts to me as they came in. Messages of wonderful meaning from college mates, Irish Army guys, all ranks from each posting, friends from home, extended family, a lot of Rita's friends; many people I had come across throughout my life. These only motivated me even more. I wanted so much to be able to one day say to all those people that their kind words kept me on the straight path. I felt like they had made an effort to reach out to me, so I should try to repay their kindness with my best efforts.

Unfortunately, all the kind wishes in the world couldn't distract me enough from the pain. The P&O crew arrived back at my bedside, complete with toolbox to administer some more torture. That's really what it was like. If you have ever seen a halo user with the pins inserted into their skull, you know it looks like a medieval torture device. I can confirm that it feels like it too.

When they had fitted my halo two days previously, it didn't seem so bad; uncomfortable, but not overly painful. This time was different. It was excruciating. I remember my father playing with us when we were kids and sometimes grabbing our head between his hands and pushing inward with his elbows out, like a vice grip. Nothing painful, but enough that you had to fight him off to break free. This was a similar kind of inward pressure, only this time it felt as if my skull was being crushed, like my head was going to crack open from the pressure and I couldn't break free. The trainee had a screwdriver-like tool to push the pins inward to the required pressure. 8lbs for each pin. The screwdriver was twisted until it made a loud crunching sound, signifying that the required pressure was reached, and then lost traction on the pin. As the pins were driven into my head, a strong vibration and noise flowed through the steel and penetrated my brain.

The trainee was very apologetic as screams of pain escaped through my gritted teeth during this procedure. John, the senior team member, ensured she moved quickly to the next pin until all were at the correct pressure. By the time they left I was in *a lot* of pain. To deal with this I just went very quiet and tried to concentrate on breathing and relaxing. It slowly subsided over the next number of hours to a more manageable level.

I had had very slight improvements in my movements by this point, particularly in my legs below the knee, but the catheter, initially inserted on the first night in ICU when I was dosed up on morphine, was now causing me a lot of distress. After day three, the nurses warned me that I would have to have it changed. Not ideal considering I had some feeling inside my penis and general core, but couldn't move an inch. Gentlemen reading this, prepare to start grimacing.

I found the catheter removal very painful. It is as horrible an experience as one would imagine. It's like something being pulled from inside your lower stomach out through the tip of your penis. Oh wait, that's exactly what it is. The nurse on duty then grabbed a new lubricated catheter and in it slid, up my tip, passing through my urethra until it reached my bladder, accompanied by my loud groans. The only benefit to this entire process was that I couldn't move to flinch and I couldn't see any part of the procedure.

It didn't feel right at all when the new catheter was slid up inside me. I had been lucky enough to never experience this process prior to this injury, so I wasn't sure how it should feel, but while it was entering through my penis it felt like she got it stuck or caught on something inside me. It didn't feel like the first time a few days earlier, although I was quite medicated then. I have so much admiration for the nursing staff in the PA, and nurses in general, but I have to say I thought this particular nurse was not very good. She seemed a little rushed yet unsure.

Later that night the senior night-duty nurse noticed that my catheter bag was not filling. She grabbed an ultrasound device and scanned my bladder, which was full. There was blood exiting from the top of my penis, oozing along the outside of the tube. She told me she would have to change the catheter again. I was not a happy camper but it was key that I remained calm, cool and accepted the pain about to come. I asked them to load me with painkillers and I stared up at the ceiling as she went at me.

'In the fell clutch of circumstances,
I have not winced nor cried aloud,
Under the bludgeonings of chance,
my head is bloodied but unbowed.'

I repeated the lines like a mantra as the nurses told me to take a breath, then breathe out slowly as they very quickly extracted the catheter. They hurriedly prepared the new catheter and, using a lot of lubrication and force, wedged it up my penis and eventually onward through to my bladder. They then watched the bag attached to my bed carefully, hoping that I would start draining quickly. Although in a lot of stinging pain, I felt relief almost instantly as the urine exited my body into the bag below.

Afterwards, I took stock of my somewhat dire situation. I was motionless on my back, in a chest brace, halo squeezing my skull, with a catheter up my bloody penis, in a lot of pain. This most certainly was the challenge of a lifetime that my dad had spoken about.

6

SCRATCH

I was crawling through the cold sludge as fast as I could, fighting hard to keep any part of my weapon dry, with my webbing, clothing and day sack, soaked through and absorbing the filthy brown water, weighing me down even further. I somehow got beached in the sludge and couldn't move. Staff started zoning in. They were screaming, bending down over me, while muddy water dripped off the front of my helmet into my grimacing face, sliding off my nose and chin.

I was leopard crawling as hard as I could, really going for it, and I reached down, attempting to get any purchase from the mud as they jeered, abused and belittled me. But I went nowhere. After enough shouting, one of the staff jumped into the pool, grabbed me by the day sack and flung me forward about one foot into the sludge. A massive sense of relief came over me as I got some purchase from the soft mud below me and managed to squirm my way out. Thank God.

I stood up and immediately felt the cold mud and water race towards the bottom of my trousers and boots. Still under intense abuse, I shuffled as fast as I could until I caught up with the rest of the course and joined in as we began raising our weapons over our heads, then out in front, then over our heads again while jogging on the spot. Once the staff were satisfied that enough pain had been inflicted with this round of exercises, we were turned around and ran back into the sludge, to crawl through again. And again. And again.

We had arrived back to the compound on the Sunday afternoon and it didn't take long to kick off. We were split into small teams and sent off out onto the Curragh plains, usually such a picturesque sight. At this stage, I felt our bodies had been almost acclimatised to a certain level of beasting. I had already lost well over a stone in weight but I wasn't as nervous for Scratch as I had been on the first night. Maybe I was gaining confidence in terms of actually passing this wretched course. I was relatively confident that I would be able to complete Scratch, even though there was no doubt that it would be horrendous.

They started by getting the teams to conduct practice drills across the plains towards the tank-tracks, as if under fire. They added in plenty of additional physical tasks en-route, such as crawling, moving heavy objects as a team, push-ups, fireman carries or anything else they could think of. At the tank-tracks, we were run around for a number of laps through the heavy sludge, muddy water and very sharp hills. These hills were usually designed to test cross-country, four-wheel driving, not two-legged nut jobs. Tank-track sessions equate to the kind of crazy mud runs you see people paying for these days, only on steroids and perhaps ecstasy too. Try doing all that with a weapon, webbing, combat clothing and plenty of soaked equipment in a rucksack to slow you down. I will never pay to do that stuff!

The actual tank-tracks are dirt- and stone-laden lanes that rise up steep inclines and then back down into large pools of ice-cold, brown, muddy water. The lanes are all linked in a sadistic route that rises and falls around the steep knolls perfectly designed to destroy the legs and lungs of anyone willing to dare attempt them. The tracks continue through the waist-deep water pools and while the centre-line of track is slightly shallower, it can be soft and thick, which is not ideal for these types of exercises. Annual rumours around the Curragh Camp prior to a selection course include that of a fire truck being seen at the tank-tracks, filling the pools with even more water.

Staff consistently tricked us as we struggled through the tests. 'Just one more lap of the tank tracks, fellas, max effort!' only to realise that even after a maximum effort we would be sent through again. But anything other than maximum effort would be noted. This wasn't just intense physical pressure, but in fact was more an intense test of mental toughness. Would you give up? Would you snap? Would you look out for yourself only? It was all an assessment. A complete character assessment. Stripping everything else away, staff needed to observe you at your weakest as only then would the truth emerge; only then would real heart – or the lack of it – be seen.

After what seemed like an eternity, we ran down to the road that runs between two of the Curragh's famous training hills, Flagstaff and Semaphore. (The latter was actually used in the movie *Braveheart* as one of the battlefields.) Semaphore Hill is over 700m in distance from bottom to top, with a rising incline all the way up to a flagpole and a copse of trees. We raced up and down Semaphore with stretchers carrying sandbags, jerry cans and ammo tins. Again, and again and again, soaked in heavy mud and filth from head to toe. My body was weak. My legs were like jelly. My back could barely remain upright as we each grabbed a corner of weighted stretcher.

We were placed in small groups and linked together, arms wrapped around the waist of the man in front, and then had to race our opponents up the hill. Leaning my head against the back of the man in front, I faced our opponents and I caught J Bag's eye. He looked terrible. Caked in mud, helmet slanted off his head, he looked in serious physical pain. As we gazed at each other we both started smiling and almost broke into a full laugh at each other. If either of us had had the strength to talk, we would have said, 'Look at the state of you!'

We finally finished the hill shuttles on top of Semaphore, which by now had been summited numerous times. Those of us who remained consolidated as a group with all the staff. After a few choice words from the OIC, the course was instructed to form into two ranks and turn to the left. Still in soggy, destroyed kit, clothing and weapons, we shuffled our way down through the back of the rifle ranges, onto the middle road that runs directly through the camp, all the way back to the ARW compound.

The eerie silence through the dimly lit red-brick camp was only broken by the shuffling of filthy soldiers carrying army kit, and random shouts of abuse. Anyone peering around a curtain from their warm bedroom would have thought this was some sort of crazy dream. Some sort of torture for the dishevelled men in helmets, delivered by the strong men in dark-green berets. One could have well thought, *I wonder what they did to deserve that?* We volunteered.

It was early morning when we arrived back into the ARW compound. We were lined up against a wall as a staff member pointed a fire hose in our direction. After a thorough spraying, we attempted to clean everything in the MTC. We didn't get much sleep before we were kicked back out to start our Ranger tests. Having completed each of the tests once already on the course, I found them relatively comfortable. We didn't get too much beasting in between tests and we were actually afforded time to get some rest and sleep. In fact, they even drove us to and from meals, which had not been the case prior to this.

We conducted two tests on Monday, Tuesday and Wednesday without too much difficulty. Usually a staff member travelled in the back of the trucks with us, but after Fore Man/Aft Man on Thursday no one jumped in. Fifteen candidates remained. I decided to say a few words in the truck on the way back. I didn't say much, other than that we were in it together, we had gone through a lot and no one should contemplate an RTU now. We needed each other for the ground phase.

That evening, the OIC gave us a fictitious situation to set the scene for our ten-day tactical exercise and then listed our initial mission and tasks. I was one of the section commanders (that being a four- or five-man section) and Doug was the patrol commander. We immediately began preparing our kit and equipment in the MTC. Doug was asked to stay behind with one of the other candidates. When he joined us after, he announced that he had been given an official warning: if the insertion patrol didn't go well under his command, he would be removed from the course.

As we continued our kit preparations, a few candidates made loud comments similar to pre-match dressing-room talk: 'Big effort guys, let's not leave Doug down'; 'Some of the guys are under pressure to perform. Let's help them out, yeah?'

As Doug delivered orders that night, I thought the task seemed peculiar; in fact I wondered whether this could be another mind trick. During the initial mission brief from the OIC, he had outlined our drop-off point and our 'Agent' contact point. The distance was 26km over the Dublin and Wicklow Mountains. I didn't need to do a detailed map inspection to understand that the task being set was almost impossible. I had heard rumours that the initial patrol during this phase of selection was usually very challenging, but this seemed extreme. I had no real context from previous courses, but I was concerned for us as this seemed like an excessive distance to patrol. We were essentially inserting from the Kilbride Rifle Range in Dublin to close to the Glen of Imaal in Wicklow. Something told me this was not normal.

Some of the guys weighed their packs before we stepped off but I didn't want to. In this case, not knowing was better. That number would only seep into your hips, shoulders and head as time wore on. Packs weighed up to 120lbs without adding the webbing or weapon. Each section also had to carry a General Purpose Machine Gun, which we rotated between us as it was much heavier than the normal assault rifle. Commanders carried baby Sincgar radios and we all took spare batteries. Having noted the kit we were carrying, and applying the most basic of maths, I could tell that this insertion was not achievable within the time frame.

***

We hit the drop-off point at 4 a.m. and kicked on immediately. Within minutes my concerns about our proposed timeline to meet the Agent were realised. As with almost every exercise I have ever conducted in Wicklow, the first few kilometres were directly up the side of a mountain. We struggled badly. We shifted from foot to foot slowly over mountains, saddles and re-entrants throughout the day. Someone would inevitably fall and have to wriggle like a turtle until they fought back to their feet. If someone else was close enough, they slowly made their way over and helped pull them to their feet. It was mind-numbing, energy-sapping stuff. Hour after hour after hour, slogging over the hills. The lonely, back-breaking plod only broken every so often by someone flopping down fifty feet to your front or behind.

Tactical movement was attempted, but it was near impossible to conduct drills correctly. I occasionally checked in with Doug to see how he was doing. He was working hard to lead the patrol but his lips were bloody and cracked and he looked pale and dishevelled. The OIC was constantly on his case that we were too slow, not conducting drills correctly and that no one was working for him. As opposed to not assisting our commander, it was more the case of each patrol member desperately attempting to remain semi-upright.

The remaining course members were good men. The course had been effective in leaving only a small number of candidates. The experience we were sharing together gave us a real sense of togetherness, even if we didn't speak to each other for hours on end during the walk.

I was extremely impressed with a few guys in particular. Corporal R was a completely wired guy from Cork, who seemed like he was on some sort of 'buzz' all the time. I genuinely thought he was a bit mad, and after working with the guy a number of years later, I can confirm a few things:

1)   Obviously, no drugs.

2)   He is an excellent operator.

3)   He is as mad as a box of frogs.

Private B was a quiet guy from Dundalk who had done time in the French Foreign Legion. Private S had been in the Irish Regiment in the British

Army, then joined the Irish Defence Forces and had only recently come through his recruit training. I thought these guys were exceptional in terms of their mental and physical fitness. Private S conducted the entire course in the old, basic-issue barrack boots. Not once did he complain. He was the complete military professional, the best soldier I had ever seen.

We kept slogging along until, at a certain stage in the evening, the course OIC pulled us together on the side of one of the mountains. We had been going for fourteen hours straight at a speed of just about 1km an hour. It was impossible to move any quicker over the terrain with the weight we were carrying. We were nowhere near meeting our Agent contact that night. We were spent. Candidates were falling over at an alarming rate.

Although I had always felt I had a strong back, I was feeling the degradation on my body. My shoulders felt like they might rip backwards clean off my body at any stage and my back was ready to snap over into a neat half. The respite of the OIC pulling us together was welcomed by my beat-up body. I looked around at the others. It was the closest we had been to each other since we began the patrol.

At this stage, I could read the facial expressions of my fellow candidates. We were in trouble. Some guys had a look of despair written behind their eyes. Doug's body looked weak as he slumped into the small ditch on the side of another heartbreaking mountain. I felt how he looked. From nowhere, a truck appeared far below us on a road. The OIC pointed to the truck and asked if anyone wanted to get in.

One candidate put up his hand. The OIC told the rest of us to confer with him for two minutes. I got on well with the guy. We had spoken at length a few times. He had attempted the previous course and almost made it. He had been through more time on selection than most, but still wanted to quit. He decided he still wanted to go after the others spoke to him. I didn't speak to him. If he wanted to go now, he didn't deserve to pass.

Some say that the idea to request to withdraw or RTU can come as a 'brain fart' to candidates. To me, however, if you want to succeed badly enough, that request never crosses your lips. Ever. If it takes external factors to realign your self-belief, then you don't have the intrinsic motivation required to be an SF soldier. Simply put, no one else should have to motivate you. Although I was in a bad way, and I knew we were failing badly at our task, I never thought to quit. I'm sure others in the group were of the same mindset.

As the OIC walked him down towards the truck, a second truck showed up about 200m further down the road. The other staff member turned to the rest of our patrol and directed us off the side of the mountain and into the second truck. Our companion gazed over in disgust as we shuffled down a few hundred metres from him while he boarded the first truck.

Then it became apparent what had just happened: we just had to keep going until *someone* gave up. The staff member turned to me and said, 'Bet he feels silly now!' It must have broken his heart and spirit. I felt sorry for him, knowing that, if he had held out, the end would have been closer than he thought.

The staff member with us during that patrol was a demon named Corporal M. He was exceptionally fit and also really smart. He also knew how to constantly mess with your mind. Corporal M would act relaxed around a candidate who would inevitably let something slip or let his guard down, and he would then smash him with this information at a later stage. He worked me over hard throughout the course but I can't say I hated him the most. I hated him, but I hated others more! He knew how to get into my head, though. He constantly told me that, as an officer, I wasn't good enough, that I was very close to being pulled off the course any day now, that the OIC thought I was no good. He would constantly critique my actions with open-ended comments ensuring I doubted myself. It made me incredibly paranoid.

We got into the truck and it drove us to a point closer to our Agent contact. When we got out, two other candidates, one from Kildare and one from Dundalk, pulled out. They were close buddies and one convinced the other that a few pints of cold cider would be better than this. I didn't wish to change their minds or give them a second chance. In all honesty, I resented their quitting. *Thanks for giving the rest of us your radio, batteries, anti-armour weapon and anything else awkward and heavy.* Not only did they lack the hunger and strength of character to stay, but they also had not a shred of empathy for the rest of us, knowing that we'd be carrying their kit for the next week.

Now just twelve remained.

Doug was still under a lot of pressure as we set off again to reach our Agent contact and eventually try to set up a patrol harbour (a hideout close to the target location). Corporal M kept it up.

'How'd you think your buddy Doug is doin'?'

'He's doin' well, in my opinion, DS.' (Directing Staff – how we addressed all staff.)

'In *your* opinion? Well in mine he's completely fucked this patrol and none of ye are helping him either.'

Back to the mind games again.

It's your fault. You're performing badly. You only look out for yourself. It is very difficult not to let thoughts like that eat at you while you're lumping the equivalent of a fridge around the Wicklow Mountains. I had to stay positive. It was very hard to tell when it was a genuine 'you're not good enough' or a mind game 'you're not good enough'. I think maybe it was half and half. I know there were plenty of times throughout the course where I did not perform well and I was deserving of a poor appraisal. But I would continue to give my best and if that wasn't good enough for the ARW then fair enough. They would have to remove me from the course.

We finally got to the rendezvous (RV) point with the Agent contact just as it got dark, at approximately 10 p.m. We managed to create a hasty patrol harbour and got an hour or two of rest before the next task. Doug thought he might have failed his assessment as the patrol commander for the insertion but the OIC left him on the course with us. J Bag and I rotated as patrol commander for the rest of the course. Doug never got another command appointment.

With around three days to go (it is difficult to recall when you are so tired) the OIC walked into a patrol harbour while I was on lookout or 'stag'. He had a very quick talk with Doug at his shell scrap (hole), and then Doug picked up all his kit and walked out.

He dropped down and touched my shoulder as he passed the 6 o'clock position.

'Best of luck on the rest of the course, Bill.'

'What's going on? They pulled you off?'

'Yep, see you on the far side.'

His face was distraught. Everyone else was dumbstruck. Disappointment and fear now consumed us. If Doug was pulled off, then who'd be next? Until now, candidates had RTUed of their own accord but no one had been removed from the course by the staff. We were bitterly disappointed for

Doug as it was very difficult to see success snatched from someone with whom you had endured so much. I knew he had an exceptional heart, even if on the course some things did not go as planned for him. It also added fuel to my paranoia.

Corporal M was staff later that day. He whispered to me, 'I told you he was going … and you're next.'

After the course, there was lots of speculation and controversy among my officer cohort over why Doug was kept on the course for so long after the insertion walk through the mountains. The most devious story was that Doug was always going to fail, even before the course started, and they had just strung him along. I don't believe that. The second was that they kept him on after the insertion as punishment and binned him with a few days to go. I'm not sure about that one either.

I don't know why Doug was kept on after the insertion. Maybe they wished to give him further exposure on the ground phase, or were just taking time to deliberate and analyse his performance. I can only imagine how difficult it was for him. He had put his 'cock on the block' and given his absolute best effort. The strength, courage and determination he displayed were outstanding, even if his application was not what the ARW was looking for. Lots of army folk talk the talk but, unless you walk the walk, you should reserve judgement on those who have been brave enough to put their hand up.

***

Throughout the ground phase of this exercise we would often do some sort of reconnaissance of an area, conduct a direct action and then insert into a new area by foot, before repeating the action. We were required to intersperse these actions with a lot of water and food patrols. Water patrols consisted of us taking a consolidated load of empty water bottles, finding the nearest clean water source and filling up, while dropping in sterilisation tablets. Food drops were placed by staff at grid references and we sent small groups out to collect the ration packs. Food drops were always booby-trapped with trip flares, so we had to be very careful when collecting them, as triggering a booby trap would mean we would have to leave the area immediately with haste, and without enough food.

It was difficult to maintain awareness of what day it was or how long was left in order to complete the ground phase. During an earlier part of the ground phase I commanded an ambush but was so tired I forgot to give the command 'Searchers out' post-ambush. This command is given after an ambush has been sprung and we are satisfied we have completed the mission. Once the command to cease fire is given, the commander will order certain members tasked as searchers out to the ambush area to inspect the battle damage, before returning and then leaving the area. I had a complete brain-freeze moment and one of the patrol had to prompt me. The staff hammered me in my debrief and they said that on the ambush initiation I had pointed my weapon at one of the other candidates. I hadn't, but this wasn't somewhere you could say you were being wronged. It ate me up that my performance hadn't gone as well as I would expect from myself.

We moved on to our last few days. I remained as patrol commander and they constantly bounced us from one position to the next, making us go through emergency procedures in our hastily constructed patrol harbour every few hours. Staff would walk in, ask a few questions then fire off some blank ammunition. We would conduct emergency rally drills, move from that patrol base to another, fighting through insane trees and terrain, then set up again, conduct local patrols, check communications, create a track plan, start digging shell scrapes, drawing range cards; essentially establishing a routine, until they came in and it started all over again. It was absolutely soul-destroying.

Some of the candidates were on the verge of mutiny.

'Why even bother trying to establish routine? They are going to come in and find something incorrect and just move us to a new location anyway.'

I found this argument quite compelling and difficult to fight against; only, clearly, it was not the right thing to do. It was a test of both our mental patience and my leadership. I told the other candidates that I agreed that we would most likely be moved on again but if we didn't try to establish a routine it would only reflect badly on us. We all knew that to be the truth – the men were just voicing their frustration.

Somewhere during our dazed and half-asleep state, we realised it was the last night when the OIC told us to start preparing our kit for the walk back in the morning. Myself, J Bag and two others got tasked with a final food patrol that night so everyone would have full rations for breakfast in the morning.

Two of us stopped short of the food drop (also known as a dead letterbox), while J Bag and the other man moved to the collection point. They came back to RV with us but didn't use the correct link-up procedure. It was exceptionally dark in the middle of a forest and we were shattered. We didn't recognise them so we laid low, let them pass and started our emergency RV drills. Wait one hour, then back to the last known RV and repeat.

Suddenly the OIC stormed around the forest, shouting for me. We jumped out of the treeline. He asked what the hell we were doing. I explained and he almost got tongue-tied.

'Eh … fine. Now get back to the patrol harbour and get some rest. NOW.'

I got the impression he wanted this patrol to be quick and easy in order to maximise our rest and energy for the following morning. Nothing, however, is easy in that state. Even climbing over the three-foot forest fence took a massive amount of physical effort and concentration, something akin to a bunch of pensioners climbing stairs. At this late stage in the course, I was so paranoid that I thought the staff were still trying to trick us by pretending to be our patrol mates and then would destroy us for incorrect drills.

We kicked off the walk back early the next morning. The 'walk back' is typical of army terminology. For something that sounds pretty innocuous, it most definitely is not. It has always been the culminating activity for a selection course. A speed march on foot from the Wicklow Mountains straight into the ARW compound in the Curragh Camp. I've walked this route four times in total in my life, and it has never been enjoyable. Speed-walk a marathon distance with full marching order after conducting a full selection course. It takes approximately seven hours. It is mind-numbing, back- and hip-breaking walking. It's not actually walking either; it's a long speedy power stride which really kills the 'short arses' (army slang for shorter individuals).

We swapped around the machine guns, and stayed in a two-man column while not leaving any space between rows, as that would seriously impede the man behind. I used high-neck Meindl boots throughout the ground phase of the course and for the walk back. They really kept my feet together. I would lather up Bridgedale socks with Dove soap the night before any speed march and it always worked very well for me. I was lucky not to get any blisters, but towards the end my feet were quite tender and I was aching everywhere.

After passing through Kilcullen, I knew we were close to finishing but, unfortunately, this knowledge didn't help the pain go away. I was confident I would finish the course but was afraid that they would still deem me incompetent or not good enough. The mind games were still zipping around in my head. One of the guys almost passed out with about 2.5 miles to go, so we gave him extra water and sugar on the go, and he kept upright, just about.

We marched straight down the middle of the camp and into the compound, along the same road we had been running down almost two weeks previously during Scratch. It felt very different now, though. This was the end, not the start. As we passed the dining complex, I saw soldiers staring out at us. They looked on in quiet amazement, or maybe disgust.

As we approached the front entrance of the ARW compound we all seemed to gain strength from somewhere. My back, which had been arched over for what seemed like weeks, suddenly straightened upright and I looked forward with my head high. The entire unit was lined up at the front entrance and clapped us in.

It felt so emotional. Without doubt it was the greatest feeling of my life. I did it. I actually did it. I was far too weak to show it, but I was ecstatic. I may have attempted a smile. The pain was gone for a few glorious minutes. After all the disappointments and distinct lack of winners' medals in my life, nothing came close to that moment. I had completely immersed myself into this course. This was a total commitment of my body, mind and soul and I, alongside some fantastic other guys, had succeeded. After putting ourselves out there, challenging ourselves beyond our limits, we stood there physically destroyed but completely unbroken.

Out of the night that covers me,
Black as the pit from pole to pole,
I thank whatever gods may be,
For my unconquerable soul.

We slid our packs off our backs and every unit member came up and shook hands with us. We got a quick course photo and went into the MTC, where fresh food and cold beer awaited us. We just sat on the benches completely spent, not saying much but absolutely thrilled.

Eleven of us completed the course. One of the candidates had to be hooked up to an IV drip once we got into the MTC. It didn't bother him too much as he was too tired to care. That night, after a fantastic sleep, we were taken out to Swifts nightclub in Newbridge by the staff but were way too beat to enjoy ourselves – we were barely able to prop ourselves upright at the bar.

It was one of the most satisfying experiences of my life but it wasn't long until I wanted more. Almost immediately after the FIANÓGLACH tab presentations, the other ranks were taken to one side and briefed on their seven-month reinforcement training-cycle continuum. As a 2nd lieutenant with no overseas experience, I knew I couldn't be selected for further training at this stage, even though I wanted to be. I really wanted to join those guys with whom I had just gone through hell. I wanted something more than just this tab. I wanted to serve in this unit. Somewhere in the middle of the course, it seems my extrinsic motivators had waned and been replaced. I had proved to everyone that I could do it but now that didn't matter. Now, I wanted to work with the best.

I had a long way to go though, to be considered: college, overseas, promotion to captain. But, for now, I had gotten the hard part out of the way: I had passed the Special Forces selection course.

The following day when we got released, the sun was splitting the stones. J Bag and I were the last to leave as MOB had given us a little pep talk about how we were so stupid to do the course as young 2nd lieutenants, and most importantly, how, now that we had completed the course, we needed to keep our bibs clean in order to ever have a chance of actually serving in the unit. I was so happy I didn't really care what he was saying. I hopped into my Fiat Bravo, put in a Daft Punk CD and turned it up loud. I was buzzing. I rang my family to let them know about this massive achievement. My mam came on the phone.

'Hey mam, I've got news, I passed the course. Can you believe that?'

'Yeah, that's great, Billy,' she replied in a very underwhelming fashion. I was a bit miffed by her reaction. I hadn't really explained the course in great detail but she had a good idea.

'Billy, sorry but I've bad news. Jeff [our family dog] is dead.' She started sobbing down the phone.

Way to kill the buzz, Mam!

7

I'M GOING TO BE BACK

PRINCESS ALEXANDRA HOSPITAL, BRISBANE, AUSTRALIA – JANUARY 2015

January 2015, what were you doing? From wherever you were, imagine you were instead in a hospital room in sunny Queensland. Smell the disinfectant, listen to the constant chattering of staff and the dinging of nurse bells. Visualise the ceiling over the hospital bed and eye every little detail on the off-white panel directly overhead. Feel the pain and discomfort across your body emanating from nowhere specifically but seemingly everywhere. Attempt to scratch your nose or wipe your stinging, watery eyes and yet remain perfectly still. Hear your wife and friends talk to you as you strain your peripheral vision as much as it can take, as you desperately believe, for a moment, that you have forced your body to reorient itself towards them. You haven't. No one even knows you tried to move. To be alive but to not be able to move is like suddenly not living, or at least not living as you knew it before.

On a number of occasions, I was briefed by spinal specialists who said that most gains happen during the initial six months of an SCI, and thereafter it would be diminishing returns. It was confirmed that I was now a diagnosed quadriplegic (or tetraplegic, as it is officially termed). I was told that I had an incomplete SCI, meaning the spinal cord was damaged but not completely severed and, therefore, there was a chance of return of function. Of course, no one knew how much function would return. My type of quadriplegia was called CCS, meaning my upper body would be more affected if my level of paralysis decreased. My level of injury was classified as 'C3/C4', meaning that the point of injury (cervical vertebrae 3 and 4 in my neck) was called a 'high-level' injury. Statistically, high-level SCIs have less recovery and more complications as more of the body is affected. All told, it was a very serious diagnosis but with some potential room for improvement.

After a week of paralysis, I knew what I had to do. I had to fight as hard as I could to get better. I was never to be lazy or allow myself to take the easy option. I was never to feel sorry for myself and would not allow myself to get frustrated or angry. The gap between what I *could* get back and what I *would* get back rested squarely on me. *It is what it is.* I could keep telling myself and everyone else how I had to stay positive and work hard, but unless I actually followed through on this talk, it was worth nothing to me. When it comes to remaining positive in times of adversity, actions do speak louder than words.

I was so uncomfortable during this period that it was difficult to sleep. I embraced the relief of being rolled onto my side as the temporary pain relief, even if it only lasted thirty seconds, and the break from my ceiling view were most welcome. I'd drift off, then wake up maybe an hour or ninety minutes later, uncomfortably numb through my neck, back and legs. I'd call for help, using the blow tube placed alongside my lips, but it might take help five to ten minutes to arrive.

The wardies who helped move me were predominantly older men, with plenty of stories and good cheer. They were employed to move fools like me around the hospital, ward or bed. There was an elderly wardie from Dublin who came to my aid from time to time. I knew him not only by his thick accent but also his distinctive multi-coloured socks that I was faced towards while they tipped me sideways so far that I was leaning over the side of the bed. A nurse would then inspect my back and bottom for bed sores or any issues before reporting the 'all clear'.

I would lie there, lifeless, in the mostly dark room, half asleep. I had no perception of where my arms were, or what position my legs were in. I was barely existing. The abbreviated phrase 'FML' (fuck my life) seemed appropriate during these long nights. Sometimes, I opted to stay lying on my side wedged up with an array of pillows. However, it wouldn't be long before massive discomfort again seeped through my body.

Throughout this period I used all sorts of mindfulness techniques to assist me in managing pain. I visualised blue skies or still open water. I worked on breathing exercises. I recited songs. These drills were re-enacted countless times, day and night, over what seemed like a haze of time.

Other patients in the ward were a frustration. There were two old ladies on the other side of the split room, one of whom was very confused and aggressive towards staff. She raised her voice a lot. She told staff they were keeping her against her will and that she was being abused. She most certainly was not being abused and the staff were incredibly patient with her. When I eventually was moved to the spinal unit I shouted over, 'G'luck Mary, don't let them get to you,' just for the banter. She hadn't a clue who had said it to her. It was a just small moment of fun for me.

Then there was The Screamer. He was aggressive and throughout the night would roar constantly as loud as he could just to be purposely disruptive. It upset everybody. He swore and called the staff horrible names. It was clear that he had serious mental-health issues, but that was little consolation to the rest of us on the ward who were just trying to get some rest.

One particular night, he roared out that he wanted water. The nurse politely told him that he couldn't drink at this time as he had a procedure in the morning and it could jeopardise his safety. It got to the stage where the conversation turned ridiculous. He kept asking for water while calling the nurse every name he could think of, as she continued to remind him that it was not safe for him. In an attempt to quieten him, she eventually told him if he took the water he could seriously harm himself or even die. He screamed, 'Give it to me anyway, you cunt.' I took this as my opportunity to shut him up, saying as loudly as I could muster, 'Yeah, please give it to him, so when he dies the rest of us can get some fuckin' sleep.' Two nurses dived in past my curtain, laughing, and he shut up a few mutters thereafter.

***

I had lots of visitors throughout January. It really helped. I couldn't move, was in constant, immense pain, had a tube wedged up my penis into my bladder and had four pins screwed into my head for my steel halo brace. So distractions were very welcome.

Army officer friends visited regularly with spouses. We talked 'shop' and just nonsense most of the time, but it was a great comfort. My direct boss (OC) and his right-hand man, the Company Sergeant Major, visited. The interaction was a little awkward but the sentiment was very thoughtful. I think they didn't really know what to say. What would I have said? *How you doing?* The platoon commanders directly subordinate to me also called in. They were all good guys and I enjoyed their company.

The unit padre, Leo Orreal, called in a number of times. He has an infectiously positive attitude. He is a big, tall, super-fit man. He talks straight and looks you in the eye when he does. He would ensure that he stood in my eyeline, as if to let me know he was there. He was so positive, full of praise and gave me a great feeling of self-worth. Through his genuine care and compassion, he made me feel loved. He told me how everyone was rooting for me back at the army base. He spent hours and hours with me displaying exceptional good will, never once telling me he didn't have time to stay. His support was incredible. He also walked our dog regularly. My family and I owe a great deal to him and, if for his sake alone, I really hope there is a heaven.

A few days after the accident, a couple of my Irish friends flew into Brisbane. Ailish and Caitriona were already on a holiday in Oz and although they hadn't planned on travelling to Brisbane, on hearing of my accident they immediately changed their itinerary and rocked up to the hospital straight off the plane.

I knew Caitriona pretty well from my college days in Limerick and Rita had gone to some fitness classes with her the year before. She has a hilariously funny stubbornness. I played some rugby and had pints with Ailish's brother, who is a very funny lad, but had only hung around a little bit with Ailish. From the little I knew of her, though, I thought she was lovely too. When they showed up it was like they knew exactly what to do, like they had been trained for something like this. They worked constantly in helping Rita at home, looking after the dog, looking after me throughout the day, getting me frozen yogurt, whatever. They were also great craic, fantastic entertainment. They fancied Joe and were joke-flirting with him constantly. When my brother, Simon, arrived on 9 January, they wanted a piece of him too (joking ... I think). They stayed for ten days and their support was immense, particularly during a time when I was in acute care. I can't put into words how much they did for us.

My oldest friend from home, Barry, flew up from Sydney to visit on a number of occasions. Another buddy from Limerick, Mark Egan, was touring around New Zealand with his girlfriend Grainne. They also re-routed their travel plans so they could visit for four days. It was an incredible gesture and the fact that he was sporting a 'man-bun' upon arrival made it all the better. Mark is a genuine, heart-on-sleeve guy, and I really appreciated his effort in visiting, and assisting while here. Sometimes a tragic event shows levels of compassion, kindness and thoughtfulness you don't realise are there in the people you know. That makes it all the more meaningful and special, I suppose. It was incredible to feel so loved and cared for.

I was delighted to see Simon on his arrival. Although we were super competitive as boys growing up, we really became close throughout our twenties and he's now my closest friend. He's my one and only brother and I love him dearly. He's an executive in German supermarket giant Lidl for a reason, but he's not domineering and reads situations well. He dealt with Rita superbly, making sure she at least tried to get some rest, while not invading the house too much and enabling her as the primary decision maker with me. He also knew how to deal with me. Like Joe, he knew to frame this not as a tragedy but as a challenge.

Simon and Rita did the vast majority of the manual care for me. If I needed my eye wiped, arms moved, teeth brushed or face shaved, they were always on-hand. I quickly became much better at articulating what exactly I needed. I was a bit uncomfortable not being able to do things for myself and, due to my own frustrations, was also probably a bit bossy as I sometimes barked out instructions to those supporting me. We tried getting into a bit of a routine, but mostly it was intense pain cycles while people stood around chatting. Sometimes we spoke about the obvious but most other times we could talk about something else, for instance when we spent hours arguing over the importance of a knowledge of history. We kept the atmosphere as light-hearted as possible and had a laugh when we could. My old rugby teammate, Joe Moynihan, visited and literally almost fell over himself when he saw me, much to the amusement of everyone else at the bedside. He had heard second-hand from Ireland that I had been injured, but this was not the sight he had expected to see.

***

More than a week after my accident, I still hadn't had a bowel movement and it was very uncomfortable. I had terrible stomach cramps which in turn completely diminished my appetite. I was being fed non-solids only, but I was done with eating soup all day. Rita or Simon would encourage me to take as many spoonfuls as possible, but I was not a great eater and was losing weight rapidly. The nurses made me a laxative drink cocktail every night and even though it tasted like absolute muck, nothing came out the far side. Day after uncomfortable day, and still nothing. I felt like I really needed to go but I had no power at all. Normally when you get the feeling that a stool is ready to pass, the body somewhat subconsciously contracts around the intestines slightly. Then, if required, one can contract further using force, bearing down. Unfortunately for me, I could do none of these things, either consciously or subconsciously.

After a few days they moved me onto a toilet for the first time. The process was so surreal. They slid a sling under each leg and around my back, then slowly used a mechanical hoist to raise me off the bed and hang in mid-air in a squatting position, with my bare ass hanging out. The hanging gave a tiny bit of relief from the stomach cramps. They put me on a high-back wheelchair with a hole in the seat and wheeled me into the toilet. I sat there for forty-five minutes. I felt so pathetic. I couldn't move at all and was just waiting hopefully for something to happen. After I was hoisted back up into bed I just lay there in disgust. I was useless, I couldn't even go to the toilet.

After over a week without passing anything it had become quite draining. All the bowel medication and laxatives with no success made for a very angry tummy. I felt like I needed to go a few times but they were all false alarms. One morning, I asked a male nurse to hoist me up on the sling and leave me hanging over the bed while he placed a pan under me. I asked him to call my brother. I didn't want Rita to see this but I was lonely just hanging there and knew I'd be there a while.

As my brother stepped past the drawn curtain and saw me I read his face. He was clearly upset to see me like this. I can only imagine how shocking it must have been for him. The indignity of it all. I was a grown man in a halo brace hanging motionless like a piece of meat over a bed, with my privates exposed, in a squat position waiting to shit. I dangled over the bed for thirty minutes as he stood to the side, attempting to ignore the ridiculous sight before him. Even though I wasn't eating much as it was very difficult to swallow in the halo, and even drinking was such a struggle that I had to make a conscious effort to force myself to hydrate (through a straw fed to me), over a week of toxins had built up inside me and I needed to get rid of them. Although hanging in that sling was quite a disheartening moment, I still had to remain focused on the goal. *Okay, this hasn't worked, but I'll sort out my bowel movements somehow. I've no idea how, but I'll keep troubleshooting until I do.*

I had another catheter change on 12 January and once again it hurt like hell. After the change I stayed quiet, focused on breathing slowly and concentrated on anything but the pain. I couldn't feel sorry for myself though. *I'm not soft*, I kept thinking. I ordered my brother to get the high-back wheelchair and to call the wardies to transfer me. Prior to the catheter change the staff had wanted me to get into the chair again for a little longer and maybe go around the ward. Due to the catheter change, however, they thought that I would stay in bed, as most patients will when having a bad day. I had to prove to myself that this was not me. I got them to hoist me into the chair and told my brother to wheel me downstairs to the front shops area. Although later that day I was very uncomfortable and desperately tired, I was happy that I had forced myself to get up. No one asked me to do it, but I was not going to take the easy option just because I was feeling poorly.

Out of the night that covers me,
Black as the pit from pole to pole,
I thank whatever gods may be,
For my unconquerable soul.

Tetraplegia doesn't just affect the central nervous system. It was also a daily, even hourly, battle of the mind. I felt as if it was designed to break one's spirit. Sooner or later, you would just give in and accept your fate. Paralysis shouts at you constantly: *'You cannot … You will never … Don't even bother trying.'*

That really positive afternoon where I forced myself to push through the pain of the catheter made me feel somewhat in control. However, it was swiftly followed by what would be one of my toughest days.

I was wheeled down to visit the Spinal Injury Unit (SIU) where I was going to be based when a bed became available. Rita, my brother, the Limerick crew and other friends of ours escorted and pushed me around in my heavy high-back wheelchair as the head nurse gave us a tour. Although it's widely regarded as one of the best spinal units in Australia, I wasn't filled with confidence. In fact, what self-assurance I had drained from me as I was wheeled around. It was quiet, it smelled of the elderly and every room just seemed to have people lying still on their beds, doing nothing. The horrible realisation came over me that I would be living here for a *very long time*, like all these people. I was a 'vegetable'. I was going to rot away down here in this unit. It looked like the kind of place where no one got better.

As I was wheeled back through the main entrance and we thanked our friends for visiting, I felt awful. The stark scene before me led to this being the lowest point so far. Not only was I sore and tired from the chair, but it just ate me up inside thinking about how I was going to be another disability in a bed. What a long way I had fallen from 'ex-Special Forces parachuting adventure racer wannabe'. I suppose it had finally sunk in that a life like that was over. This wasn't just some sort of sports injury. I hadn't broken my leg or popped my shoulder. This was a full-on life-changing accident. *I was fucking paralysed.*

***

Two days after my visit, a bed became available in SIU and I was transferred. I was rolled directly into the acute room where they monitor patients closely and have a dedicated staff. They put me into the intensive care bed, which is located by itself in a room within the acute room. Bed number forty of forty unfortunates. There was a nurses' station directly outside the window looking into the room. It felt a bit like being in a goldfish bowl, even though I could never see the nurses' station as it was over to my right.

The nursing staff in the unit immediately forced me out of my comfort zone and started challenging me. I didn't enjoy getting put into the high-back wheelchair because it hurt so much, but I knew I had to start building up my resistance. They started me on a more solid routine, which had not been the case in the previous ward due to what seemed like a severe shortage of staff. Every morning I would be tilted forward onto a hoist and lifted off the bed onto a shower-chair, taken to the bathroom to be bathed and left to attempt to go to the toilet, then hoisted back into the bed where I was then fed breakfast. A spinal unit OT would visit for an hour to attempt to reduce the rigidity in my hands and arms, making splints for my hands at night and attempting exercises to move something.

A spinal unit physio would also arrive at some stage during the day to conduct 'ASIA testing' (assessing sensation via pinprick) and do some work on my lower limbs, which included attempted foot movement, lower-leg raises or the physio manually moving my limbs through a range of motion. By now I had regained some movement in my lower legs and faint movement in my wrist. I could bend my knee slightly and straighten, but lifting a leg off the mattress was still very difficult.

My bowel and bladder troubles were at their very worst during this time. One Saturday, Barry was up from Sydney, visiting for the day. He and Simon were with me as they transitioned me from the high-back wheelchair back onto the bed for lunch. I was eating in bed as I still found it difficult to swallow, so I would eat at a heavily tilted position. I had to start developing adaptation strategies to overcome issues with the tasks of everyday living. Someone would feed me a bite of food, immediately followed by water through a straw to assist it down my throat. I ended up doing this for months. I couldn't eat things like chips as they would get caught in my throat and I'd end up almost choking.

As the nurses hoisted me up using the sling and automatic hoist to put me back into bed, I felt a throbbing pain in my penis. Already I was on my fourth catheter, each one getting wider in size to try to stop the urethral bleed by outward pressure. I was like a broken record every time I was being moved in any way, telling staff to be very cautious of the catheter. As soon as they lowered me onto the bed I could tell something wasn't right. Both the nurses hoisting and my brother seemed concerned. One scurried outside before returning promptly with the nurse team leader for the acute ward. I was bleeding heavily through my penis. Very heavily. Barry stuck his head into the room, took one look at the carnage and said he had to leave to catch his flight!

I was in a lot of pain but I couldn't see what was going on around my waist, which was a very weird experience, I have to say. Simon stood up next to my head looking down the bed, grimacing, while attempting to describe to me what was going on without alarming me too much. The nurses came back with ice and essentially had to hold it around my penis to stop the bleed inside.

After an hour, they were happy the bleed had stopped and wanted to clean the bed. The on-call urologist came in to survey the scene. He told me the only way to stop these bleeds was to keep pressure from the inside out, and calmly mentioned that he was going to insert a twenty-gauge catheter.

To put that into context, guys usually get a twelve or occasionally a fourteen-gauge with women using a sixteen gauge. But if it was going to stop all these bleeds, then it had to be done. *Right, let's get on with it.*

I kept my focus between my brother's horrified face and the ceiling.

I am the master of my fate:
I am the captain of my soul.

It felt like the most gut-wrenching interrogation I have ever received, but I was still not going to give in. *I can take all this punishment. I'm tougher than this.* Of course, that didn't stop me letting out a roar as they slid the old one out and then proceeded to stick a goalpost inside me. This was followed by hours of Zen-like breathing and quiet time. The resident psychologist had been very helpful in outlining techniques to deal with pain, such as mindfulness, imagery and breathing strategies, which were all put to use at this point.

Right what's next? Oh yeah, I still haven't gone for a shit in two weeks.

The previous day I had said to my registrar doctor that I wanted to get my bowels sorted and needed a clear out, that at this stage it was untenable. I had severe bowel cramps. She was happy for me to up my dosage of laxatives, which I had been taking twice daily. That night I took eight sachets of the strong laxative mixed into water, which tasted like shots of Jägermeister mixed with Buckfast tonic wine, albeit without any of the positive side effects.

The morning after the catheter drama, my bowels finally decided to open, with no warning. I could feel the warm liquid-like substance filling the lower half of the bed, but I was worried it might go near my penis and get it dirty. I didn't want my catheter to be removed again for sure. But I also kept pushing as hard as I could, not that it worked as I still couldn't bear down at all. The relief was amazing. It was absolutely disgusting but by now I was far from worrying about my dignity.

Simon was looking after me while the Limerick girls were out in the shops with Rita. I was glad they were not in the room for this. The smell was repugnant. The nursing staff were awesome throughout as they swarmed in and quickly tidied me up without batting an eyelid.

Two days later I was moved from the intensive care bed out to bed 37 in the acute room. I was slowly working my way up the ward, it seemed. I was feeling a little better, with less cramps and less urethral pain. I was still getting loads of visitors and my dad arrived to take over from Simon. I was gutted to see my brother leave, as he had been exceptional during my greatest time of need and managed everything just right. I was also a little disappointed for him, as the day he left I stood up for the first time. After completing a two-day handover with my dad, he had left early that morning and missed it. After all his excellent efforts during my most acute period, he wasn't present for what was clearly the most visual improvement to date. I wanted him to see it, as he had been an integral part of getting me to that point.

That makes it sound like I just casually stood up, but I can assure you that wasn't the case. I had been doing an hour in OT and physio daily. I never missed a session, no matter how difficult it was. I was hoisted into the chair from the bed and then Simon, Rita or, latterly, Dad would push me down from the ward to the physio clinic. I was building up my tolerance of sitting in the chair and was up to over five hours. Sitting with a pillow on your lap to prop up your hands, how easy it sounds! I also managed to eat my first meal in a sitting position. It was all so very basic, but every day was a progression. I worked hard in every single session. *No point in doing a session if I'm not fully committed,* I thought.

A few days before standing up, I was placed on a tilt table and the physios were very pleased with how my body responded. We also did a number of lying leg exercises to build up to the action of taking weight over my feet again. Each evening the staff placed electronic wraps around my legs to ensure blood pooling did not occur, while knee-high socks were a constant feature of my stylish attire. I had now graduated from a purple hospital gown to cheap, loose-fitting shorts and large vest tops to fit over my space-station upper body. We conducted basic leg and arm movements repeatedly with assistance. I worked as hard as I could to lift something or to move a finger, or to contract a muscle. The day prior to standing, the physio asked if I felt confident enough to attempt to stand. I told her that I would be standing above her the next day. I had been asking her all week to give me an indication of when she might allow me to attempt to stand. So, when she finally said that we would attempt it, I was excited, I was confident and I was absolutely determined to get my weak-ass body off the seat.

I stood four times that day, with Rita, two physios and my dad assisting. I utilised a rocking motion to tilt my centre of gravity forward before pushing through my legs. It was extremely difficult to straighten up as my lower back, hips and knees all desperately wanted to cave in, while I fought to respond to each and every sense I could feel. The physios had a standing armrest in front to assist in displacing the weight through the arms, but as I couldn't move them very well, they had to be placed and almost balanced on top. I looked out and downwards slightly as my backside stuck out behind me. Although I was confident that I would succeed in my attempt to stand, it was a relief to actually do it. I was very grateful but I wasn't satisfied. We were very happy that I stood, yet I was determined not to celebrate my achievement. Deep down I knew I could do it. *'Four was my number today, so tomorrow the minimum is six,'* I said to myself.

The following week I took my first incredibly wobbly single forward step. It was tiring and I was aching all over. It felt like at any second I could just crumble forward or backwards. Everything was so difficult to control: my back, pelvis, knees, feet, arms. The feeling is that of losing bodily control similar to what might happen on a very drunken night out, except without the blurred memory. Nothing wants to do exactly what you want it to do. Every joint feels as though it is contemplating whether it is going to be the one that gives up. My actual posture and form were terrible as all I wanted to do was to throw that leg out there, using whatever momentum and sense of direction I had. *Adapt, improvise and overcome.*

January was coming to a close and I was progressing nicely. The next priority would be to get my bladder to work properly again and recover more arm movement. My CO and Regimental Sergeant Major (RSM) from my home unit, 6 RAR, visited. It was a nice gesture but more importantly the CO told me my job was safe and any equipment or assistance I required would be taken care of. I told him I hoped I wouldn't need much and that I would be back at work as soon as possible. I know it didn't matter when I got back but I needed him to know that I wanted to return. To me, it was a matter of pride and self-worth. I would show all the medical staff, military members and anyone else what I was made of.

I'm going to be back in uniform someday, I know I will.

8

CHAD

We touched down in Goz Beïda in Eastern Chad and I felt the heat immediately when I exited the C130. I was met by my OC, Dave, and my company second-in-command (2IC), Conor. They had been part of the first chalk, while I took the remainder of the company with me on the second chalk.

It was early October 2008 but it felt like the middle of summer. In fact, as we stepped off the aircraft, I thought that the immense heat pushing against my face was emanating from the engine, but as we were guided away from the rear ramp I realised I was very wrong. Eastern Chad was heading into the dry season and we would be the first battalion from Ireland to experience it.

I was exceptionally lucky with this, my first overseas deployment. The vast majority of officers and other ranks listed on the deployment were from the infantry unit in Kilkenny, so I knew them quite well. After commissioning, seven years earlier, I had been posted as a 2nd lieutenant to the 3rd Infantry Battalion (3 Inf Bn) in Kilkenny. I was very nervous starting in the 3 Inf Bn or, as the unit was commonly known, 'The Bloods'. However, the crew of young officers, coupled with an overall relaxed atmosphere, really settled me. James Stephens Barracks was very close to Kilkenny city centre, and as junior officers we made the most of any opportunities available to sample local establishments such as Matt the Millers, Langtons, Biddy Earlys and Lenehans – the pub with 'the best Guinness in Kilkenny', which just happened to be a sum total of twenty feet from the front gate of the barracks. I quickly became comfortable in my working environment and established a good relationship with most officers and other ranks within the battalion. I was a 'pure-blood' in so far as I was there from 'birth', i.e. from my very first day as an officer; therefore, the battalion had essentially raised me and I knew it in intimate detail.

Although I had been sent to Limerick during the college semesters between September 2004 and May 2008 to take a degree in Physical Education (PE), I remained with 'The Bloods' throughout, working in Kilkenny during all the college breaks and summer periods, thoroughly enjoying my time in the battalion. I was thrilled to be going on my first overseas mission with the unit I had been serving in since 2003.

As we drove from the red-gravelled engineer-made runway to the camp I found myself growing extremely excited. After years of deployment virginity being held against me, I had finally gotten overseas. This was my opportunity. From the early days in officer cadet school everything revolved around leading troops. Being in charge. *'What do you do now, cadet?'* It was always seen as quite significant for a junior officer to be given command of troops overseas.

My civilian friends used to ask often what exactly I did as a junior officer. It was tricky to explain. I was busy, but a lot of the time I was doing nothing of real substance. I used the sports player analogy. 'He begins by learning his craft and hopefully shows some flare for his sport. Then he transitions to the ever-long training continuum in order to be the best when selected for the championship game.'

We trained a lot in the army: courses, exercises and physical training. However, until you finally went on an operation, you were still in the training paddock. You were never playing championship. Imagine years of training without ever being able to use or properly showcase your skills. It can be very disheartening. Hour upon hour of exercises for what?

As our convoy, bound for the camp, spun the African dust into the midday sun, I felt that I had finally put on my championship jersey. After seven years, I was finally getting to test myself. Until you get on the pitch, you can never know for sure how you will go. It didn't matter now how I had performed on any course or exercise. This was real. This was what I had trained for. I was a leader on a real-life operation. This was no UN Charter Chapter 6 'peace-keeping' mission with weak rules of engagement. It was a European Union Force mission with UN Charter Chapter 7 'peace-enforcement' rules of engagement, allowing us to shoot first if required. During pre-deployment briefings the battalion commander and intelligence staff had warned of the high likelihood that these rules of engagement would be tested, due to the fast-approaching dry season. This improved movement corridors for the Janjaweed militia which was attacking the population of Eastern Chad, and we were told that we should arrive under the understanding that we would be fired on at some stage. It was nerve-racking but very exciting.

As part of the EU Force mission to Chad, the Irish element was officially named as Multinational Battalion South, a force comprised of approximately 450 soldiers based in Camp Ciara in Goz Beïda, Eastern Chad. Other than administrative and logistic staff, our main forces were two distinct manoeuvre companies (approximately 120 personnel each), with a Dutch marine platoon (approximately thirty-five personnel) attached. My official job was weapons platoon commander for the Armoured Personnel Carrier (APC) Company. I was also promoted to the rank of captain for this mission. This meant I was in command of thirty soldiers, all qualified in various infantry light-support weapons, such as 84mm anti-armour weapons, Javelin heat-guided anti-armour rockets, 60mm mortars and 7.62mm sustained-fire machine guns. A lot of fancy terms, but, to put it plainly, I was in charge of a group of guys able to use high-quality anti-tank weapons, small-range mortars and large machine guns, who could also act as normal foot soldiers as required.

We drove around in large, heavily protected eight-wheel vehicles called Mowag APCs, with mounted machine guns. My guys were able to be used as a basic infantry platoon but could also be detached as required for specific missions or tasks. For instance, if my boss wanted an over-watch to guard an area ahead of the main body arriving, or required lead elements of a convoy to protect against potential vehicle or armoured threats, then I might detach some of my guys carrying the anti-armour weapons to the front of a convoy.

My knowledge of the soldiers aided me during our initial manning discussions with Dave as I managed to slightly shape my platoon staff. Of the three platoons in the company, I had mentioned which sergeant I would prefer. All three were very capable but I had dealt with Sergeant Fla on a number of occasions in Kilkenny and I really liked his leadership style. He was very calm, astute and mature for his age. He remains one of the most professional NCOs I have ever worked with. We maintained an excellent relationship throughout the mission. He would regularly advise me or give me the inside track on platoon issues, and would often deal with them accordingly before they needed to come to my level. Most importantly, the guys in the platoon respected and listened to him, mostly because he was fair and honest with them. He didn't fly off the handle much and his calm demeanour suited my leadership style. Often I might have some outcome or issue I wanted raised within the platoon and he was the go-between. I might direct the plan but he, with buy-in from the other NCOs, would sell it. I was happy that this was the case, as a leader always has concerns that he may be undermined, particularly in the military where a young junior officer with no overseas experience is thrown into that position.

My command mantra was pretty simple: I would be myself, always attempt to make the most rational decision with the facts I knew, and maintain an objective mind as best as possible. By doing this I felt the guys would judge me fairly too. If I made mistakes (and I had made plenty during my time as a newly qualified junior officer in Kilkenny, such as being late for parade or forgetting to book enough transport for an exercise), then it would be more easily forgiven by the group if I was honest in my endeavour and had the platoon's best interest at heart.

The camp was as expected: relatively basic but with most amenities. In fact, we had a pretty decent gym inside a large marquee-style tent. Two main command-post containers sat side by side where our operations centre was constantly maintained. A large tented accommodation village in perfect lines housed the entire battalion. Numerous containers situated as far as possible from the aforementioned accommodation stored all of our extra explosive ordnance and ammunition. Engineers had built protective bunkers around empty forty-foot containers on the fringes of the camp for us to run into for protection if we were bombed. Vehicle workshops, weapons workshops and a transport yard maintained our various capabilities, as required. They were kept busy by the damage that the desert-like terrain caused the Swiss-built Mowag APCs.

A main square of sand and gravel with a large Irish flag alongside classic Irish signposts greeted you on entry to what had been named Camp Ciara. We had a basic dining hall with a kitchen and cleaning area at the rear. A welfare room with a few Internet-connected computers was also built, although the connection was very slow. Each company also had its own tents for planning and administration, as did battalion headquarters (Bn HQ), with a number of makeshift staff offices, the largest and nicest belonging to the battalion CO. I had actually expected worse.

The camp was surrounded by a large eight-foot berm (dense, wide clay wall) with a trench either side with wire obstacles. The camp guard consisted of a full platoon rotating between the main gate and the various lookout posts built on top of overlook positions on the berm. The camp guards would also patrol the top of the berm by day and night.

During a down day early in the deployment, I was out on the sand-covered square pucking a sliothar around with Mo, a cavalry captain who happened to be from my home village. There we were in the fifty-degree-heat desert of Africa, two boys from Watergrasshill, with its one shop and three pubs. Mac, who was in the tent next to Mo and me, and one of my closest friends from my initial officer training, came sprinting across from the Command Post (CP). It was unusual to see Mac sprinting for any reason, but when he started roaring 'STAND TO, STAND TO' I knew something was wrong. *Shit, it's kicking off,* I thought as Mo and I raced from the square to our tent and immediately swapped our hurleys for our rifles and body armour.

I didn't even know if I had time to get into uniform. I ran, still in my sports gear, to the rear of my APC and loaded my gear in quickly, then made a snap decision and darted back to grab a uniform as I heard the unmistakeable thud of ordnance exploding in the distance. Everyone was spinning around the camp. I got dressed at my APC and began chasing down the platoon.

As our platoon had such a large portfolio of additional weapons it took us a little longer to load up into the vehicles than it did the rifle platoons. My NCOs were working the guys hard, and in turn I was working them hard. We had been warned about how volatile the area was. We had been told that when the roadways and riverbeds dried up the Janjaweed would start moving again, and they had no fear of us. Rounds started landing on the hill just outside the camp. We loaded up, reported ready and waited for our next order.

Mo and his cavalry troop ripped out of the camp in their cavalry variant APCs at breakneck speed to investigate. We waited in the back of our vehicles, sweating heavily. I hopped out of my APC and walked from the back of one APC to the next, staring in at my sweat-drenched soldiers. Some were jovial and excited, some were very inquisitive and hungry for information, while others just remained quiet and looked a little nervous.

Initially I was a little displeased with our reaction speed, but we could easily fix that some other time. For now, I was just happy we were poised and ready. I checked in with my OC to get any updates. As the minutes ticked by, the group broke out into banter, displaying the dark humour that only army people truly appreciate. After thirty minutes, Mo and his troop arrived back on base. As it transpired, it was the local Chadian Army attempting to scare and test us, so we were stood down. *What in God's name is going on here? Aren't they supposed to be helping us?*

After a few days we settled into a 'Battle Rhythm', which is just another excellent military term for routine. We would spend a week on a long-range, company-sized patrol, driving from town to town within our area of operations, followed by a week on camp guard, or as a Quick Reaction Force (QRF), which was on a constant ten-minute recall to be deployed at short notice to the township of Goz Beïda.

Our OC, Dave, was very passionate and I really appreciated his loyalty to us. Although there were times that I may have questioned his demeanour or temper, I learned a great deal from watching his command. It was widely acknowledged around the camp, and in particular among the Bn HQ staff, that he was willing to back us and protect us against anyone else. The company responded so positively to this display of affection that it made everyone want to work for him. A leader who shows loyalty to his subordinates gets it back in return. In my opinion, one must look to consistently evolve their leadership skills, and this was a great practical lesson for me.

Dave had no fear of Mission Command. Most western-style, modern warfare utilises the 'Manoeuvre Theory', which heavily encourages the tenet of Mission Command. This is where your higher HQ tells you what effect they want, but not how you should conduct the mission. Essentially it is trusting your lower commanders to do what you ask without dictating how to do it; therefore, it is a display of loyalty and trust. Although most militaries will say that they employ Mission Command, in reality, due to a risk-adverse culture, this is very rarely the case. However, I felt that in general, Dave did enable his lower commanders on operations to follow their own instincts.

For example, it had been dictated from Bn HQ that all long-range patrols had to be conducted at company-level strength as a protection measure. That gave platoons little scope to plan and conduct independent actions. However, Dave was keen to give his officers exposure to higher-level activities. He would regularly give tasks to various platoons while we were on patrol. He might order one of the other platoons to move forward to the next village ahead of the main body to conduct reconnaissance. He did not tell us how to do it. Other times, he might order Conor or me to organise a snap defensive posture around our nightly patrol base including the employment of various larger weapons. He would then wait for us to return and back-brief him on where we had pushed out the anti-armour sections, mortars and sniper observation posts. I loved the buzz of planning things and then executing them. Sometimes it may have been the simplest of tasks, but just leading without anyone watching over your shoulder felt liberating. Dave never belittled us or stood over us as we conducted the tasks. I really appreciated that level of trust.

There were three platoon commanders in APC Company and we each had our own way of leading. We were given the scope to be ourselves. Barry was full of banter with his platoon. But they absolutely loved him and trusted him deeply. They all grew horrible moustaches to annoy the Bn RSM, with Barry's black, rodent-like 'tash' leading the charge. Kieran, in contrast, had very little time for bullshit. He cut away any 'fluff' from his orders and was quite direct and blunt. But he wasn't a 'hard-ass' to his platoon; in fact, he tried at all costs to shield them from anything he thought was a load of rubbish. Again, they really responded well to his style. He also wasn't shy about having a bit of fun, and was known on occasion to swap his APC driver into his commander's hatch while he ripped around the dust in the APC. I was taking my platoon out to a training area outside the camp one afternoon as his platoon vehicles roared past ours in the opposite direction. I thought it was a bit strange to see Kieran give me the middle finger from his commander's hatch as I waved at him, although he swore he knew nothing of this event when I asked him about it later that evening. I'm sure No. 2 Platoon got great mileage from that one!

***

Mix one part *Groundhog Day*, two parts stupid tasks and one part the wearing of woodland-coloured uniforms in the oven-like desert heat and, congratulations, you have arrived at Camp Ciara. Long-range patrols were enjoyable mostly because they meant we got outside of the camp. Although we ate dust for hours a day driving in convoy from village to village, at least we were out from under the watchful eyes in camp. It was extremely hot while on patrol, and the APCs gave our bones a good rattling, but it was much better than the alternative as far as I was concerned.

As the car commander, I would stand at the rear right section of the vehicle, half out of the rear hatch, speaking on internal communication to the gunner who was located high in the cupola (the 'mini turret') of the vehicle, with the driver located forward left half outside his hatch. I could talk via external communications to either the other car commanders, or if required, the operations staff back at camp. I used goggles and a shemagh to protect my communications headset and to cover my face during transit.

The rest of the soldiers were all located in the rear with me, sitting on canvas bucket seats facing inwards, with a massive load of supplies, equipment, weapons and ammunition stored in the centre and behind the seats. We learned the tricks of the trade quickly. I would take my water bottle and cover it with a thick army sock. I then wet the sock and tied it off the edge of my commander's hatch. Although we were driving through immense fifty+

degree heat, convection would keep the water slightly cooler. Guys would, on occasion, throw on their baker's hat and treat the rest of the car to a homemade 'combat cake' consisting of ration biscuits, water, sugar and cocoa powder, sealing the mixture in a ration tin on a stationary APC in order to heat to perfection. Small acts of sharing like this most certainly enhanced morale, while increasing cohesion and bonding even just within the APC itself.

We would patrol in a company-level convoy with a support element of a few large trucks carrying extra vehicle supplies and fuel. I was tasked with leading the convoy and navigating for the first number of patrols. I also took my two vehicles to scout ahead into villages on occasion as required. The villages and townships were very basic – clay-walled streets with mud/clay huts and straw roofs. The women wore long, sometimes bright, sheet-like clothing, while the men predominately wore traditional white Islamic clothing and sandals. Old rusted vehicles were interspersed with both camels and donkeys, while children roamed free and wild through the gaps between street walls, which was of constant concern to our Mowag APC drivers. One could smell the lack of sewage facilities, and we regularly interrupted people using the roadway as a toilet, who would then finish by wiping with the left hand without too much concern for the enormous APC behind.

We sometimes patrolled through on market days, when colourful spices, nuts and vegetables were located next to an array of meats strewn across the side of the road. I didn't know where any of these had come from as the soil seemed completely adverse to any type of crop growth or animal farming. As we meandered past, I was conscious not to kick up dust or make a scene as people attempted to make a living. We were, after all, there to help protect them. And they were poor. Very poor. Kids played with the most basic of items, if anything at all.

On one quiet patrol, one of my drivers asked if it would be okay to muck around with the kids as we had stopped in an over-watch position on the outskirts of Goz Beïda. He proceeded to attempt to organise a game of rugby with them using a flat rubber ball. They were so excited by his inter-action that no one actually followed the rules, instead running around and jumping all over my gleeful driver and a few other willing patrol members as the rest of us chuckled, sitting atop the APCs. It was on occasions like that I felt truly happy that we were doing a good thing here. These were poor and vulnerable people and, as fellow human beings, the right thing to do was to protect them from the potential dangers caused by the militias encroaching from Sudan, looking to overthrow the Chadian government by any means.

Our usual plan to discourage any ill-behaviour towards the population was an overt show of force in the villages. Dave and a command group, including a local interpreter and civil military liaison team, would meet the village chiefs (sous-préfets) to discuss security concerns and garner any information on potential rebel activities. We were there to create a safe and secure environment, so a lot of this posturing was to dissuade any rebel contingent from thinking that coming through our area of operations was a good idea. It made sense. I would not have fancied driving a land rover with makeshift small and medium-sized weapons against us. We looked professional. We were professional. We were dressed correctly, we carried our weapons at the low ready position, we deployed our forces rapidly around the villages showing our tactical awareness and set up some of our support weapons if we really thought it made sense to, such as pulling out our quick action mortars for all to see. We found areas close to high ground to bed down while on patrol. We tried not to stay in the villages but remained close by to conduct night foot patrols or react to something in the village at short notice. We regularly deployed our snipers and Javelin sections (equipped with thermal imagery) to over-watch position as we maintained a basic company all-round defensive position. Then out came the single-man tents in a line left of the vehicles, with the driver and commander sleeping alongside the car. The guys would usually congregate at the back of a car, sitting around the back ramp while getting a brew or food before racking out or going on night guard duty around our hasty base camp. Platoon commanders and company HQ maintained the command post from the OC's vehicle, sending back various reports to the camp throughout the night.

This was our general routine, but we regularly had issues that required assessment and adaptation, such as a broken vehicle, a punctured tyre, an obstacle on the road, or rapid re-tasking from the camp. For example, a French fast helicopter in direct support of our patrol may have wished to liaise with us, or an increased threat in an area may have required us to re-evaluate.

Sometimes, in the dead of night, I would lie on top of the command car I was manning and look up at the clear sky. It was my own little 'quiet time'. I would reflect on how crazy it was to be in the middle of nowhere in Africa, listening to various insect and frog noises, staring up at the same sky as everyone back in Ireland. My home was so far removed from this kind of existence. I wondered what everyone was doing while I was here chewing my muesli bar. I pictured friends on nights out in Cork, my family watching *The Late Late Show*, or teammates finishing up training on the rugby field. I wondered how my (then girlfriend) Rita was enjoying her exploration around southeast Asia. I didn't necessarily feel homesick or lonely. I just found it interesting to contemplate and speculate what others were up to at that very moment, and how our current existence here in Eastern Chad was so different to it all.

***

By December we had conducted a number of long-range patrols and Dave gave me the opportunity to plan and command a company patrol to the border. I would have to plan and deliver orders to the company and foreign attachments coming with us. I would then command the patrol from the OC's vehicle while he would watch on and guide me as required. I delivered orders to a combined group of almost ninety Irish and French soldiers before we conducted various rehearsals and then headed off the following morning at first light. It was one of the few times I truly felt like I was a commander.

As we waved to the camp guard on our exit from the camp, I had to pinch myself. I was a genuine leader on operations. Not only that, but I was quite comfortable in my surroundings. I wasn't overwhelmed or in doubt. Through incremental exposure to a life in charge, I had no fear of making decisions. I was confident in my ability and I felt that my guys respected me. From watching and learning from Dave, I also gave them enough trust and responsibility, I hope. In fact, I really enjoyed it. The patrol proved relatively uneventful but I still loved every minute of it. Dave even allowed me to act as the company leader during some meetings with local village elders. It is said that experience cannot be taught and I was subconsciously learning more about leadership in the fifty-degree dust of Goz Beïda than I did from any lesson or lecture I ever received on the matter.

Due to my platoon's slow reaction to the earlier camp 'stand-to', I wanted to run a trial call-out for my platoon. No one directed me to do so. I wanted to be personally satisfied that my platoon could get into action quickly. I was accountable for the poor performance so it was up to me to remediate it. Of course, my NCOs were also disappointed about our reaction time and were fully behind further practice runs.

As we had a large number of weapons and ammunition to load into our APCs, I wanted to be able to test our timings for loading, getting out the gate and immediate action drills. I got the go-ahead from Dave and ran the exercise. We sprinted down the camp, got into uniform and ran to the containers, quickly drawing our kit, then carrying it all to the vehicles and loading up. Some of the logistic and administration staff chilling in shorts and T-shirts looked on in disgust as we tore around the camp in great haste, pushing each other with roars and shouts. I even saw the odd giggle from some HQ staff.

We drove out the gate and I ordered our guys to debus (rapidly exit the vehicles as tactically as possible) and begin setting up our mortar line, anti-armour line and machine-gun line. We set up on the edge of the airstrip outside the camp. I used the APC, which was parked halfway down the airstrip, as a reference point for the weapons and to begin practice drills under NCO direction.

All was going well until I noticed one of our anti-armour privates opening a Quiver (a container designed to hold two high-explosive (HE) anti-armour rounds) and begin to load an HE round into the 84mm anti-armour weapon. When we 'calmly' asked him what he was doing, it turned out that he actually believed we were going to fire the HE round at our own APC. *Christ, this is what I'm dealing with,* I thought. This was one of those occasions when I felt that, as the officer, I needed to take a step back.

I looked at Sergeant Fla and he nodded. I didn't need to say or do anything else. The NCOs would fix this. This private was a little nervous at the best of times. He didn't need to be screamed at or given extra physical training. He needed to relax and think clearly. I trusted my staff. I felt that Sergeant Fla was not going to 'destroy' the guy and I needed to display trust in my subordinates' ability to realign him, so I left them to deal with him. When we returned to camp I reported back to Dave and Conor that we had had a very beneficial run-out, one so realistic that one of my soldiers thought we were under attack by our own APCs!

I can only imagine the teasing he received within the platoon thereafter.

***

Ade is a town located right on the border between Chad and Sudan. To the north of the town was the Moydona pocket, an area within the Chadian border utilised mostly by rebel forces. Recent intelligence reports stated that a French Special Forces team had gotten into significant trouble up there.

On approach to our first patrol into Ade, the atmosphere seemed slightly uncomfortable. The local Chad Army commander decided to conduct some live-fire training close by as we were driving in convoy towards the town, even though he knew we were en route. We arrived at the meeting with the sous-préfet and he came across as arrogant, rude and aggressive. He told us if we drove any further down the road we would be shot at. He didn't say by whom. I felt as if he was trying to act like the Alpha male. Dave recognised this and stroked his ego. I was very alert.

I stood behind Dave as my platoon conducted the protection and link-up between the meeting place and our convoy which was located some 600m away. I noted the village leader carried a pistol, the first leader I met to do so. Some of his staff carried rifles (mostly AKs). I was concerned about the situation. I wasn't overly happy to have the OC buried in passionate conversation with this guy. I wanted the meeting to hurry up and finish. We were offered a local form of tea, as was usually the case, but it seemed to take a prolonged period to show up.

Suddenly, a number of Chad soldiers, who until now had been posturing outside and staring at us from their four-wheel drive Toyotas, bustled towards the meeting, carrying one of their soldiers. I began to step forward to intervene when the sous-préfet beckoned them forward and I noticed the soldier was injured. He had bandages wrapped over his hands and forearms.

Dave understood that this was an opportunity to show some good faith and turned to us to fetch our patrol doctor. He was a civilian doctor promoted into the army with very little military experience. He ran into the meeting and immediately began treating the man. I'm not sure if the doctor understood the political and tactical struggle occurring before him. His primary concern was the treatment of this man. He turned to Dave and requested that we take him back to camp with us to continue treatment. The sous-préfet had no English but understood perfectly. We were in the awkward position of either taking a soldier from the Chad Army, something which the rebels would clearly use against us, or not taking him and incurring the wrath of the local army and village leaders.

In my opinion the doctor was asking the OC to break clearly defined rules and was doing it in front of a very interested audience. I thought we were being played by the locals, that they'd brought the injured man here on purpose to see how we'd react. This situation was very sticky. Dave apologised to our 'friends' but outlined how we were not allowed to take the soldier with us; however, he gave a list of options as to how we could help. The doctor openly disagreed in front of everyone. After a small chat, the clearly dissatisfied doctor returned to the convoy.

We finished the meeting soon after as the village leaders had become disengaged and quiet. As we quickly mounted up into the vehicles and drove out of Ade, a number of Chad Army technical vehicles straddled us, swerving throughout the convoy, driving erratically. Both our drivers and gunners acquitted themselves well and I never feared we would initiate anything. Our soldiers understood the posturing and chest-banging being displayed. As I sat in our company patrol base later that evening, I thought about how easily that situation could have gone sour. This gave me much more confidence in my soldiers as no one panicked or did anything rash or inflammatory. We kept our cool and remained professional.

***

Non-governmental organisations (NGOs) had compounds and aid stations throughout our area of operations. Since the outbreak of the Darfur conflict, there had been a massive influx into nearby refugee camps and internally displaced person (IDP) camps. A refugee camp situated alongside Goz Beïda actually held more people than the town itself. IDP camps were situated in every village and town that we visited during our long-range patrols. Wherever the camps were, NGOs would set up too, including Concern, UNHCR, Médecins Sans Frontières, Save the Children and the Red Cross to name a few. All these were in compounds located across Goz Beïda and beyond.

If the hoisted NGO flag wasn't a location giveaway, then the high clay walls with big steel doors and local security most certainly were. I knew all of the NGO locations throughout Goz Beïda in intimate detail. On our alternate week from long-range patrolling, we either conducted camp guard or QRF duties, where our platoon was on a constant ten-minute call to get out the camp gate. As a show of stability, the QRF was also required to conduct three two-hour patrols every twenty-four hours, two of which had to be conducted during the hours of darkness. I ran our APCs through the emergency evacuation routes and NGO collection points countless times. I believe I ended up conducting over forty QRF patrols during my time in Chad. If the Janjaweed rolled over the hills and we got the call to evacuate NGOs, I was satisfied that we could begin collecting their members within fifteen minutes.

With these conditions in place, one might think NGOs would be friendly towards us. Not so much. It was more like they ignored us completely, unless of course they wanted our assistance. One day, while on a QRF patrol, we received a message from higher HQ to visit an NGO compound where a four-wheel drive had been stolen at gunpoint. I asked over the radio how this pertained to us, but we were ordered to investigate, so, of course, I directed my patrol to do so. We managed to locate the whereabouts of the stolen vehicle, but after giving chase for a period of time, I called off our cat-and-mouse caper as the skilled driver in the four-wheel drive easily escaped our sights across the sand-covered tracks.

Upon our return to the NGO compound we were treated as though we had taken the vehicle ourselves. Somehow this was our fault. I reminded them that we were not the local police and left the compound soon thereafter. My soldiers were quick to point out that it had at least made an otherwise boring patrol more interesting.

My company took the long-range patrol over Christmas week. On Christmas Eve we were close to Goz Beïda conducting a day patrol. The operations staff back at camp contacted our OC and revealed that an NGO compound in Goz Beïda had just been attacked. We loaded up into the APCs and headed to the town centre with immediate haste. When we got there the situation became clearer. Bandits had gone into the compound and stolen the staff's Christmas bonuses at gunpoint. The NGOs wanted us to track them down, stating that we were clearly not creating the safe and secure environment that we were mandated to.

Hold on, Christmas bonuses? For aid workers? I had been driving around Eastern Chad for the last three months and had seen a mass of poverty, but here we were chasing down Christmas bonuses for some of the only other white people present. I thought it was bullshit. The other officers were of the same opinion. We conducted foot and vehicle patrols throughout the night to keep the NGOs satisfied but I can safely say I didn't look too hard, nor did I order my platoon to do so. I have no doubt that there is superb work conducted by NGOs worldwide, but, unfortunately, my views on the actual work conducted by NGOs in Eastern Chad were tainted by my experiences during my time there.

***

The exposure to all these new experiences enabled me to learn and develop as a junior leader. I felt I was looking at situations through a different lens. I felt more confident in questioning the 'why?' behind certain orders. In essence, I started to act like a captain and do things that a naive lieutenant would not.

On one occasion I was left behind on a long-range patrol to supervise the guys within the company who were unable to go due to a lack of functional APCs. The NCOs and privates were immediately snatched up as a work party for the camp RSM before I even knew it, as I was busy doing paperwork. I found them filling sandbags and dumping them into massive Hesco bins being built as protective bunkers, a task formerly given to the Engineers to complete. I was the senior representative of the company in camp but I knew nothing of this task. So I grabbed a spade and joined in, and enjoyed talking rubbish with the guys.

We worked through the task all day until I was called to the CP as the company representative for the CO's daily meeting. I was covered from head to toe in dust. It didn't go unnoticed. In fact, the CO commented on it immediately. One of the other senior officers mentioned that it wasn't appropriate for me to have been doing that task. I apologised for my tardiness but stated that my guys were very busy conducting a task for the RSM, doing an Engineer job all day, and that if they were doing it, then so was I.

In late January 2009 I was tasked with taking a platoon to Abéché to conduct camp guard duties for the French camp. Our mission was strictly without alcohol, but in this camp the French ran a number of bars. Word from other platoons was that locals had stolen a number of very large and expensive items from the camp during the tenure of previous camp guards. I did not wish for a repeat performance and our guys did a wonderful job. We repeatedly thwarted innovative attempts to break into the camp.

However, on the night after handover to the ongoing French platoon, two of our guys (attached to my platoon only for the duration of this task) took it upon themselves to drink a number of alcoholic beverages and then stumble around my bed space in our transit tent late that night. I waited until the following morning, then gave them stick. I was so disappointed and angry. *Why did they think they were better than any of us and that they deserved to drink?* As they still appeared to be the worse for wear, I told them to run off the booze and then assist the others in the clean-up before we flew back to the Irish base, when I would put forward discipline charges against them.

On return I did not get the response I expected. The battalion commander immediately summoned me into his office on my arrival back at base and proceeded to question my actions. Later, the RSM approached me across the parade ground. He also challenged me about my actions, saying that I had used abusive words and that I had already punished the guys by ordering them to run around the camp and clean toilets. I disagreed with his suggestion that this was punishment, as the run was conducted as a health measure, because alcohol does not mix well with Lariam (a potent and controversial anti-Malaria drug we had to take). Also, all platoon members had been involved in conducting cleaning tasks, myself included, before we left the French camp. I asked the RSM if he acknowledged that the guys had broken the rules of the battalion and, by drinking alcohol, had disobeyed a specific direct order given by me. I then asked if he thought that conduct of this nature was acceptable.

I would not have done that had I not been confident in my ability as an officer. The RSM is the highest rank below that of a commissioned officer. The rank deserves the respect of all junior officers for sure. Had I still been a doubtful lieutenant, then I might have backed down. But I believed I was right and wasn't afraid to stand up to anyone to justify my point. The soldiers were eventually given a caution by the CO.

Although at the time I was nothing but furious about this incident, it ultimately assisted greatly in boosting my confidence and also my development as a leader. It was a challenge of my moral compass as a commander, but I believed in my actions and backed myself, which allowed me to stand my ground. I was adamant that I owed it to all the other soldiers, who had performed with excellence throughout the mission, to ensure justice was served on those who deliberately broke our trust.

I had been an officer in the Irish Defence Forces since 2003, but most of my experience was forged through training exercises, courses and on low-level on-island operations. There is no comparison to the experience of leading in real scenarios. No one is standing over you, assessing you, no one is there to tell you that you did the right thing, or that you could have done or said something differently.

On many occasions I reflected on whether or not I had made the right call during patrols or even interactions with soldiers in my platoon. One of my soldiers lost a good friend back in Cork while we were deployed. He wanted to fly back for the funeral at his own expense. As it wasn't immediate family or within the normal flight patrols, our higher HQ refused the request. I had to deliver the news to a clearly frustrated, angry and hurt soldier. He was outrageously insubordinate to me as I delivered the news. I let it slide, though, as I felt he was just venting his anger. He was bitter to his chain of command from then until the end of our deployment. I could have gone hard on the guy but I gave him the benefit of the doubt this time. Unfortunately he acted with contempt thereafter. I had to address his behaviour a few weeks later, but by that stage I felt my command of him had been compromised as I was being inconsistent with him, which in itself was unfair. I felt bad for the guy, but I couldn't have one rule for him and another for the rest. I dealt with the situation as I thought best and didn't dwell on it too much. I couldn't afford to.

This was only one of many daily issues we commanders dealt with. Overseas missions are filled with relationship breakdowns and internal conflicts, coupled with loneliness, homesickness and the family dynamics of each of the thirty soldiers for whom you are responsible. I learned that it is up to the commander to keep the platoon together and to ensure that this group is still able to function as its job demands despite any 'problems and issues'. It is always tougher than it seems as leadership books only list the skills – it was up to me to actually apply them in Chad.

An overseas deployment where one actually gets to act as a true commander is a rare experience, but I was fortunate enough to be able to reflect on my faults and successes in order to improve my capability thereafter. I learned so much and enjoyed my time there thoroughly. Chad shaped my attitudes, values and ability as a leader, which from then on I could take with me and use wherever and whenever I needed to.

9

GOOD MORNING, ROGER

PRINCESS ALEXANDRA HOSPITAL, BRISBANE, AUSTRALIA – FEBRUARY 2015

Although I didn't realise it at the time, the end of January and start of February were where I made some of my most significant improvements. Medical staff began discussions about removing my 20-gauge (6.6mm diameter) catheter. The issues were firstly the immense pain caused by removing it, then a subsequent trial by void in which I had to empty my bladder completely within four hours. If I was unsuccessful, from then on I would have to have daily catheters put in. No thanks!

Early one morning they whipped out the shotgun from inside me and started the stopwatch. I was on my bed half asleep for the first couple of hours. The pain of the removal had tired me a bit. Rita's sister, Una, who had arrived in Australia not long before this, was at my bedside, and I kept asking her to give me water, even though the doctors had advised me to drink normally. There was no way I wanted something else stuck up my penis. Three hours passed and still nothing. I started to get a bit worried as it approached three-and-a-half hours. I was determined to do everything I could to assist my bladder. I began wriggling around in the bed. The head of the bed was raised, so I managed to fling my left leg out over the side of the bed and slide my head down towards the right side. I didn't really know what I was trying to do, but I felt I had to do something. Una was in silent shock, probably concerned that I may have been spasming and moving around the bed involuntarily. Then I just stopped, half-splayed across the bed, and out it came. The physical and mental relief was immensely satisfying. I saturated the bedsheets but I couldn't have been happier. It was a particularly positive, if undignified, result.

By early February I was in room 3, where I was bunked in with a seventeen-year-old, a twenty-year-old and a twenty-six-year-old. They had received their respective devastating injuries by way of a car crash, swimming-pool slip, and a fall from a height. Two of the guys were high-level quadriplegics. The lives in this hospital room were now changed forever. I found it difficult to sleep in the complete lockdown of a halo brace but when I did sleep I would breathe and snore loudly as my head couldn't move so my jaw would drop open, which was not ideal for the other guys in the room.

My father was ever-present and focused. He was over here to do a job – that is a direct quote from his own lips. He didn't care about anything else, and anyone foolish enough to ask if he was going to see a bit of Queensland while he was here was soon set straight. What my dad lacked in tact, he more than made up for in effort, positivity and love. He brought his familiar level of intensity to the hospital ward, but knew he never had to push me – more like facilitate me. It was interesting, as I think he always knew I had strong mental resolve, but he hadn't seen it in action until then. Outside of a small circle, I don't think many have. So maybe it was good to be able to show Rita and my dad some of my inner strength.

Rita's sister, Una, was superb, though I knew she would be. She gave us excellent respite, looking after Rita (who at this stage needed it) and nursing and assisting me, even when I was my demanding and grumpy self! As a social-care worker, Una reads situations excellently and, like Simon, gauged the situation perfectly, while also dealing with my dad.

I still had lots of issues with my bladder and bowels, but we all remained positive as things were improving all the time. Over the next few days, every time I urinated, the staff would ultrasound my bladder to ensure that I had emptied it fully. They also put a condom with a tube linked to a bag onto my penis so that when I did pee, it didn't go everywhere. The urge would come on very suddenly and I couldn't hold it for long before I would have to go. This was due to the fact that I hadn't used or been able to use my urethral sphincter muscles until now. After a week of condom use, they started getting me to use a bottle. I would regularly get my dad to rush me into the toilet in the wheelchair, then pull my pants to one side, hold my penis for me and let me go into the bottle. As time went on I also got my mother (she arrived just after Valentine's Day) and Rita to assist in my peeing. Usually I would attempt to anticipate the urge, and actually go before then. I had to train the muscles to work again, so I would have to try to break the flow constantly, which was quite difficult.

One afternoon, while I was in my chair sitting across from my father in the hospital café, the urge suddenly came over me. I told my father that I wouldn't make it to the toilet and, unfortunately, we were sitting in the far corner of the open café, right alongside the glass partition to a busy hospital corridor. My father grabbed the bottle from the satchel at the back of my wheelchair, sat alongside me, and reached under the table, placing my penis into the bottle while he spun his eyes around the room and through the glass, hoping no one would notice the man in a wheelchair peeing into a container while another man held his penis. Without batting an eyelid, my father then fixed my shorts, stood up and carried the bottle past the other customers out to the toilet. We laughed hysterically upon his return.

I would get my dad to do the pee bottle just before I went to sleep. He would lift up the sheet and I'd just go into the bottle on the bed. Usually I would then require one call to the nurses overnight. I still couldn't feel anything with my hands, even if my movement was becoming better, so there was no way I could self-administer peeing.

Sometimes it didn't go so well. On the night before Valentine's Day, I called for a nurse at around 1 a.m. (I still was getting very broken sleep throughout the night, as the halo and lack of movement were quite awkward. I'd regularly have pains in my back, neck and shoulders, or maybe I'd mistakenly move my leg, removing the sheet from over me and, as I couldn't move my arms particularly well or feel the sheets, would then spend the next hour or so fighting to get the sheets back in situ.) I used the plastic blow-tube rigged up alongside my mouth to call for assistance. I felt a dull urge to urinate and had realised early on that when in doubt, I should act early, as otherwise accidents would occur.

No one came. The 'binging' alarm rang and rang for over twenty minutes. I was wriggling around, trying not to release. I couldn't hold out any longer. The bottle was on a rack at the side of the bed. Maybe if I swung around I could get my legs out and then stand up and somehow pee into it. I was able to stand and transfer from bed to wheelchair by this point, and take a few unassisted steps. I wriggled around and got my two legs out over the side of the bed over the side protector. I wrapped one of my legs around the outside bar and tried to sit upright on the bed, pulling with my leg. I was extremely close, just falling back onto the bed at the forty-five-degree point. It became a serious leg and ab workout! I tried a few more times but the panic was setting in and I couldn't hold on any longer. I just relaxed and peed everywhere. All over my bed, all over my sheets and all over myself.

I lay back down in my own puddle, with a leg wrapped around the side of the bed, with the nurses' call still beeping. I was devastated. I could tell the other guys in the room were awake but they didn't say anything. The room was open plan, with four beds separated only by a U-shaped curtain around each bed space. When someone else in the room was being treated throughout the night, we would usually all be awake. It actually led to a real sense of solidarity and friendship. Eventually, after the warm wetness had subsided to a cold stink, a nurse arrived to find a patient soaked through and half hanging from the bed. She began to chastise me but then thought better of it and just went about her business getting me fixed up. She assisted in transferring me from the bed to a chair alongside the bed, where I sat in the darkness as she scurried around changing bedsheets, wiping the mattress, cleaning me down and changing my underwear. (I had gone back to wearing underwear once I could pee again.) I didn't feel angry. I didn't feel embarrassed. I just felt hopeless. I couldn't even go to the toilet. I was happy to be put back into a fresh bed as I just wanted to go to sleep and forget I ever wet the bed.

***

Having been moved from the acute room to room 3, I was then moved again to room 4 in early February. In this room were two very different characters: Roger and Nick. Roger was approximately fifty years old and had been paraplegic for almost thirty of those. He was very jovial and happy around us but at times quite short with certain medical staff, so much so that he was told off on a number of occasions by the head of nursing and the senior unit doctor. He was there as a sore on his lower back had developed into an open wound and he required a lot of care and attention for it to heal. In fact, he spent over nine weeks completely bedridden during this period. He was transferred to the toilet on a waterproof mattress each morning, grinning towards me as he passed my bed space on his side, with his ass cocked out behind.

Roger was quite strong in his arms but was carrying a little weight around the belly. He told us stories of his life in Bundaberg with his family, of investments gone wrong, of how he played high-level wheelchair basketball, and how he was pretty much a recovered alcoholic and had previously suffered from depression. Overall, it was an amazing exposure to a lifestyle I had never fully appreciated. It hadn't really crossed my mind before. I had never been friendly with someone in a wheelchair. I had no appreciation of the daily struggles they faced, the lifestyle changes and improvisations they made. For instance, a lot of paraplegics have to self-catheter. I never knew that. After a few beers it would be a terrible struggle, which Roger said at times in his past had led to injuries. In my fit and healthy state, I had never thought about how different a paralysed life is. 'Respect' is too small a word when it comes to my feelings towards Roger. The mental toughness required to live that sort of life is just mind-blowing.

Next to Roger was Nick. He (or I should say his mother) was the reason I was moved to room 4. I had been next to Nick for a while in the acute room and his family and mine had spoken a little, as had Nick and I. They had seen me working as hard as I could in physio and OT and I felt that

Nick wanted to work with me. I had no problem with that and thought it was a good idea. Although Nick's injury was different to mine, our recovery paths were similar. Nick had injured his spine slightly lower down and was also diagnosed as an incomplete quadriplegic. He had surgery on his neck and did not require a halo. He was as immobile as I was to begin with. People will always say no two spinal cord injuries are the same and I agree, but our recovery did track similar lanes.

Nick was twenty-two years old and lived close to the army base in Brisbane. He had fallen into a swimming pool, broken his neck and taken on a lot of water. He almost died but his girlfriend saved his life. He was unconscious in ICU for a number of days and when he woke up he found his mother and father side by side for the first time in years. I found that Nick liked to chat (as did I) so we got on quite well. I liked both sides of his family and his girlfriend, who was always excellent with him. They were lovely people, although I was present to see Nick's mother challenge a few nurses/doctors and she was not a woman I would have messed with.

During our daily grind, Nick would inevitably bring the conversation back to his or my injury and how we were progressing in certain areas. At times, I felt very conscious speaking about my standing or progression to walking with Roger around. What astounded me most, though, was Roger's genuine thrill to see each level of our progression. He would congratulate or cheer us if we did something of note during the day. How incredible to think that a complete paraplegic for thirty years was watching others gain function around him, but couldn't have been more supportive. I saw a level of selflessness that I could barely fathom. It constantly reminded me to be grateful for everything I had, and to continue to work as hard as possible.

Nick had played rugby prior to his injury and was most definitely competitive. This wasn't necessarily a bad thing, though, as it must have helped us both. He liked to let me know how he was progressing: how his bowel function was improving, how he had only one arm with reduced movement, etc. He openly laughed at me a few times when I tried picking things up and couldn't after multiple attempts. Had I the ability to pick up any one of these items, they may have been used to stop his bowel movement! But I still liked Nick; he was friendly, helpful and positive. He and I had good discussions about how, if we worked hard and stayed motivated, we would see great improvements. He showed determination and strength of character throughout and that I must commend. That was the key: to remain determined and focused on achieving maximum results. We both agreed that attitude mattered most. Even from an early stage, when others had better functional movement than us, our progression was tangible. Positivity and resilience aided us, I have no doubt to this day. I am grateful to still have Nick as a mate, and I still love winding him up by asking how much weight he lifts, then adding a few kilos to my own reply.

Throughout February I had improvements that in the spinal injury world would be seen as massive achievements, but I saw as small progress towards the next step. It was never about 'high fives all around' when I achieved something. In my head, each success was just another piece of the rock being chipped away, another step on the very long road ahead. In physio, I progressed my standing into stepping and assisted walking. We worked on core stability a lot. One of my favourite exercises included standing next to a raised physio table with bean bags placed on top. I had to stand up and pick one up and then throw it into the bucket below the table. There were so many challenges within the activity, but over time I got slightly better. Every day I wanted to go further than the last. 'We walked four steps yesterday, let's do eight today. How many stands do I need to do to beat my PB?'

In OT we worked on the many different tasks of everyday living. The OTs were very resourceful and creative, and could manufacture items to suit and assist specific needs. I started in the chair with weighted pulleys raising and lowering my arms, like a puppet. They loaded a game onto my iPad called 'Fruit Ninja' and built a retracting metal-arm assist onto the left side of my chair. I then would be given homework of slicing the moving fruit on the screen with my fingers and besting my score each time. Over time they kept adapting the exercises as movement and strength returned. Once I developed enough strength to hold something in a pincer, they made me attempt to pick up utensils. On one occasion, my primary occupational therapist, Glenda, cut a piece of cylindrical hardened foam and inserted the handle of a fork into it. I could barely lift it with a child's grip, and manipulating the fork's prongs to pierce into any food seemed near impossible as I slowly chased a soft banana slice around a raised counter-top. But I eventually got it. I stabbed it, lifted my arm as much as I could as the shaking mouthful came ever closer. Of course, I couldn't reach down to meet it, so the last thrust was a hit-or-miss type flick, but I made it, just. I chomped the banana as the therapists began their slightly patronising celebrations. I knew they didn't mean to be patronising, of course. Yet in my mind I had already moved on to the next task that I couldn't do yesterday but was going to do today.

I wanted to get out and about. There was no way I was rotting inside the walls of this hospital. Once I was strong enough to stand assisted, the next progression had to be a focus towards transferring. In the world of paralysis, a transfer is getting from any surface to another. It is absolutely key in order to enable mobility beyond the bed. People work incredibly hard to transfer, as doing so opens up access to the world again.

First up was conducting a successful transfer from my bed to my chair and then eventually into a car. Everything was incremental. The chair takes you far from your all-too-familiar bed space; a vehicle can take you to the realm beyond your ward. With staff assistance I could rock my upper body forward from the side of my bed, flinging my centre of gravity over my feet as I pushed upward with my non-existent leg muscles. Although the halo kept my upper body from slouching, my arms drooped forward from my torso as I made a number of jerky leg shifts until I had turned ninety degrees and could begin my descent into the chair. To complete this, I lowered my ass down a little before flopping into the seat. All the while nurses and family guarded me with hands out to catch any wobble. Over time I got more skilled and my speed of transfer improved. But even a good transfer was not to be celebrated. There was an acknowledgement on my behalf, but then I focused on the next step. *So, when can I transfer into a car?*

The process to transfer into a car was just as challenging. One day, my dad drove our Yaris into the spinal ward car park, as I was wheeled out by the physio and Rita. They removed piece after piece of the chair as I was squeezed up alongside the open passenger door. Then, with assistance, I stood up and bent over, arching my ass into the car seat. But the tricky part was still to come. Once I was on the seat I had to swing both my legs, and my head into the vehicle. I slowly placed my right foot up and over the lip of the door, then leaned forward to attempt to bring my satellite dish head into the car. It was a little strange attempting to work out the spatial clearance required, but slowly and very awkwardly, I managed to scrape in.

I lifted my other leg in slowly and I was there, sitting in a car. I was mobile again.

As we pulled out of the car park, I was thrilled. A little nervous but excited to be outside the walls of the hospital. I thought how strange it must have looked to any driver who pulled up alongside us, but it didn't matter as I couldn't see them anyway. To be mobile was an excellent progression. It was great mental therapy to know I could get out if I wanted to.

Once I could get out and about, we organised a day trip into Southbank, a beautiful pedestrianised area in the city along the Brisbane river, where I met two former Irish Army mates who had flown up from Sydney for the day to see me; John Boylan, from my old section in the officer cadet school, and Ronan Purcell, from my days in Kilkenny. It was very thoughtful of the guys to make the effort, along with Barry, who at this stage was on his second trip up from Sydney. I really appreciated the visits and it showed how people can be so supportive during tough times.

It was great to feel a little more normal again, even though I felt pretty conscious of people staring at the guy in the wheelchair with a halo brace around his head. I noticed almost immediately how difficult life is in a wheelchair. Everything takes much more time. Route planning, foresight and adaptability are key to getting around. As I was very fragile and in body lockdown, the vibration from uneven surfaces shook me to the core. I was in immense pain while moving across the tiled stones around Southbank. It gave me such an appreciation of the struggles facing wheelchair users every day. It made me feel like it was almost too much hassle to go there again. For someone to apply that level of effort every day for forty or fifty years seemed unfathomable. Exposure to life in a wheelchair puts the everyday trials of a walker's life into sharp perspective.

On Valentine's Day my dad dropped Rita and me to the cinema. Again, it was very challenging but excellent for our well-being. We saw the romantic classic that is *American Sniper*. As we waited in line for our tickets, I felt like people in the cinema were staring a lot and I gained further appreciation for the difficulties wheelchair users have in everyday living. Various surfaces caused vibration and pain, and the awkward set-up of the cinema was astounding. All the entrance doors were upstairs and the lift had to be activated by key by a staff member. Not a major issue until halfway through the movie when I had to go to the toilet, and we had to wait for almost ten minutes to find a staff member to get the key as the toilets were downstairs. This was less than ideal when I was still at a very awkward and rushed stage of my bladder control. How I didn't have an accident is still beyond me. It also meant that we ended up missing almost twenty minutes of the movie.

I was very self-conscious in the wheelchair. I felt like a freak when out in normal society. I knew I looked pretty banged up. My own niece didn't like looking at me on Skype. What if I saw a young man in a wheelchair unable to move much with a halo brace on? Would I stare? I probably would. I would probably feel sorry for him, thinking of the various terrible types of accident that may have caused such a dramatic injury. I didn't want anyone's pity, though. Maybe that's why I felt so self-conscious.

I had a few interesting altercations during this period which certainly added to my perception of how busted up I appeared in the halo and wheelchair. One day, a guy in the main hospital reception approached me with his young child. I was sitting in the chair, watching the people come in and out of the hospital. I enjoyed doing this with my dad or Rita, just people-watching. This particular guy seemed a bit on the rough side. He bluntly asked what happened. He quickly turned to his son, loudly stated 'That's what you'd get if you're not careful in the surf', then grabbed his son by the arm and powered off.

Later, we attended a Queensland Reds Rugby Union game in the club president's box thanks to friends of my father. Although I met and socialised with the club president and some players, I felt a bit patronised, as if I was one of the 'special kids' they look after. I was older than most of the players but I felt like I was spoken to like a teenager. Sometimes I felt as if I was being treated like a child. Not just by Reds staff but also by the hospital staff, and even my parents. It wasn't anything obvious or overt, and maybe I was hypersensitive to it, but because I was mostly being aided and because I was seated while all the others stood, I felt childlike. It frustrated me and at times I had to grit my teeth as I thought of the juxtaposition of occasions where I was leading SF soldiers on high-risk activities. No one ever meant any offence and the Reds game was a lovely experience, but it gave me the feeling of pity from others which I really didn't want. I was going to get better, and the next time I went to a Reds game I would be standing at the bar. One comment I did really appreciate came from the club president who said, 'Billy, you're more than welcome to come in here, just let us know. But if your level of recovery continues, then I hope to see you in here without that chair. We'd love to see that.'

In mid-February we went to a local steakhouse to bid Una farewell, just before my mother arrived. There was an adult family eating and drinking wine next to us. Rita and Una went up to order dinner, while my dad went to the bar to order drinks. The elderly father sitting opposite our table had clearly been drinking red wine, as his upper lip and teeth attested. He got up to go to the toilet but leaned over the table to me in my chair. 'Hey buddy, do us a favour and stop staring at us,' he said jokingly, thinking that this would amuse and cheer up an incapacitated quadriplegic faced in his direction. Off he stumbled as the others returned to the table. My dad queried what he said but I kept it vague. I didn't want him to kick off at the guy, which I am absolutely sure he would have if he had been present during the remark. I didn't really let that type of stupid ignorant shit bother me too much. Anyway, I was more concerned with not choking myself while attempting to eat steak for the first time in a halo.

I knew I looked messed up. I couldn't get away from it. Even if I caught my reflection somewhere it disturbed me. I didn't look like myself. My face was gaunt and thin, I had longer, unkempt hair and large black circles under my eyes. The circumference of my upper arm matched the size of my wrist. My legs had lost all muscle tone and my glutes had completely vanished. My body appeared to be eating itself. Consequently, there are not many photos or videos of me during this period, other than media I mostly used for my own analysis. But although I was conscious of how I looked, I wasn't too upset and I didn't let comments bother me at all. I just blocked it out for the most part. If I delved into it too much, it would only drag me down. Was I conscious of this because of my own personal vanity? Or because I was embarrassed by the accident? Or because I appeared so helpless? It didn't matter. I didn't want to answer that question. It was best to just realign my focus to more pressing matters, like trying to walk again. *Who cares how you look, Bill, just get on with it!*

By late February, medical staff and I had conducted a home visit where they determined whether I was safe to be allowed home for a weekend and whether I required any additional aids. It went well and so, a week later, with the halo still firmly embedded, I spent a weekend at home where, much to my mother's disdain, I managed to drink two bottles of beer. I lay in my bed for the first time since the accident. It felt surreal. I sat in my favourite armchair and took a deep breath. I soaked it all up.

I had done well so far. I had made some good improvements. I asked the staff to discontinue my daily blood-thinning belly injections (used to stop blood clots) as I felt that I was moving around enough to keep my blood flowing, which they did in late February. By the end of February I was able to feed myself certain foods and perform some simple tasks of daily living like brushing my teeth (with adaptive utensils). The simplest of everyday tasks had become long, drawn-out puzzles that I had to solve, but if I thought there was something I might be able to do, then I tried it. I also began to stop asking for help. For quite a while I had been requesting assistance for literally everything. I now had to remind myself to break that cycle. Even drinking that first beer, I had asked my dad to open the bottle, but then, with two mostly paralysed arms, I pressed inwards and managed to grasp the bottle off the table and lift it towards my mouth, where I tipped a small amount in. As I couldn't tilt my neck, I had to lean back slightly as my parents and Rita watched on, all waiting for the bottle to fall. I was clinging on for dear life, but it still appeared that the bottle would dive to the ground at any second. Thankfully, and to our delight, it did not. Of course, that is not to say that I didn't drop or could lift many other items. I did and couldn't. But I always tried. Over and over and over.

There were still a lot of challenges during February. I was constantly tired and found it difficult to sleep. The re-tightening of the halo every two weeks was very unpleasant. The P&O girls would come in and it is as crude as one can envisage: they pull out a tightening tool from the toolbox, set it to 8lbs of pressure, then tighten each pin until it makes a loud grinding sound signifying that the required pressure has been reached and the bite is released. All of this results in immediate head-crushing pain, which takes a day or two to settle down. I also started picking up a rash on my back underneath the vest, as I had lost a significant amount of weight and my shoulder blades were rubbing off the vest and creating sores. The P&O girls would open the vest slightly in order for the nurses to dress the sores, then tighten it again, but it did make lying a little more uncomfortable and a little more frustrating.

Almost everything was frustrating. Like not being able to open or manipulate anything. I would try to open a chocolate sweet and I would drop it five or ten times. My dad often said he didn't know how I never freaked out. But I never did. I remained calm and composed during the most menial tasks. I never got upset. I never threw something across the room. I never screamed out in anger. I kept control of my emotions and just stayed focused. Yes, it was annoying, and yes, at times it was disheartening but I would just take a loud, deep breath, stop for a few seconds, relax, and continue. In my mind I was resetting the task each time. Like a computer game where you keep failing at a particular point, but you just press pause and reset, then go again … and again … and again.

Sometimes I had no idea where my arms were. I couldn't really feel them, they were difficult to control and if they were below my peripheral view then I couldn't see them. When they were in front of me and I could see them, I could concentrate on moving them as I wanted, but if I couldn't see them, or feel them, then God knows what they were doing. It sounds funny, and sometimes it was, but at other times it was very gloomy. I recall asking Rita one night to take my arms off my chest and place them down by my sides. She quietly said they were already there. She smiled at me with sad eyes. Certain small events like this had a habit of keeping me grounded and letting me know not to get ahead of myself or be overjoyed with feeding myself a slice of apple.

I despised the wheelchair. The first chair I used in acute had a high back and I was in constant pain when in it. In the spinal unit they gave me a pink/purple chair for a few weeks, then transferred me to a yellow chair and altered the seat. I needed armrests as they could hold my arms in place, and I couldn't push myself around anyway. It was a heavy, awkward chair but I didn't care. Once I started standing and transferring from bed to chair I didn't want to use it. I'd actively discourage my dad or Rita from keeping it by my bed. I'd get them to park it outside the room. When I was told that I wasn't meant to transfer without a nurse's assistance, I did it anyway with my dad. When they said I could do it with a family member present, I started doing it by myself. Roger would provide nervy commentary when he saw me swinging my legs out, standing up with no one around and taking a step over to my cupboard and then back to the bed, resting the halo back on the raised end. 'Christ, Billy, take it easy!' It was all part of the process, all part of me staying outside of my comfort zone. Never satisfied.

Different doctors and nurses would comment on how well I was doing, how I could now do this or that, as if I was meant to be thrilled with it. I was most definitely grateful and very pleased with my progress, but not so much as to think that I was some sort of hero because I could walk again. Once, when a temporary nurse gave me a scolding for walking around my bed without an assistant nurse holding my safety belt, I came very close to telling her where to go! I understood it was a safety protocol but the way I saw it, it was my body and my choice. *I'll determine the risk and if I feel it's unsafe I'll stop. After all, if I fell I would be the one dealing with the consequences.*

Was it worth the risk? Absolutely. Recovery is not just physical. Mentally, I needed to be continuously challenging myself. I needed to know I could do it. Push the limit every day. In all my knowledge from years of sport, exercise, study and experience I know this: in order to improve we have to go further than we did before. The overload training principle. You want to run a quicker mile time? Then train at a faster pace than your mile pace. You want to lift heavier? Then train out of your comfort zone. You want to win championship games? Then train at and above championship intensity and speed. You want the best recovery possible from a SCI? Then every chance you get to stand up, walk to your locker or pick something up, you do it. I didn't care if ten nurses told me to use an assistant.

I stopped using the chair as often as I could. One day, and without warning, I told my dad I was walking to lunch, a sum total of about thirty feet. He knew not to try to convince me otherwise and I could tell he was proud. My mother fretted about my not wearing the belt and I told her off a few times, though I completely understood that she was just worrying as mothers do. My dad never told me to wear it, because he knew that the act of walking unassisted was very important for my mindset. I needed to believe I could become completely independent. My biggest arguments with people usually stemmed from them trying to assist me. 'I've got this,' I would say through gritted teeth.

I told my parents and friends that if I needed assistance I would ask. And I did, regularly. It is a very fine and difficult line for people assisting others with paralysis. They want to help so badly. Some could hold back and watch me try and fail repeatedly. It must have been extremely difficult and heartbreaking for them. I get it. If it were a loved one of mine of course I would want to dive in, assist as much as I could, do anything and everything for them. To fight against that instinct of love must have been very tough. Those who couldn't resist would rush in and hand me the straw, or pick up the towel, or hand me my phone. But they were told quite clearly that I did not need assistance in that instance. My mother and father may have gotten the brunt of it on occasions! 'Let me try it, then if I can't do it I'll let you know,' I would say.

The challenges were as simple as you could imagine. For example, every morning I would attempt to transfer from my bed to my shower chair mostly by myself. Over time, I asked my family not to be present first thing in the morning as I would then have to work something out myself, no matter how challenging. I would assist the nurse in washing me in the shower. I might stick out my legs so she would not have to bend down, or ask for the cloth to scrub my own crotch. (Occasionally the cloth would fall from my grasp, and not noticing this I would continue to scrub until this was pointed out by a smiling nurse.) I would assist the nurse dressing me by transferring back onto the bed, then swinging around on my back and creating a bridge to aid her as she pulled my underwear and shorts up. Even gripping the toothbrush and manoeuvring it around my mouth was a painstaking experience. I would finish my morning routine by clumsily shifting around my bed, pulling the corners of the duvet to make my bed correctly. As US SF Commander Admiral Bill McRaven advises: start the day right, make your bed!

I was constantly challenging myself and never took a break from it. I never gave myself an easy day. One morning I was due to go to OT at 10 a.m. I was in severe pain. The back-right quarter of my head wanted to explode. It was an eight-out-of-ten pain, and that would be rare for me. I remained calm and composed, though it hurt like hell. I asked my dad to get a nurse. I had gotten myself off Endone painkillers (morphine) as quickly as I could but I had the option to request them if required. I had resisted the urge many times, but this time the doctor and nurse advised that I take it and so I did, at 9.30 a.m. I rested my 2kg halo down against the raised bed, and my dad and I discussed not attending OT. I hadn't missed a single session, ever. I lay down and relaxed for thirty minutes, then sat back up. The drugs had taken effect and, after a horrendous morning, there was no way I was hanging around feeling sorry for myself. 'Dad, get my chair, we're going to OT.' He was shocked. He thought I was down for the day. But I had never missed a session, and never would. Never. Once there, I apologised for my slightly late arrival and we cracked on. I knew both staff and patients hadn't seen much of this behaviour before. My brother actually said to me before he left: 'They have never met someone like you before, Bill. I honestly believe that.'

An enduring side effect of paralysis is a spasm, which happens when a number of muscles contract for a period of time. Spasms can occur to complete or incomplete quadriplegics and can be as violent and dangerous as they are uncontrollable. I was very lucky in that I only spasmed when I woke in the morning, and although the contraction could be quite strong, it would only last for a few seconds. Post-morning spasm on a late February day, I stood up from the bed. I was very stiff and walking like a robotic zombie. I shuffled around my bed and swung my arm around the side of the curtain and walked the curtain around, opening my bed space out into the room. Roger almost fell out of his bed as he loudly exclaimed, 'Holy fucking Christ, Billy … are you fucking shitting me?'

'Morning, Roger,' I calmly replied.

That was it, every morning from then on I opened my curtain, made my bed and then sat on the side of my bed, ready to work. *No one will fault me for lack of effort.*

10

THE VALUE
OF FRIENDSHIP

CORK, IRELAND – MARCH 2009 AND
LIMERICK, IRELAND – NOVEMBER 2013

I have decided to tell the stories here of the deaths of two of my closest friends for a specific purpose. I am not looking for sympathy in recounting these. Instead I am highlighting how I selfishly used their stories for my own benefit during my recuperation.

Every day that I woke to the delayed realisation that I was paralysed, I thought of how lucky I was to be alive when my friends were not. Why, like my cousin who was killed in a car crash in 2006, was it their time but not mine? I still feel guilty sometimes when catching up with their respective parents, telling them my latest life news, when we all know they will not hear the same from their sons. What right did I have to live when they hadn't?

When I dive even deeper into these feelings, my guilt fades. I knew these guys. They wouldn't hold it against me for dodging death. Instead, I began to use their tragic circumstances as ammunition in my fight against giving up. Every time I ever thought about feeling sorry for myself, I reminded myself of how I was luckier than them, and how I must never take anything for granted. When I was in the physio gym, straining to hold a standing position, I used their loss as my strength. I thought that if I could get through those times, then I would get through these. It's not anything near the level of the pain and suffering of their family and other friends – all I'm saying is I used their memory to help me, and when I feel guilty for doing so, I picture them telling me to shut up and stop being ridiculous. It might sound strange, but even though they have passed away, both Aidan and Alan continue to help me through every challenging circumstance I face. In a way, they are still looking out for me like the great friends they always were.

Aidan

My buddy Aidan Connolly died by suicide on 27 March 2009. He had been suffering from PTSD following an unprovoked assault in Cork eighteen months earlier. He was one of my oldest and closest friends.

Nowadays, it seems everyone knows someone who has mental-health issues. It is a truly gut-wrenching experience for all concerned. All you want to do is help, but you are afraid of saying the wrong thing, and you fear that, if you do, you might lose the person's trust. And then, if the worst happens, other questions arise. Why did they do it? Could I have done more? Could anything have been done to stop it? Why could they not see what is clear? That you and others cared. That things would have got better.

Aidan and I were in the same class from the age of twelve onwards. At first, we were friends without being close friends. When we were fourteen years old, I persuaded him to come out to Sundays Well where I played my rugby. He was put on the wing and, although enthusiastic, he had a lot to learn. He rubbed some guys up the wrong way because he wasn't afraid to be vocal and criticise others during training. Also, he thought from a very young age that he knew better than any referee. He held that thought to the day he passed away! He was a very good tackler, though, and even when I thought I was the best thing on a rugby field since sliced bread, he would regularly and actively seek me out in training and smash me as hard as he could. It hurt, too. Aidan was an only child and he had something to prove, it seemed. He was tough and could fight his corner on the field, but sometimes he was a little bit argumentative. I never got into a row with him, thankfully, as it would have been awkward with his mother and mine alternating lifts to training.

During my last years in secondary school I was changing physically and also in terms of my values, attitudes and even who I hung around with. I drifted slightly from those I had been closest to when I was younger, as Aidan did with his close friends, and the two of us started hanging out with another mate of ours, Barry, to whom we also became really close. It wasn't that we had a falling out with anyone, we had just drifted into a new friendship group which became quite solid. Bar was great fun to be around and we enjoyed each other's company very much. Even after we had finished school, we maintained our friendship, which probably said a lot as I was in Kildare in the army while everyone else partied as 'Freshers' around Cork city.

The three of us and our other close friends used to frequent the city late at night a lot. After I finished my training in the officer cadet school in 2003, I would regularly take the trip down to Cork from Kilkenny or Limerick and usually ended up in Fast Eddies nightclub. Markie was our man. He's that friend with a lot of nicknames, who's in the clubbing scene and a 'head around town'. It seemed as if he knew everyone as he always got us in free to the clubs – mostly by wearing down bouncers' resolve enough for them to let us off. We thought we were 'Big Dogs', walking past queue lines getting into clubs. I was one of the few my age earning a solid wage and I happily bought 'Fat Frogs' or 'Toilet Ducks' (made-up expensive drink mixtures) all round. We became regulars in Costigans pub in town and usually took over the corner under the stairs so we could call our rounds through the little hatch at the back of the bar. It was a fun existence. We had countless nights out when banter was flung like mud at a festival. From 2003 until 2008 I have no idea how many boozy nights we had, but my liver must have been under pressure.

In 2006, while I was taking my college degree, Aidan convinced me to come out to Old Christians RFC in Rathcooney, only 500m from his house. As soon as I stepped out onto the training pitch it reminded me of all those years ago in Sundays Well. In fact, I felt a little guilty playing with another club, but the guys at Old Christians were really down to earth. No egos, just a lot of hard-working rugby players mostly from around the northside of the city. After games or training I might hang around with Aidan and his dad or we'd head into town and meet the lads.

After I completed my college degree in May 2008, our group had a few great nights out in the city to send me off before I left for Chad in October. Aidan was living in town with his girlfriend Keara and he seemed happy. He had his loud shirts, spikey hair and cheesy smile on parade most nights. He would often banter or argue with us over some stupid issue or tell hilarious stories of the mischief he got up to as a teenager.

Aidan was so passionate about rugby it almost embarrassed me. He would roar from the stands in Thomond or Musgrave Park, or at the pub TV as loudly as possible, telling off the referee or explaining in great detail how the opponents were 'constantly offside'. Aidan and I went to a number of Munster games with our mates Bar and Bucks, and we even made it to the 2008 Heineken Cup final in Cardiff, where we had a great buzz, even though I was on driving duties.

Post-Chad, in February 2009, I had one night at home before I was due to head for Australia on leave to meet my girlfriend Rita, who was over there on the final leg of her travels around southeast Asia. Aidan and Bar met me and we went into town for pints. Bar mentioned in confidence that Aidan was a bit sick and had been very down lately. I hadn't noticed anything of note but I took his word for it. Aidan did seem quite pale and he was a little quiet too. But he still showed off that gleeful grin and, as I had maybe got a bit too much sun in Africa, gave me some grief about doing nothing but sunbeds while I was overseas. Before I left for Australia I told Bar to keep me informed as, although I couldn't put my finger on it, Aidan just didn't seem fully present.

Almost a month later, on my way back from Oz, I called Bar from Thailand to deliver a warning about my impending arrival home. Ireland was going well in the Six Nations Rugby Championship, having beaten France, Italy and England already. I had watched the France game in Chad, the Italy and England games in Oz and would be home for the Scotland game. While we were talking, Bar told me Aidan had been admitted to a mental-health ward in a hospital in town but was being released prior to my arrival home. He said it was serious. I was told that his girlfriend, Keara, was being very good to him but that it was very worrying for everyone, especially his mum and dad.

When I got home we went on a night out with Aidan and had no real issues, although he was still pale and not his usual boisterous self. I had been told that he was on medication but he seemed pretty chilled. I invited him up to Watergrasshill to watch the Scotland game with my family. He sat in the sitting room with my parents and me, commenting on the match as he always did. My mam made steak sandwiches and we celebrated Ireland's win after wolfing them down. Ireland only had to beat Wales in Cardiff to win the Grand Slam, for the first time in over sixty years. Bar rang me and floated the idea of us all going to Cardiff for the game. He then rang Aidan's dad to clear it with his family, before asking Aidan if he was interested in going to Cardiff to be present for a potential Irish Grand Slam, an idea which made him smile broadly.

Aidan and I walked out to his car and discussed the trip to Cardiff and options for a new car I was going to buy with my overseas money. The conversation then quickly changed as I wanted to talk seriously with him. I remember that discussion vividly as I've played it over in my mind many times since. I told him that any time, day or night, no matter the circumstances, he must pick up the phone and ring me if he needed me and that I'd be there. I asked him straight out not to hurt himself and that if he ever felt that he might, he should call me right away. I put it as bluntly as I could. I pretty much begged him not to do it. He didn't open up too much but I hoped I had reached him, or helped him somehow. I worry sometimes that I may have said the wrong thing; that, because I mentioned hurting himself, he shut me out. But I walked back into the house thinking that I had done the right thing, that I had done a good job and that if he did have an issue he would talk to me.

The weekend of the Cardiff match, Bar, Aidan and I drove from Cork to the ferry in Wexford. The plan was for Bar and I to have a few drinks on-board and Aidan would drive the car to Cardiff where we would meet Gregs. On the ferry, Aidan went missing for an hour or two. Bar eventually found him sitting outside on one of the upper decks by himself in the freezing darkness. He was bent over with his hood up to shield himself from the bitterly cold sea air. We were happy to find him but Bar was a bit excitable when we docked and told us that he would drive to Cardiff himself. Later that morning I found out that Aidan had told Bar that he had been up on the outside deck contemplating jumping off. Thankfully Aidan had phoned his dad, who talked with him until he felt calmer. I imagined the absolute horror had something of that nature occurred. How we wouldn't even have known for hours. How his body would most likely never have been found. How seriously sick was he to consider this as an option, I wondered.

The weekend hadn't had the desired effect. The planned party weekend was now more of a rescue mission. When we arrived in the hotel in Cardiff the rest of us held a quick meeting in the corridor as Aidan slept. By this point he hadn't slept at all in two days. Bar called Aidan's mam and briefed her on the situation. We talked about the best option going forward. We decided that we'd still go to the game but we would monitor him closely. Our mission was clearly defined by his mam: 'Get him home, no matter what.' We had sobered up pretty quickly, as we knew this was serious. Aidan's mam and dad and Bar were all very upset. I took Aidan's threat seriously; however, I wasn't outwardly upset. Worried but not upset. I was hugely concerned but it wasn't a tragedy. He didn't go through with it, so that was a positive. He was still alive so he could still get better. We just had to make sure we kept him alive. Maybe that was callous. I felt he was sick, very sick, but he was still with us and could get better as long as we got him back home to start with.

We got out to the city centre early the following morning. Did I mention that none of us had tickets? Bar's brother-in-law met us for a few drinks. We had no clue how we were going to get in to the match, but Aidan had picked up and was in very good form that day. Almost his normal self. We kept talking about the game, and how it was going to be an amazing feeling if Ireland won. I could see it in Aidan's face. He was really invested in this game. Bar's brother-in-law called a ticket tout over to us. He asked how much for four tickets (he had one for himself already). The tout was asking for something ridiculous like £250 a ticket. Bar's brother-in-law asked to see the tickets, then grabbed them by the stubs. He told the tout that we'd pay £150 a ticket or he'd rip them right there. Sale agreed.

Of course, Ireland won an incredibly exciting game and the Grand Slam. I often wonder if the players realise how their actions on a rugby pitch can have life-changing consequences. I thought about writing to Ronan O'Gara, Paul O'Connell or Brian O'Driscoll to let them know that what they did that day was not just win a game. They also gave Aidan Connolly the best last weekend of his life. Sometimes I think maybe Aidan had already decided on the deck of the ship, or that the game gave him so much joy that he was then happy to leave us. All I know is, he was absolutely buzzing like the rest of us. We hugged and danced and high-fived all night long. The rescue mission relaxed back into a party atmosphere. We celebrated long into the night and Aidan and I were among the last to leave the Cardiff nightclubs in the very early hours. We headed home the following morning and I really thought he might have turned a corner. We had one of those great car journeys when everyone is a little worse for wear but in high spirits. Even though it subsequently transpired that he hadn't turned that corner, I am so happy we got to experience a great Irish occasion with Aidan before he left us. But more so, I smile for him knowing he felt such delight and joy so soon before his death.

The following Thursday night I drove to rugby training in Rathcooney. I had bought a beautiful BMW 318 coupe and contemplated calling into

Aidan's house afterwards to show it off, but thought better of it. I didn't want to be rubbing it in to a mate who was having a tough time. Then I remembered that he was out playing poker that night anyway. Early on Friday morning I was at home, just about to head to the army training camp in Kilworth, when my dad came down the hall. His facial expression was solemn. He told me Bar was on the home phone and then followed me up the hall as I approached the kitchen.

I knew something was wrong. I picked up the phone and I could hear that Bar was crying. He blubbered and whimpered as he told me that Aidan had lost his battle with depression in the early hours of Friday morning. I was in complete shock but coherent. I told my family what had happened, immediately got into my car and drove down to Bar's house in Glanmire. I parked on the road and walked towards the house and that's when it first hit me. I was greeted by a visibly shaken Barry and his girlfriend, Deirdre, in fits of tears. Everyone in Barry's house was very upset.

It was real. This had actually happened.

Later that morning, we went up to the house. We met Aidan's mam and some of their family and friends. Aidan's dad had been up the country with work and was on his way back down. Aidan's girlfriend was numb. Massive bear hugs were given with people desperately attempting to hide their scrunched-up pain-faces. My stomach was in knots. I wept again and again. The wails, screams, sobs and blubbers were coupled with bouts of intense silence. Aidan's parents were obviously distraught. His mother was broken, as she had found him that morning.

Every twenty minutes or so, someone else would arrive up and another bout of loud cries would bounce around the house. Aidan's mam cried out for her beautiful boy. We stared at the floor and at cakes in the living room

Commissioning day with my family at the Curragh Camp in July 2003.

At the Millennium Stadium in Cardiff in 2009 with Bar, Gregs and Aidan – less than a week before Aidan (*on the right*) passed away.

At the summit of Kilimanjaro in 2006. Alan is beside me in the light blue coat.

An ARW selection course at the tank tracks, *c.* 2004. *Courtesy of the ARW*

Siting an over-watch position near Goz Beïda, Chad, in 2008.

On foot patrol in Chad on Christmas morning in 2008.

Post-resistance to interrogation training on a SERE instructor course, 2011.

ARW counter-terrorism training during the reinforcement cycle, *c.* 2010.
Courtesy of the ARW

The staff and successful students from the ARW selection course 'Victor 1' in 2012.
Courtesy of the ARW

Baldonnel 2014. I squeezed in a jump on my last week in the Irish Defence Forces.

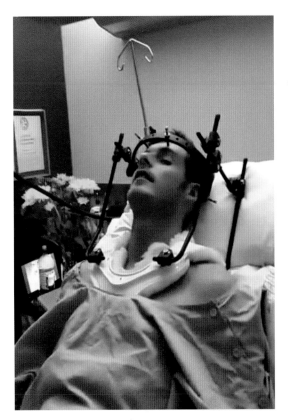

Nine days post-accident and still in acute care in the Princess Alexandra Hospital, Brisbane in January 2015.

Occupational therapy, January 2015. A weighted sling was used to raise my arm, while I attempted to grip a sponge ball at the limit of my field of view.

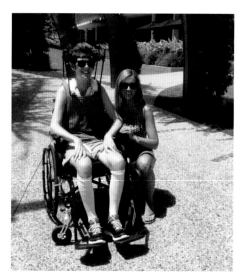

Rita and me in Southbank, Brisbane, on my first trip outside the Spinal Injury Unit.

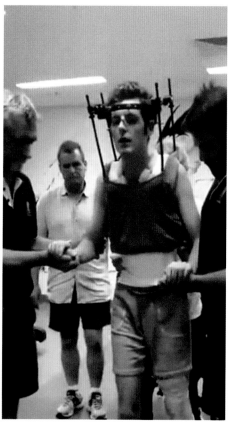

Preparing to stand for the first time, as my father watches from behind.

At a physio session with the amazing staff of the PA. Tiff, my physio, is behind me, holding my belt, as my dad follows with the wheelchair.

Left: The shackles coming off in March 2015 – the real work was about to begin.

Below left: My arrival home to Mitchelton, Brisbane, in April 2015. Time to start eating!

Below right: My return to skydiving as a recovering quadriplegic at Toogoolawah in January 2016.

Back on the beach in 2016. My tattoo of The Vitruvian Man is encircled with a Gaelic translation of part of 'Invictus'.

with glazed red eyes, as more people shuffled into the kitchen to console a heartbroken mother. I was so upset for Aidan's parents. When people you know so well display such raw, unfiltered despair, it is awful. It is a tragedy. It is horrible. I also felt so sorry for Keara, as she had fought so hard for him when he was sick. I thought about how she must be feeling. I wanted her to know she did everything she could but I couldn't say anything like that. All I could do was give a hug, hold her hand, make tea, catch her eye and give a slight nod. The *we're here for you* nod. The entire scene was just a terrible experience.

Over the next week we drank a lot, too much I would say. The week ended up blending into a myriad of half-drunken days in the Connolly's house or in pubs such as our old haunt Costigans or the Widows in Glanmire. I would wake up so hungover that I would just get more upset. I cried into our fridge at home while my brother and his girlfriend were eating breakfast.

After about two weeks, Aidan's death settled with me. Our group of friends had talked and talked and talked and I came to my own peace. In my mind, Aidan was sick. Not selfish, as some would like to say. I know how precious life is, but the illness is not being able to see that, not being able to see how it will affect those closest to you. So I refuse to believe that Aidan's suicide was a selfish act. He was sick and unfortunately didn't get better in time. That's how I started coming to terms with it. But I was so upset that I hadn't been able to help save him. I could and should have done more. Did I not take his situation seriously enough? Why didn't I text him on Thursday night? I had the phone in my hand when I finished training and thought about it but just didn't bother. I knew there was most likely nothing I could have done. I knew he may have decided it all well beforehand and was looking for his peace and freedom. But still.

This is the complicated nature of depression and anxiety. We can never know why. That doesn't mean that I don't ache whenever I think of him or feel sad when I visit his parents, but I've come to terms with his actual death and I did so reasonably quickly. The entire thing shaped all of us in that group a little differently, but one thing that is certain is that I take Aidan's memory with me everywhere I go.

***

Alan

By the morning of 11 November 2013, I was getting accustomed to the ridiculous timing of my alarm clock. I had spent the first half of 2013 on an overseas deployment in Bosnia and my return posting did not go as planned. By now, Rita and I were living together in Castletroy, Limerick, and I wanted to live out of my own home for a while. We had just gotten engaged and wanted a bit of normality after my time in the ARW. But even though there was a vacancy in the infantry unit in Limerick, I was posted to the Brigade Training Centre in Cork, against my preference. As a result of this posting, I was up at 5 a.m. for the drive from Limerick to Cork, where, on my arrival, I would do a session in the gym, then work from 8.30 a.m. until 4.30 p.m., when I would jump back into the car. Because of the early start I would fall into bed by about 9.30 p.m.

After a typical gym session in Blackpool that November morning, I made my way up to the barracks to start preparing my uniform. Donal Mealey rang. I knew before I picked up the phone that something was not right. Donal and I are good mates but he wouldn't ring for a chat, and definitely not at 8.20 a.m. He began talking, initially quite calmly, but then he ended up being very upset. He told me that Alan Feeley, our best buddy from college, had had a brain haemorrhage in the University of Limerick (UL) gym the night before and was in intensive care in Limerick. He said they were keeping him alive but there was not going to be a good outcome. I excused myself from work and immediately drove back up to Limerick to the hospital. I remember stopping for petrol in Mallow and talking to Alan aloud, asking him to hold on and not to die. When I got there I met Alan's youngest brother, Liam, as well as Donal and Louise, Alan's girlfriend. Liam gave me a big bear hug and told me Alan was going to die.

I was shattered. Rita met us in the hospital soon after she excused herself from her teaching duties at nearby Laurel Hill Secondary School. We were just numb. It was so out of the blue. So mad. So disappointing for him. I cried like a fool. He was without doubt one of the most genuine people I had ever met. I know it's a strange thing to say about someone but I thought he was the nicest man I knew. Not to mention awesome at everything. No joke. I was so upset for him.

Alan and I had been great buddies in UL, where I completed a BSc in PE in May 2008. He was one of only a very few from my time in college with whom I had stayed in contact. Throughout college, we had a great crew in Limerick, mostly from our PE university class who were very tight as a group. There were approximately thirty students in PE Group 'C', the geography (our minor subject elective) dumb-asses. We did everything together. Even between and outside of classes, we'd organise soccer games, tip rugby, tennis, gym, or anything at all to keep us going. We played a lot of Pro-Evo Soccer on the PlayStation and later maintained incredibly serious full-time leagues of Super Mario Kart on the Wii. I made some great friends and it was completely different and refreshing compared to the army stuff.

We took college seriously too. We never missed any lectures, labs or tutorials and we always did our work. PE is like a class of positive, competitive, eager dickheads who are great buddies with lots of in-jokes. We'd go to Mollys, The Icon, or the epic hole that was The Lodge. There were insane house parties, crazy drinking games, hot chicken rolls and plenty of Dutch Gold. I could tell hundreds of stories from nights out and of great fun we had knocking around UL and the city, but they were mostly 'you had to be there' situations. In our first year in college we started calling Alan 'Touchy' as it was funny to be called Touchy Feeley, not to mention the fact that as an aspiring PE teacher he didn't like it, so naturally it stuck! So much so that by our last year in college there were many people around UL who didn't know his first name.

In 2006 Alan, our buddy Ross and I climbed Mount Kilimanjaro together for a charity that built schools in Nairobi. Suffice it to say, we were pretty good mates at this stage. The visit to the school located deep within the city slum was a profound experience. Although the scene was quite disconcerting, we were also very proud that we had each raised €5,000 towards the school and were honoured to actually see where our money would be going. The initial four days of the subsequent climb up Kilimanjaro were very pleasant and incredibly easy. However, above Kibo (the last base camp), things were much harder and we had to zig-zag across a slope covered in steep shale to reach Gilman's Point, which is the crest of the crater. Once you reach this point you have officially climbed the mountain but not reached the very summit. We had left Kibo about midnight and moved dead slow, but by the time we reached Gilman's Point I was feeling less than fresh. I leaned over a rock and puked my guts out, down the mountain. I told the guys (Alan, Ross and two army mates) that I didn't think I could continue to the peak. It was Alan who gave me a little kick in the arse. He told me I would regret coming so close but not finishing, and then jokingly smiled when he said that they'd never let me live it down if I chickened out. He knew I would hate myself if I let something as easy as this get the better of me. He challenged me to push on. Challenge accepted. We kicked on and moved to the summit within thirty minutes. Cue obligatory photos and handshakes.

Alan, Ross and my other close buddies would also often support me when I was playing the drums in various establishments around Limerick with the band Zenith. I joined this rock covers band in my first year of college and have been great friends with the existing members, Cormac, Keith and Gar, ever since. I used to play the drums when I was younger, but had failed to keep it up. After I answered an ad in a music shop in Limerick, we hit it off. We had some great times and became relatively successful for a small-time band, if I may say so! It was so different to both my army life and my college life that I really enjoyed it. There were a number of occasions in the beginning when the entrance of Alan and the UL crew into a bar around Limerick may have doubled our audience, and I really appreciated it. Zenith played at the 2008 University of Limerick Education Graduation Ball, with Alan 'Touchy' Feeley and co. right up the front bopping away to songs they must have heard hundreds of times.

When Rita and I got engaged in 2013, I had asked Alan to be a groomsman. He travelled from his hometown of Claremorris, Mayo, to Cork for our engagement party in August and spent almost the entire night chatting with us in Watergrasshill after the nightclub. We would meet up in the gym or just call to each other's house in Limerick. A seriously talented sportsman, he began trying his arm at full 15s rugby with Old Crescent in Limerick that autumn and was superb in any of the games I went out to watch. He even tried coaxing me to join so that I could play with him, his brother Liam and friend Dave Egan. He had come down to Cork for the Jazz Festival on the October long weekend, where I met up with him, Liam and the Egan brothers. So staring at Alan on the bed in the intensive care unit less than two weeks later seemed so surreal when thinking of the pints we'd enjoyed in The Castle Bar in Cork city.

The day after we had gathered in the intensive care unit, Alan's parents arrived back early from the holiday they had been on and asked us to say our goodbyes before they turned off the machine. I stood at the foot of the bed, with Rita behind me, and Alan's parents, friends and girlfriend gathered around the bed. I didn't want to stay for long so as to give his family and Louise the time they needed. But as I put my hand on his leg, I broke down. I wailed and cried hysterically. I was embarrassed that I couldn't control myself while his parents seemed composed. But I just couldn't stop myself. I was just so gutted for him. Alan's mother consoled me. It should have been the other way around. I said my goodbyes and left the room. It was all over.

I met my buddy Cormac in the hospital car park. Cormac, an awesome all-round musician and just another superb individual, had been Zenith's lead guitarist. As with Alan, I had asked him to be a groomsman for my wedding. His dad was very ill and close to passing away, so to say the mood was sombre in Cormac's car would be an understatement. But that's another time when I have seen the worth of true and meaningful friendship. Here was a guy who was dealing with his father's terminal illness but was willing to sympathise with Alan's tragedy.

We went to Claremorris to attend the removal and funeral. Rita and I stayed in a B&B with old college friends. We were in Alan's house for the majority of the time. Lots of people were around the house. There was a massive crowd at the removal. I was asked to be a pallbearer for the funeral along with Donal Meeley and Alan's three brothers and father. It sounds weird, but I was so proud to be carrying him. As sad and disgusted as I felt, I had a sense of unbearable pride. He was such an awesome guy and everyone knew it.

Even in his death, Alan drew people towards him. A day after the funeral I got up from the living room in the Feeley's house to open the front door. I was met by Taoiseach Enda Kenny (the Irish prime minister), who proceeded to stay in the house for a number of hours, talking to us all (he knew Alan's father). I met most of my college group that week in a pub in Claremorris. It was great to reminisce but very upsetting to see everyone under these circumstances. The whole thing was just so low.

I didn't make the same mistake I had made after Aidan's death. I didn't try to drink my sorrows away this time. I knew from previous experience that it only made matters worse. I just mourned as people do. I was also embarrassed about some of my own feelings. I selfishly thought of my own situation. I thought of how crazy this all was and how fickle life can be. How we don't know how good we have it at times. I thought about my job in the Irish Army and how I wasn't happy. I thought of how Alan's life was taken from him well before his time. How we can't take our own life for granted. I had been looking into leaving the army and doing something else. I had already applied for a transfer to the Australian Army and was awaiting an offer from them. I felt really selfish for thinking these things at this time but I also felt as if this tragic event had helped to make up my mind.

Looking at Alan's grave after he was lowered down, I thought that I had to take control, because we can never tell when it will be our turn. To quote *The Shawshank Redemption*: 'Get busy livin', or get busy dyin'.' Not that it mattered much in those moments. I felt so bad for his family, particularly Liam, who idolised him. I felt bad for Louise, who was such a strong and focused person but who was clearly gutted without him. I also felt bad for Vivian, his old girlfriend from college and another good friend of mine. I would have loved to have talked to him one more time. Just to let him know how much I thought of him, how highly I regarded him and how honoured I was to be his friend.

Probably while looking down at us all, he also managed make sure that I met all his friends in our combined grief. I knew most of the boys but, other than Donal and Conor Daly, not very well. In death, Alan brought us all together and, as these were Alan's friends, they were of course lovely people. A group of us in Limerick, led by Liam and Louise, started to plan an awareness activity to commemorate Alan's life but also to show his awesomeness in death – the fact that he was an organ donor and saved the lives of six people through his donations. It was as much therapy for us as it was actually about the activity. We eventually ran an event called 'Alan's Sports Extravaganza' in Limerick in August 2014, combining a sports day and tag rugby tournament with a charity ball. The committee met almost every week from some time after Christmas until the event. We grew close and it was good for all of us. It ended up as a massively successful event. So many people wanted to help, once again attracted by Alan's gravitational pull.

By the time we ran the event I had one week left in the Irish Army. I wore my dress uniform to the charity ball, knowing it was the last time I would ever wear it. It seemed fitting, as Alan had played a part in me making that decision. Like when he helped me on Kilimanjaro.

When things get hard I think of Alan watching me and telling me to push on. I know Aidan would too. Maybe it's unfair to use their deaths as my motivation. But I'd like to think they would want me to. After all, that's what friends are for.

11

MY LEADERSHIP LEARNING CURVE JUST GOT STEEP

KILDARE, IRELAND – 2010–2013

This chapter is a synopsis of my service as an officer in the Irish SF. In order to maintain operational security for the ARW and the Irish Defence Forces, I have deliberately kept dates and certain locations vague, used pseudonyms for ARW members' names and omitted certain aspects of my service within the unit. I discuss tactics, techniques and procedures that have been published as open-source information only. The views expressed within this chapter are mine alone and do not reflect official DF policy, and the details listed are my recollections only. Throughout this book, some of my views on the ARW and the Irish Defence Forces may come across as bitter, but this is not the intent. I simply hope to illustrate through an honest, personal account, the highs and lows of an SF commander, and my own progression in building resilience and self-confidence as a leader.

2010 – Learning

I was twenty-six years old when I was called up to work in the ARW. I was petrified. I had broken a leg in September 2009 and was still recovering, but when I received a phone call out of the blue from the CO ARW in November, I told him I was honoured to be considered to join, and that I was fit and almost fully recovered. I hung up the phone and hobbled around my kitchen, absolutely ecstatic. Had I just conducted the biggest bluff of all time?

I met the CO and 2IC in early January and was to be introduced to the unit at a morning parade immediately thereafter. Even walking into the compound that morning was nerve-racking. *Do I wear my black (Regular Army) beret or go without any head-dress? Do I salute people?* SF units don't usually salute, as an operational security measure to keep rank anonymous. I felt eyes all over me as I wandered into the main building looking for a familiar face. I was escorted outside by one of the other officers for morning parade.

The entire unit paraded every morning outside the front of the main building. The officers stood off to the side. Very few people were in uniform that first morning. In fact, other than the guy taking the roll call, who seemed to be on duty, and me, no one was correctly dressed. The unit 2IC strolled out in front of the parade. He was dressed in running shoes, jeans and a unit jumper. With his hands firmly in his pockets, he motioned for me to come forward. The silence in which I was being judged was deafening. I sheepishly nodded as if to say hello as I was introduced. There was a large 'woop-woop' from someone in the crowd as I walked away, followed by a few low giggles. For the rest of the day, I tried not to make eye contact with anyone and stayed almost completely between my locker space and the office my predecessor was working from.

I was earmarked to take over the Special Operations Task Unit Land/Air, (SOTU-L/A) or, as it was commonly known, the 'para' sub-unit. A mate from Kilkenny was the current commander and I'm sure he had endorsed me to take over. I was still a lieutenant at the time, as the moratorium on all promotion in the public sector had stopped my promotion to captain in mid-2009. It was awkward walking around for the first few days, not knowing what was going on, and it felt a lot like my first days as an officer in Kilkenny. As I had completed my selection course years previously, and as a lieutenant without a completed reinforcement (Reo) cycle (a seven-month SF specific training course for those who have passed selection but require specific skills before they can fully join the unit), I felt incredibly conscious and underqualified. I saw some staff from my selection course around the unit, some of whom barely acknowledged my existence. Even though I was coming into this unit to lead, I felt judged. I was a little apprehensive that maybe I was not what they were looking for and that they had made a mistake. At the same time, I was buzzing at the thought that I was in the SF. Back in my tiny rundown room on the other side of the Curragh Camp, I sat on my bed thinking how cool this was.

The unit immediately set me to task, saying they needed me to get some qualifications, so they sent me on a Live Fire Tactical Trainers (LFTT) course. This was run through the infantry school at the far end of the camp and some of my original cadet school classmates were both students and instructors on the course. I was a little embarrassed to wear the green beret I had been given by the unit CO. I had pictured this, how amazing it would be for me, a simpleton from nowhere, to be an SF officer, but in truth I had not earned it yet. The CO only gave it to me as it was a number of months until the next Reo cycle and he didn't want to send a unit officer on an external course without the beret.

The significance of that beret was huge, and not lost on me. Only fully qualified members should wear it and I was very conscious of this. Some non-qualified members who served in the unit for extended periods were given the right by the CO. I disagreed with non-qualified guys wearing it but it is, after all, at the CO's discretion. I had passed a selection course and was attending a Reo cycle, but if I hadn't been told to wear it, I would not have done so. I was uncomfortable wearing it until I had passed my Reo cycle and fully earned the right.

I quickly noticed that the wearing of the beret brought a certain level of scrutiny with it. Suddenly people around the camp stared at you. During the LFTT course, I felt that both classmates and other staff viewed me differently. All my moves were noticed and commented on. 'Why does he get a different pack and boots?' I learned quickly through a few small mistakes to be very careful of what I said and how I acted, as everyone watches SF guys.

Throughout 2010 I was sent on a number of courses that would usually be conducted post-Reo, but as I was waiting for the next course to begin in late October, I got my job-specific qualifications while I could. I was run through a suite of driving courses, some weapons courses and of course parachuting, specifically working up to military freefall. Although I had a higher number of skydives than a lot of my sub-unit, I had not conducted a jump in over a year and, therefore, was not current. Freefall-qualified guys in the unit were all too keen to point that out to me. During the first parachute training block, I was required to jump with coaches until I regained my currency and competency. I kept quiet and observed a lot of the training procedures and drills. I also took note of the group dynamic of the guys I was meant to be leading. What else could I do? I wanted to let people know that I was the boss but I wasn't fully qualified, which was an awkward position to be in.

I got to know a few of the guys a bit better during this time and slowly I settled down into the unit. My officer cadet school buddy, Mike, had also just been posted into the unit and it was great to have a close friend to confide in. I had assumed command of the sub-unit in April and, even though I was tied up with courses, I still had to maintain all the usual administration that every commander does – appraisals, leave, career progressions, welfare, injury issues, etc. A working day for me usually started at 8.15 a.m. and could easily go until 8.30 p.m. or later. Each night I crawled into my prehistoric bed in the tiny room in an unkept and filthy excuse for accommodation on the other side of the camp. I lived the life of a hermit mostly, sometimes not speaking to a single person outside of work. It was a lonely existence at times and I resorted to single-person cinema trips, hoping other army cinema attendees didn't recognise me.

My simplified definition of SF is that they are uniquely able to do stuff that the rest of the DF can't. A bespoke asset, one might say. In September I was involved in a joint exercise with the Naval Service and Air Corps, conducting a maritime takedown of the Gas Rig Platform Alpha off the coast of Kinsale, County Cork. I was very excited, but nervous too. I was commanding an SF sub-unit conducting a maritime counter-terrorism exercise 30km off the Irish coast. As I still hadn't completed my Reo cycle, I was lacking confidence about my knowledge of even the most basic skills and drills. But I had an excellent 2IC who assisted me with my planning and delivery of orders, as well as keeping the guys aligned. 'Killer' was older than most of the guys in the teams, but vastly experienced and intelligent, and he had an excellent attitude towards officers in the unit. He was an absolute pro. As the air assault guys, we would hold off until our Special Operations Task Unit – Maritime (SOTU-M) brothers contacted us. (Due to their general grumpy demeanour, some of the guys called them 'the dark side of the Force'. We decided that their grumpiness was most likely due to the fact that while they conducted combat dives in the freezing black water of Blessington Lake, we would high-five, then freefall out the back of aircraft into the beautiful sunny atmosphere. They were wet and cold. We were ice-creams and high-fives!) We then charged forward in the choppers, touch-landed or fast-roped onto the ship, then burst into the main structure, clearing it level by level. Cue 'Ride of the Valkyries' music.

One of the other unit officers gave me some advice beforehand. I had voiced my concerns over being new to this, so he kept it simple, noting my habit of having 'blonde moments': 'Let the guys do the work, you just guide them. KISS – Keep It Simple, Stupid. All you need to do is tell a team when they get to a junction left or right. Remember; you are just pulling the strings, you are never first in the door.'

I took his advice and let the execution flow. Killer and I had delivered the plan of how we would assault the structure, and went into great detail on each level, using blueprints of the gas rig, with actions on various possible issues. We then had to trust the guys to get the job done. We didn't need constant chatter or shouting as the teams moved through. Once on-board, everyone slid around the structure, taking up shooting angles, moving silently and smoothly. All things considered, I was pretty happy with my performance, as I successfully planned and delivered orders which were then executed as planned. Although I had been nervous about messing up or looking silly, I gained confidence and learned a lot during my first big unit exercise. I wanted to do this stuff every day. I was also getting to know my guys more, and (hopefully) they were happy to work with me. I knew I wasn't the most experienced at this stuff but I was trying hard and I hoped my honesty of effort could be seen.

Murphys' Law also applies during the execution of missions. On our second day of running through the exercise, just as we began our run in, the pilots in our lead heli got very chatty over the radio and told me there was a 'problem' and they were turning us around to land. Naturally I was unimpressed. After a minute, the pilot came back on internal comms to me. 'Bill, we're gonna have to divert back to land immediately, we've lost one turbine and if we lose the other we'll fall into the sea. I obviously can't take the risk of landing it on the platform. Sit tight, I'm getting us over land ASAP.'

I briefed my guys and, very casually, we started unslinging our MP5 assault weapons. One of the guys jokingly pointed towards the exit handle as we mentally reminded ourselves of the heli underwater-evacuation training we had conducted earlier that year in Cork. Helicopters invert quickly when they hit the water. We stared out the windows looking at the freezing ocean zipping past us and I gauged reactions through the balaclava-covered faces. I also thought about the guys left assaulting the platform without us and how frustrated I'd be if we had been left to fend for ourselves, under-strength. We made it over land surprisingly fast. The pilot told me he was aiming for Collins Barracks in Cork city as the heli would be secure there. We ripped in as fast as we could over the base. I looked down and could see the barracks square filled with guys in their number 1 uniform delivering marching lessons. It appeared that some form of important course was in the middle of conducting a drill assessment day.

The heli banked directly into the middle of the square and spat out a bucket load of annoyed, tooled-up SF operators, clad head-to-toe in black counter-terrorist kit. I could almost hear jaws dropping over the rotor sound! I casually walked over to an officer friend of mine who was assessing the soldiers. I apologised for the interruption and, in typical army fashion, we started abusing each other.

The second heli, which would re-insert us into the operation, was at least twenty minutes out, so my guys chilled out on the edge of the square. I went up to the barrack adjutant's office and apologised for the unintended 'show of force', and to ensure that the General stationed in Cork didn't get too upset that his lunch was most likely interrupted. We boarded the second chopper and made it out to the platform in time to be greeted by very sweaty and breathless assault team members who told us we were a bunch of chickens who only came out for the free lunch. To be fair, the food on the gas rig was superb.

In October 2010 ARW ran its annual selection course, called 'Tango 1'. I was directed to understudy the OIC of the course, give lessons and act as DS. The course OIC made judgement calls throughout the course that I may not have agreed with. Although I had my opinions, as did every other DS, ultimately it was his call that mattered. I learned a massive amount from the OIC and staff, while I also formed my own thoughts towards selecting SF soldiers, having now experienced both sides. I didn't like the idea of interrogation on a selection course (i.e. it should be done during the Reo cycle) and I didn't like the thought of being responsible for the serious and/or permanent injury of a student, as he would be no good to the unit if he arrived broken post-selection. I also made a mental note to myself: *no one performs well on a selection course.* Prior to my posting to the ARW, I had worked with some of the candidates on the course and knew them to be excellent at their job. However, on selection, they had performed to an assessed average standard. Initially I was a little surprised, but I reminded myself never to forget how difficult it is on the other side of the fence. It always looks easier from the top of the hill.

Five non-officers passed 'Tango 1'. The general progression then is to roll into Reo cycle thereafter for seven months, then continue upskilling in your respective platoons after completion of the course. Most other top SF units worldwide have a much longer Reo, but due to the small numbers and limited resources in Ireland, guys get pushed out to the teams earlier and catch up afterwards on insertion skills, advanced driving and other trades. Along with the five guys on this Reo, there would be three officers: Mike, J-Alpha and me. It's funny to think how I started my very first day in the army alongside Mike, and here we were together on Reo.

The guys on Reo with us were all unique characters. We had a stocky guy from Cork, whom I had known as a boy growing up in the local area. One of ten boys, he was built like an inverted pyramid and was very upbeat and an absolute gent, unless we managed to get him angry. He could have easily ripped my arms off if he wanted to, so I was glad that he was on our team! We also had a quiet guy from Kilkenny who I'd worked with in 3rd Battalion and in Chad. He was a former barber, smart and jovial. Our band of merry men was rounded out with Private P, a young guy from Kildare who looked like a 60kg pre-teenager, and a crooked-eyed guy from Mayo with a tendency to be about as tactful as a sledgehammer. Our last member, from Cork, left the course early and the unit soon after. It is funny how people have a preconception of what an SF guy looks like or that he is 'forged from steel'. However, it really is an eclectic mix. Yes, there are absolute Spartan-looking guys but, in truth, body shape, size and looks don't matter. Only performance and heart matter, as we were about to find out.

SF tasks are much more complex than I have depicted here, but simplified, the course worked off two distinct phases: 'Green' and 'Black'. Green was everything from advanced marksmanship on a vast number of weapons, to long-range recon patrolling, to survival and much more. Black was everything counter-terrorism related. There was crossover between the two. For instance, Special Recon ('to find out something'), Special Recovery Operations ('to get something back') and Direct Action ('to use force for some reason') missions could potentially be a mix of both Green and Black skills.

The senior instructor was superb and another absolute pro. I felt it was tricky for him as he was training three officers, two of whom were the task unit commanders, and though we didn't always perform well, I really appreciated the fact that he treated us like adults and not like students on an induction course. He let us organise most elements of the small-scale activities and focused on the actual teaching points. I had been told by other officers that Reo was the best course they ever did, and I have to say I completely agree. But it was tough. There was a constant self-induced pressure that would eat away at you every day. The staff would rarely give you a real strong talking to because if you shot poorly or did a drill incorrectly, you knew, and you would be furious with yourself, particularly as a commander. All any of us wanted was to do everything absolutely perfectly.

We conducted two full mission-profile Green exercises that did not go well and they still bother me to this day. Both were conducted in very challenging weather conditions, which degraded us severely. Our first full mission exercise was in late 2010, when it was snowing heavily and minus seventeen degrees throughout the activity. Our boat insert had to break the surrounding ice close to the pick-up point on Blessington Lake to get to us. In our planning and analysis, we underestimated the conditions and we were not issued the appropriate cold-weather gear.

We were attempting an infiltration patrol at night over Black Hill in the

Wicklow Mountains, but it became a very slow plod. Movement in such conditions was energy sapping. Each time I lifted my boot up, out and over the foot-hole I had just created, and attempted to conduct a single leg step up, it felt like there was a baby elephant on my back. Halfway through any given step up my foot would squash the snow, crunching my body back down to earth and reminding my knee, hip and back of how great it was to be called 'Special'. All this, while I was trying desperately to remain tactical, navigate and not freeze. In fact, the only morale boost was watching one of the other members of the patrol flopping into the snow, then wriggling like an overturned turtle before finding his feet with murmured expletive moans thrown in. Over the duration of the exercise, we all picked up frost nip, which has left my fingers quite susceptible to moderate cold weather even today. I suppose it should have been obvious that I was going to pick up frost nip when I was making mock-up models from snow, but our minds were too weak to even notice.

We had decided during planning that, as a patrol in deep reconnaissance, we would not cook hot meals (this is called hard routine). This was a big mistake. Our bodies were shutting down slowly but we were too focused on doing what we thought were the correct drills, not realising that first, and most importantly, we needed to be fit to fight. It was so cold that most of our battery-powered optics and radio equipment didn't work. After a few days of gathering information and planning, we conducted the slowest raid on an objective known to man. We snatched the target and were stepping off, having picked up our wardrobe-like backpacks, when the staff decided we were moving too slow and too close to the objective and started to shoot blank rounds in our direction (commonly known as 'contact'). We attempted to return fire and manoeuvre as best as possible given the two feet of snow, 100lb+ packs and the degraded state of our bodies after over three days' exposure to temperatures lower than minus seventeen. The guy acting as our High Value Target (HVT) was the transport sergeant in the unit. An old-school former team member, he seemed to want to give us a hard time. When we were securing him, the staff directed us to leave him uncuffed for exercise purposes. He kept giving us abuse and was acting out. We pointed out to him that in real life, we would have *quietened* him by now.

Mike had gone on a close target recce two nights previously and when he returned to greet me at the final RV some nine hours later, both he and Private P were in a bad way. They were slurring their words and unsteady on their feet. I gave Mike some biscuits and we escorted them back to the patrol harbour ASAP. During the raid, the tables turned. Now I was the one really feeling weary, lightheaded and dazed. I was disorientated and had to ask Mike which way we were going. Two days previously I had given him a dig-out on his return, but now I badly needed his help. The buddy system was still as applicable, almost a decade since Mike and I used it for the very first time as young officer cadets.

As we were just about to break clean from contact, one of the patrol members shouted at me. Private P, our 60kg child from Kildare, had momentarily let go of the HVT, who proceeded to run away, back to the objective. I was furious with the team member as we manoeuvred back to the objective. He maintained that the sergeant acting as HVT had told him he would 'play the game' as we say, then ran off. I approached a four-wheel drive parked alongside the objective. I could see a figure inside and, thinking it was our guy, I screamed at him to get out of the car. I was two seconds from putting my rifle butt through the window and dragging him out through the glass when the window came down and I saw that it was our senior instructor observing the entire episode. He told me in expletive terms to go away and find the HVT, and not to miss the extract at first light.

What an absolute mess. We swept the objective and I made the decision to move off before enemy reinforcements arrived. We started trekking towards the heli pick-up, knowing that we had failed in our mission. It was soul-destroying. I tripped, fully face-planting into the snow with my backpack over me, so I couldn't even move to a side. The DS near me had to roll me over so I could find my feet. We plodded off into the distance until eventually I got word on the radio to turn around, as the heli was cancelled due to the bad weather and the exercise was now over. Our bodies were destroyed. I was gutted that we had failed our mission so badly. I attempted to take learning points from it in the immediate aftermath, but I was just so disappointed that I couldn't muster the enthusiasm. I questioned my self-worth and felt shame. *Should I even be here? Am I good enough for this?*

We sat down in the office back in the Curragh and debriefed our performances. The unit 2IC spoke with us the following day and he told us to work harder and act like officers. I wanted the ground to eat me up as I walked gingerly around the unit. But the 2IC was right. If I was staff on the Reo cycle I would not have been impressed. I needed to act like a commander. I needed to be an SF officer, at all times.

Two nights later, the three officers on Reo were ordered to attend the Curragh Camp Officers Mess Christmas Dinner with the CO of the unit. Our bodies were still messed up and we were in no mood to be jolly. The CO noted our very heavy drinking and general pissed-off demeanour, and stayed well away from us three stooges propped up at the bar, warming ourselves up with the water of life.

During our next full mission profile, we conducted a live-fire (i.e. with live ammo) withdrawal from an underground observation post, then moved to an emergency RV and began our exfiltration through our designated area of recovery corridor. The only problem was that the corridor was across Cavanagh's Gap to Tonlegee car park. This meant walking up and over Table Mountain and then subsequently over Conavalla Mountain, the most peat-soaked, featureless mountain in Ireland, by night, in strong sleet, gales and bitter cold that played havoc on all battery-operated items such as night vision and GPS. I usually layer down when patrolling, but on this occasion I wore every item of clothing I had and was still freezing as the wind chill factor was immense and we were painstakingly slow due to the underfoot conditions. I took the lead scout position for the patrol and had to use the old-school navigation method of map and compass as all GPS systems were unworkable. I'd like to say I used my paces to measure distance, but it was impossible due to the conditions. Everything took more time. A map check would take three times as long as I fumbled with my compass, while the others shook violently behind me. As visibility was close to zero, we stuck right up onto each other, in a very untactical conga line. Every few yards I'd either get stuck in soft black bog up to my knee, or attempt to dodge around it, while trying to stay on bearing. A number of times I blindly stepped straight off a four-foot drop and clattered my way to the peat below. I got stuck up to my waist on one occasion and two of the guys had to lie down alongside to pull me out, with the DS assisting. After ten minutes of wriggling, I got out and lay on my back for thirty seconds to catch my breath. I stood up, whispered 'moving now', took three steps and sank again. The phrase 'FML' was designed for instances like this.

We finally made our RV some fourteen hours later, soaked, frozen and shattered. But something remarkable occurred towards the end of the patrol. As we came off the mountain and headed toward the RV, we began patrolling correctly. As opposed to feeling sorry for ourselves, we broke from self-preservation back into military mode, conducting marry-up procedures, obstacle crossing and basic hand-signals correctly. We made contact with our Agent, before we were then extracted back to the Curragh for a debriefing. The staff were unhappy with certain aspects, but were very pleased with the heart and determination shown.

Reflecting now, this was an excellent mental challenge. I'm not sure if we made massive learning strides in terms of SF skills for long-range patrolling, but maybe that wasn't the point. At one particular moment very early in the morning, the group was getting immensely frustrated with the conditions and had a quick discussion on top of Conavalla about turning back off the mountain and attempting a 5km hook-around. But we persevered. We kept going, and going. We managed to remain fit to fight this time, our determination was proved and I felt that both the other officers and I had shown we could lead and bring the guys with us. Although I was still a little disappointed with the construction of the observation post, the effort and will were superb and I felt more confident in being there. As part of the debrief, one of the staff actually gave me some praise. During our little team meeting on top of Conavalla, amongst the peat, sleet and gales, when some of the guys thought it might be easier to walk down off the side of the mountain and traverse from the north, I argued against this and said either way was extremely harsh terrain but we just had to continue on and get through it. I backed myself, and my navigation and my moral courage were noted afterwards by a DS member. The perceived easier way may not be the best.

After conducting an unpleasant survival and interrogation exercise, we moved into the Black role phase of the course and the dynamics changed rapidly. Black role is based around counter-terrorist actions but still quite flexible as the spectrum of conflict is not simple. One could argue that it's an additional layer of skills as opposed to separate. All exercises were short and sharp but the intensity was immense and the margin for error was minimal. We used training paint rounds, had live enemies and worked on a lot of live-fire practices. We fired live ammo every day. We would be taught a drill – a basic room entry for instance – then repeat it over and over until it was conducted with live ammo, over and over. More difficult tasks were incrementally but rapidly added in and repeated over and over. I loved it. Shoot/no-shoot targets, hostage scenarios, working on methods of entry into buildings, trains, buses, aircraft, abseiling through windows, fast-roping onto objectives, mechanical and explosive entry; if this sounds cool, it's because it is. I got a head shot (with paint round) on a terrorist holding a hostage. It made my day. The following day I missed a terrorist behind a door upon entry and I was disgusted with myself. The DS didn't need to reinforce the points – you knew if you had done well or not. One or two of the guys were under pressure at this stage. Top tip: don't shoot hostages and particularly staff acting as hostages.

On one particular paint-round serial, we moved together as a team, flow-ing through various scenarios in each room. We neutralised a live terrorist in a room and he lay down. As we moved past our downed terrorist (one of our DS), one of the students cracked two rounds into his head and one into his body. The DS jumped up and almost began a full punch-up. The student maintained that the terrorist had moved, but our sore DS was not convinced or impressed. We all thought this very funny, except for the student in question, who was sentenced to a paint-round barrage in the buttocks from his fellow team members.

Our final exercise of the course was a heli fast-rope insertion into our live-fire kill house where, after an explosive method of entry, we would storm the house, seize the box in the last room and then conduct an exfiltration. The entire unit came up to the viewing stand that overlooks the house. I was the team leader for the exercise. By this stage I had grown in confidence and felt happy with my ability. I was able to lead the team comfortably. I enjoyed the planning, delivering orders and directing the guys during execution.

We circled over the Curragh Camp, heavily kitted up, before we made our insertion, and then came the butterflies as we screeched down to hover above the range. We fast-roped down and entered the range with smooth haste. We engaged a number of steel targets on the move outside the house around some busted-up cars. We then set up to storm the house in the range area as the ordnance officer joined up with us from the rear, before he stepped forward and blew the doors. *Wooah, he used a lot of dems!*

We burst in and worked through the building, moving quite well as a team. *Slow is smooth, and smooth is fast.* We were fluid, taking up angles with minimal talk and a lot of anticipation. Although we were lobbing stun grenades and firing live rounds inches across or over one another we had complete trust in ourselves and each other. We worked through the building until we reached the last room, collected the box and exited the house.

The CO met us outside the building as we removed our helmets and balaclavas. He opened the box and pulled out our green berets. I was now a fully qualified SF officer of the ARW.

A dream was realised.

2011 – From Learning to Leading

If 2010 was my 'learning the ropes year', then 2011 certainly was not. The unit maintained its breakneck speed throughout the year. The personalities involved both internally and externally made for some tricky exchanges. But I was confident enough to voice my opinion and enforce it when necessary. I got a slap on the wrist for telling guys outside the unit to stop trying to interfere with military freefall activities. I had a few awkward conversations with unit members who had no issue with challenging me in front of others. I wasn't trying to push my weight around, but I was not afraid to disagree if I felt there was a better way forward. Although I was pretty easy-going, I wasn't just going to go with the flow or be a pushover. I most certainly wasn't acting all 'Alpha dog' either, as that tough-guy image just isn't really me.

Around this time, the unit focused attention towards maritime counter-terrorism as we had certain capabilities and capacity that no other Irish agency could bring to bear. We worked off the premise that the next large-scale activity in the region was the London Olympics, and therefore one aspect we analysed was maritime interdiction (intercepting to prevent movement) of a large vessel under subversive control, as it entered Irish waters. The set-up for our initial exercise was to interdict the Stena *Adventurer* (a large passenger ferry) from Liverpool as soon as it hit Irish waters en route to Dublin. This, along with subsequent cargo-ship interdictions in 2012, were some of the most complex exercises I was involved in.

The nicknamed 'dark side of the force' (SOTU-M) used rigid-hulled inflatable boats (Rhibs) to speed in behind the ferry as it powered towards Dublin Port at twenty-one knots. The guys hoisted up an extended pole and hook while the Rhib ploughed alongside the ship. The team then hooked the top of the ladder to the steel lip on the ship's deck and retracted the pole, leaving the wire ladder of approximately 25cm in width flicking off the ship's side, daring those in the Rhib to climb it. The operators duly obliged as the best climbers set off first up the wire ladder. Transferring from Rhib to ladder was ungraceful at best, then the operator would haul himself up the side of the moving ferry as smoothly as possible, concentrating on arm and foot placement to prevent entanglement. Once aboard, they began their assault as directed by Mike (who by then was the commander of the maritime sub-unit) and the respective team leaders.

As the air element, we roared in as the heli loadmaster gave the thirty-second signal. I removed the aircraft headset and donned my helmet. We unbuckled our quick-release heli lanyards and conducted last-second moves. We tightened fast-rope gloves, checked snag hazards on our neighbours' belts, then shuffled towards the doors as the loadmaster slid them open.

The pilot banked hard and slid the aircraft behind the ship's bridge as the rope was quickly deployed. One by one we scurried to the edge, placed our feet either side of the rope, grabbed onto the rope at eye level, then pushed off with a slight rotation away from the heli to avoid a potential catch. I was the last man out of the first heli. My feet were happy to feel the solid surface of the ship as I flung the rope away and immediately lifted my MP5 onto my right shoulder, adopting a high ready position. I tagged in directly behind the first team, which was already advancing on the rear of the bridge as I joined the snake. We moved with purpose towards the rear door. As the first team began assaulting, I remained at the doorway ready to direct the already advancing second team on entry and task any team thereafter. I crossed decisive events or persons off my armband as reported, and key areas were secure within minutes. I then met up with Mike (fresh-faced from his ladder climb and run around the ship) on the top deck to conduct a quick analysis of the situation before sending back the various reports to both the naval and air assets on station.

We recocked the exercise throughout the week to refine timings and, as the maritime guys were giving us a lot of abuse about not climbing the ladder, the sub-units traded positions in order to give all the members exposure to both methods of inserting onto the ship. We had all done the required work-up training but I have to say my technique and strength on the ladder were not good. If I'm honest, I was very nervous.

We loaded onto the boat and tore into the middle of the deep Irish Sea. Once we reached our stand-off point, the engine was turned off and we bobbed around as I stared into the dark, cold water, listening in on my radio. When we eventually got the call, the Rhib flew over the surface until we ripped in alongside the ship.

Jesus Christ, I thought as I craned my neck up at the moving steel mountain. My 2IC and I were last after the first team. My 2IC had also been struggling with the ladder in work-up training but I think he felt he needed to show me some strength, so he pushed past me and grabbed the ladder. He started well but then began to struggle badly. His arms gave up about halfway up the ladder and he clung on for his life. We pulled the Rhib out from the ship so if he fell he wouldn't land on the boat, while the safety guys on-board attempted to sway the safety line his way. Eventually he got it, hooked on and they lowered him back onto the Rhib. I took the carabiner, clipped it on and grabbed hold of the ladder. I stepped off the Rhib and placed my foot onto the highest rung possible. I was petrified but just started pumping my legs, kept my body close to the ladder and climbed for dear life. It came easier than I expected as I had been practising all week back in the base after hours. All in the legs! Halfway up I stopped, as I was moving too quickly and tangling the safety line at my feet. I looked across the side of the ship. I could see safety boats in the middle distance staring right at me, with the nearby naval ship holding its breath. *'Don't fear fellas,'* I thought as I scurried up the ladder to be greeted by Mike asking what had taken me so long.

I felt bad for my 2IC. He was leading by example while I had hesitated and yet I was on-board. I learned some very valuable lessons that day. *Never let your fear take over* and *there are always better people than you out there,* I said to myself during a quiet moment in Keogh's pub in Dublin the following evening over some well-earned pints of Guinness with the heli pilots and unit officers. As happens so regularly in the unit, the exercise wrapped up and we quickly moved on to the next item while the ink was still drying on the exercise debrief points.

The unit was well aware, before any official announcements, that Queen Elizabeth II and the President of the United States were both visiting Ireland in May 2011. It was very exciting for us. This was shaping up to be a real operation, and on home turf. I was the heli-borne QRF tactical commander for the operation. Unfortunately, this would turn into the biggest disappointment in my time in the unit. From external sources to the DF and within the general staff, there seemed to be a massive reluctance to utilise the ARW in any way. People seemed to have the impression that we were some sort of rogue and lawless outfit that daily came up with ways of trying to kill each other. I was dumbfounded that the police didn't want to work with us and didn't want to use us in any way. We would have done anything to assist, and we had plenty to offer.

However, our CO, a very smart man, understood that we could still create an effect on the battlespace. Media photographers were somehow excellently located at Baldonnel Aerodrome (Air Corps Base) to picture our snipers covering the Queen's entry into the state. One could argue that the task served no tactical relevance, but the pictures made the front-page news of *The New York Times*! We were also photographed getting in and out of the helis all tooled up and looking mean, even though it was a transit flight for us to sit in Baldonnel hangar while we watched the Queen strutting around Dublin with the plainclothes Emergency Response Unit following her around. That photo was also plastered all over the news.

We didn't like the fake photo parades but I saw the relevance of it. The CO may have been as pissed off as we were but at least he had a strategy to combat it. One could also argue that it was a deterrent in itself, as it showed us being busy and let the general population know that things were safe and in hand. The police even attempted to arrest our unit 2IC, who was driving around sites in Dublin conducting area surveys. Even after he outlined who he was, they persisted in attempting to arrest him, and it seemed to me like they wanted to make him look silly.

In actual fact, we already felt silly. We were Ireland's premier DF unit, the country's SF, and we were being shunned by the very state we were employed to protect. We were scrambling to find relevance with no guidance or direction. It was in that moment I knew that the Irish government, the Department of Defence and senior management in the DF didn't – and still don't – take the ARW seriously. They like flaunting the name of the unit around but, in reality, they see it as a liability or, at best, a 'zombie-apocalypse' last resort. Someone needs to realise that direct action is only one very small feather in the cap of the ARW. I was very disheartened by the whole operation as we sat in Baldonnel and Cork for the duration of the visits. I remember thinking afterwards: *have I wasted my time, punished my body and compromised my lifestyle for no actual real reason? Have I been fooled by years of military exposure so that I actually believe in our relevance?* It was very demoralising both for the guys and for me personally. How could I ask guys to work hard, stay late and perfect all these high-risk skills when we couldn't confirm that there was any significance to any training we did?

I was lucky to do a few courses when in the unit but I didn't actively chase courses like other officers I've seen. In 2010 I refused an officer who wanted to do an Accelerated Freefall course internally during our freefall training block. He was posting out of the unit soon and didn't want to pay to do it in a civilian drop zone. He later rang me and gave me a bit of abuse. I told him I had made the decision myself and that was that. Had it been 2011, when I was much more confident in my abilities, I would have told him to go fuck himself and to stop looking out for his own interests. To me, it didn't make sense for an officer to go on a course when he wouldn't plug back into the unit or the DF. However, I did attend the wider DF version of the Survival, Escape and evasion, Resistance to interrogation and Extraction (SERE) instructor course in 2011. Certain voices in the unit were not happy with me. 'We run our own course, what would they know?' was the rhetoric I heard. My aim in conducting the course outside of the unit was twofold; first, to get an officer qualified in SERE so we could have officer supervision over interrogation, to protect not just the students but also the staff in the event of any complaints, and second, I wanted to show that the ARW was an inclusive organisation within the DF, willing to learn from others. Less than two months after my qualification as a SERE instructor, Killer and I ran an ARW SERE course and restructured the entire ARW SERE training continuum. The way I saw it, the unit had put me on the course, so upon returning from it, I should plug it back into the unit.

2012 – Leading and Let-downs

By 2012 I felt like I had a good grasp on the capabilities, personnel and equipment within the unit. I was confident in my decision-making and working well with both my superiors and subordinates. Our operations officer had graduated to become the new unit 2IC and I thought he was superb. His attention to detail, knowledge and understanding were outstanding. He regularly corrected or advised but never demeaned and never forgot any detail. There are few officers I ever met whom I really admired, and to this day, when in certain situations, I find myself wondering what he would do, as a guide.

Quite early in the year, the unit got an exercise call out to conduct an aircraft takedown. With the London Olympics approaching, it was good to be fresh in both aircraft and maritime takedowns. As the tactical commander, I was relatively at ease with the process whereby we would analyse the situation, develop a plan, then deliver orders to the guys and enablers. We would then rehearse the process as much as possible before moving to a staging area. This would be a 'cold exercise', i.e. no practice runs on the aircraft in Dublin Airport prior to the takedown. We drew a chalk mock-up of the aircraft in our training hall to conduct rehearsals – real old-school – as due to the tight schedule we felt time was best spent practising rather than attempting to build or find something similar to the aircraft at such short notice.

We arrived up to Dublin Airport and received updated information from guys already monitoring the situation. The officer cadet school had kindly volunteered its students to act as hostages ('Hotels') while some of our unit guys acted as terrorists ('Tangos'). We let them stew there for quite a while before eventually moving in and assaulting with speed. By the time I got into the aircraft, it was already secure. Tangos neutralised and no hasty evacuation required. This was yet another excellent learning activity as I was exposed to practising command in a different environment. Being in command for yet another large unit activity gave me the feeling that the exposure was making me a better planner and leader. I was more assured and less stressed under the duress of decision-making. I felt much more confident.

Post-activity, we were allowed to do a few practice runs on a new, larger Airbus 320 in a secure hangar. We got the guys to rotate around each part of the aircraft in small groups as I monitored the training. The senior ground-crew member from Aer Lingus approached the unit 2IC. 'Is that kid in charge or something?' he asked while pointing at me. 'He is indeed,' our unit 2IC replied with a grin, to the astonishment of our Aer Lingus friend. I had heard comments of this nature before; in comparison to most of our grizzly middle-aged operators, I looked like a failed boy-band member. I had attempted to grow a beard, which was a disaster, and was in the process of growing my hair out a little but kept needing to cut it for various reasons. I remember one night in Kilkenny while I was socialising with Mike, a guy came up and started talking crap to us. Out of nowhere, he mentioned the ARW. We hadn't even told him we were army. He was a police officer, but most definitely off-duty. He said that 'the Army Rangers were as tough as nails; serious guys not to be messed with'. I asked him did he know anyone in the ARW. He lied. I started having a bit of fun and asked him what they looked like and he proceeded to describe the cast of the movie *300*. I asked him if he thought I had any chance of becoming one. He laughed and looked me up and down stating that I hadn't a chance in hell. We left him at the bar soon after.

Despite the lingering disappointment of the previous year, when the unit was not properly utilised for the major overseas visits, morale was boosted in 2012 when HQ started talks about potential overseas missions. Now this was something we could do. We got as far as names on boards for a deployment to Somalia to imbed as UNHCR ship guards to protect against Somali pirates in the Gulf of Aden. Ireland was one of a very limited number of EU states not providing assistance and all signs were good for us to deploy. I had even investigated buying a standalone container of gym equipment to drop onto the ship as we would be the security detachment for approximately four weeks at a time as ships sailed from Mogadishu to Djibouti. We got some info from the Dutch marines that it was a tedious operation but we were really looking forward to any kind of deployment. Then it fell through. Once again there was not much appetite to use the ARW, it seemed.

Things only got worse when our attempt to participate in a high-altitude military freefall training symposium in Spain with other SF units from across Europe was also knocked back at short notice, as our own General Staff didn't like the idea. I was later told that a very senior decision maker had been on a recent holiday to the French Alps and felt dizzy during a road trip, so he thought that working at high altitude would be too dangerous. I personally drove to DFHQ in Dublin to hand-deliver a full risk assessment and training instruction outlining in detail the work-up, networks, cost analysis and Defence capability benefits of attending this symposium. I even went as far as to explain that after the symposium Ireland would have the ability to insert medical teams into anywhere in the world from a substantial stand-off distance, to assist Irish people as required. I couldn't fathom why someone would say no when there was pretty much no cost involved and we were trying to improve capability for the DF. The Air Corps maintenance facility for the CASA CN-235 maritime aircraft is in Spain, and they were due to fly close to our intended exercise. The exercise was cost neutral. It was called off two weeks prior to the symposium, even though we had been given money to conduct hypoxia awareness training (a pre-requisite for high-altitude oxygen military freefall) in the Netherlands earlier in the year. All unit-developed networks were immediately broken and our reputation around the European SF community was in tatters. Counterparts across Europe stopped replying to my emails.

I had become so invested in unit and sub-unit matters that it really bothered me we were being treated in this way. I felt the lack of explanation from DFHQ on decisions affecting us was disrespectful of the hard work we put in, and that the time, effort and work we carried out were being neither realised nor recognised. Not to mention that the pay scales given to unit members were (and I'm told still are) disgraceful for a force committed to constant strategic force projection or, as it is commonly known, 'call-out'. Unit members are not dumbass 'killers'. They are intelligent, articulate and highly skilled assets who should be treated as such. These guys are genuine professionals who commit their bodies, minds and hearts to the unit and to the defence of Ireland.

A unit member approached me one evening with genuine upset etched across his face. He had been scheduled to conduct a promotion course outside the unit, but had to cancel his attendance due to an early injury on the course. He almost cried in his apology to me, discussing in detail how he didn't want to let the reputation of the unit down and how he would now do everything in his power to fix his injury and get back on course as soon as possible. The guy had pretty much ripped his own hip clean from its socket from overwork, yet he was visibly more upset about the unit reputation than his own welfare. He was as tough as nails, as fit as a national athlete and as skilled an operator as you are likely to ever meet. He was both humble and completely committed to service within the unit. The fact that his commitment to the unit and selfless devotion to his comrades and country were neither understood nor fully appreciated was more than disappointing.

I don't think anyone in the country would argue against paying ARW members a significantly higher wage due to the sacrifices and commitments they adhere to as a constant national strategic asset, as with most other SF units worldwide. Just because we were really passionate about doing what we did, it did not give the higher echelons of Defence and in particular the Department of Defence the right to walk all over us. As best I could, I attempted not to let the guys see my frustration. I tried focusing on *well if we should be doing this stuff, then we need to be the best we can be at it, because we are professionals.* In trying to make our unit the best it could be, both Mike and I would comment regularly to each other on our sleep difficulty due to our frustrations.

I was fortunate enough to be the OIC of the unit selection course in 2012. ARW selection course 'Victor 1' was due to kick off in late September. I was very excited to be at the coalface of recruiting and screening for the unit. The course syllabus in 2012 was still a little old school. We had discussed potential course alterations at length, and we had guys going on an exchange with our British counterparts to confirm how they selected. We felt that, in the current format, our selection course was outdated. We wanted to run more self-motivated testing, not just 'beasting', as we could see that any super-fit individual could apply themselves enough when shouted at, but the lonely walk for 20km+ with no appraisals was a real mental challenge. The unit was already planning for the next course when we began this course. I still wanted to bring in some small changes. No interrogation whatsoever was to be conducted during selection. I also wanted to conduct a number of individual tests using a time/distance/weight, with no positive or negative reinforcement – this is called 'silent running'. *Be there, within this time, carrying this weight, cheerio.* We needed a team member to be very fit; however, we didn't need a team member who was super fit but only did what they were told. We needed intelligent, mature people whom we could trust when sending them off alone for days at a time. Fitness can change with training. Skills can be worked on with training. But attitude, resilience, toughness, determination and self-belief are more difficult to coach.

Throughout the course I reminded myself of things that I had learned, having had previous experience on both sides of the fence. As we progressed through a series of testing and monitoring exercises, I noticed the staff were 'out for blood' at times. It was a challenge reminding them of how we all performed on our courses. I made some tough calls during the course. I removed candidates for poor performance, including one candidate who had completed all but the very last activity on the course. I had to live by the very construct I had created in terms of assessment. I also had to put my trust in the staff I employed to assess. If I overturned their assessment of the candidate, which I could have easily done, then I was telling them I did not trust their impartiality or judgement. I removed him with fourteen hours left on the course, but was concerned about the optics of this decision. The Irish DF is not an enormous organisation, and details of those who pass or fail selection are a topic of interest during the month of October. I knew that people would argue that I should have let him complete the course and then recommended him 'not fit to serve', but that had the potential to create longer-lasting damage both to the officer and to the reputation of the unit.

Ultimately it was my call; standards are standards and I trusted my staff. The decision to remove him was probably vindicated by the way the candidate acted thereafter, or maybe he was just furiously angry. Either way, I do not regret removing him from the course. There were other occasions during the course when I made what I thought to be the most fair and objective decisions possible. Some were close calls and were not taken lightly, but I was in charge so I had to make that call, and I did so each time with the conviction and confidence gained from the previous two years.

Seven hours after removing the unfortunate officer from the course, I decided I had to show the remaining candidates that I could do the entire 45km walk back with them, carrying the same weight. Without hesitation, the course sergeant decided he would accompany us, as did most of the staff.

2013 – Leaving

I left the ARW in late January 2013. I had only been overseas once and was top of the list of my cohort to go again (in actual fact I was quite overdue), but had held off under the assumption that we'd get a deployment while in the ARW. The CO came to me in early 2013 and said I needed to look at deployment opportunities. The usual cycle for an ARW officer is between two to four years, then to move on as others who have passed selection are waiting to get their chance. Thereafter, who knows, maybe back to the unit as the CO someday?

An officer pulled out of a deployment to Bosnia at the last minute and so, with nine days' notice, I was offered the job and I didn't really have a choice. It was a very abrupt end to my SF career. I felt like I was doing well in the unit, but I really wanted to follow through on things like the projects we had been working on for years, my personal relationship with the guys, and helping and assisting careers. I was so invested in the unit and the guys, I just wanted to make sure the right things would be done. I felt really frustrated that I hadn't fully delivered on things that we had set out to achieve. I almost felt like apologising to the SOTU as I was leaving without finishing what I had started. I was just another ex-member now. As the unit members always joked: *When you're in you're in but when you're out you're out.*

What had I taken from my time there? There were many positives. I had really developed and grown in confidence. I doubted myself less. During my first year I was stressed as I felt I was constantly being judged by everyone and at times I was found badly wanting, but I tried not to hide behind my rank or my office and I wasn't afraid to look foolish, weak or substandard. I had failed in some things but at least I bloody well tried. And I got better. After one particularly embarrassing attempt to climb the wire ladder, I spent the following week in the gym hall practising by myself after hours. I developed more confidence throughout my time there, probably linked to the greater exposure to command in an SF unit. I also became much stronger in terms of my shooting, physical training and parachuting.

Most importantly I became a better leader. When you are in charge of the best, you need to be the best. I wasn't afraid to voice my position and develop new methods and processes within the unit. I went as far as bringing in PT assessments for assault team members. We would conduct a PT assessment every few months to assess our standards. All assault team members had to do it. There were no pass/fail criteria, but it was a best effort, individual test. Assessments ranged from some of the selection course tests to combat swimming to assault course assessments. I wasn't the best on them either, but that wasn't the point. We all needed to have a certain physical standard as 'the tip of the spear' of the Irish Defence Forces; no one ever argued with that point. I would never have thought of bringing something like that into the unit in 2010, but by the end of my time in ARW, I had no problems taking it on and justifying it to anyone who wanted to discuss it. I felt my leadership was stronger and more definite than before. I felt at ease with my job, which I hadn't in the beginning.

I was lucky to have been placed at the tactical end of the ARW for the entire time that I served in the unit. I gained excellent exposure to a range of mission profiles throughout my time. I was more comfortable with my tactical command acumen by the end of my tenure. No more was I a 'rabbit caught in headlights'; instead I would think of the simple things. When something came up, I just made the obvious and simple next move. The KISS (Keep it Simple, Stupid) principle; don't overthink it.

Lastly, the challenges in dealing with a lot of strong people, egos and divisive personalities helped me learn new management techniques. The vast majority of the guys were absolutely incredible to work with but, as seems to be the case with SF units, this job attracted people with strong personalities. I had a sergeant who was quite brilliant but challenging to work with; he was argumentative and blunt. At the start I found him very difficult to deal with, but over time I think he warmed to my style and I to his. As opposed to my telling him the way I wanted something done, we would mould his way (which may have been similar to my way) as the way forward. We ended up working very well together. I felt it taught me that there are many ways to skin a cat. It wasn't as simple as just telling someone what you wanted done. I felt more confident in myself and I really enjoyed working with these guys.

Unfortunately, it is not all sunshine and rainbows. As was apparent during the on-island security operations for Queen Elizabeth and the President of the United States, there appears to be a certain level of distrust of the SF within the realms of DFHQ and the Department of Defence. The best trained, most motivated, most skilled and best equipped element in the DF, which DFHQ and the Department of Defence were too afraid to use.

We live in a risk-averse culture, which often leads to decisions driven by fear of failure. Brave decisions are less likely because of the fear of the responsibility and accountability that the decision brings. I don't know if general staff in Dublin have had a chance to browse McRaven's *Spec Ops* and the theory of relative superiority. I don't know if many senior government staff or Department of Defence members have Petit's *Going Big by Getting Small* on their reading list, or if they appreciate 'phase zero operational planning' and the application of Special Operations within that spectrum. I know I probably seem like a bitter ex-SF grouch, but I get the feeling that people are afraid to use what they don't fully understand. Maybe some thought could go into raising a Special Operations Command with a headquarters linking the strategic (government defence strategy, Department of Defence military strategic commitments, DFHQ directives) to the tactical (ARW, new task-specific specialised units in areas such as Electronic Warfare, Special Operations Engineering, Special Operations Logistics, Cyber Warfare, Human Intelligence (the Irish Defence Forces don't even have a specific Intelligence Corps), Special Operations Air Corps and Naval Service sub-units – streamline the force to make it more relevant and fit for purpose, while achieving the intent of the higher echelons of DFHQ and Department of Defence). It's just a thought … one of many!

One last warning to any SF wannabies is you should understand the toll it takes on your lifestyle, assuming you are committed and want to be the best you can be. I lived the life of a hermit. I worked crazy days and nights. No one told me to, I just had to. I loved the unit. I rotted in the Curragh Camp and ate poorly. My daily diet would inevitably include a flapjack, banana and a can of Monster! I was tired any time I went back to Limerick to see Rita, would arrive late on a Friday night and leave on Sunday afternoon if not sooner. I'd smash a six-pack of Corona on the Friday night and watch crap TV or sport on the Saturday, but was always thinking of work stuff. When I did go out, I would let loose. I had to blow off steam so I got pretty drunk a number of times. It seemed unsustainable. Maybe I was too invested, or not managing my time well, but I found it was all-encompassing. Of course, I loved my time there and I have such pride and honour to have served there, but anyone thinking of this type of job should know that you need to be prepared to go all in. But what else would you expect, only to give: *'The cleanliness of our hearts, the strength of our limbs, and the commitment to our promise'* – the ARW motto.

12

LET'S GO TO WORK

PRINCESS ALEXANDRA HOSPITAL, BRISBANE, AUSTRALIA – MARCH 2015

A sharp, full body spasm let me know it was time to wake up. My spasms consisted of an immediate and aggressive contracting of major muscles throughout my body, shooting my legs and arms straight for an electric-like shock before subsiding after a number of seconds. Sometimes, I felt as if my hip or foot would dislocate from the ferocity of it. From time to time I could feel when it was coming and, through relaxation, make the spasm shorter and less powerful. On certain occasions it might be one leg first, then onto the other, or maybe only one arm. There was no real pattern to it. Others, with much less return of function than I, could have violent spasms during sleep or showering. One of the guys had to be strapped to his bed so as not to fall off during the night. My leg spasms shook my bed to a rattle in the morning. In some instances, it woke the others.

At approximately 7 a.m. every morning, the nurses could be heard moving through the ward on the hunt for light switches and curtains. Each morning I slid my legs out over my bed and used momentum to rotate myself and sit upright on the side of the bed. I weakly stood up with a shudder. My robotic, zombie walk around my bed space served to shed some natural light as I used my arm to drag the curtain around to the side. I then shifted my food table and returned to my seated position at the side of my bed.

The food delivery staff dropped my breakfast onto the table as the nursing staff moved from room to room conducting the morning handover with the incoming staff. 'Here's Billy, he's doing superbly, no issues last night', would be the usual commentary, as I might get a small audience watching me attempt to open a sealed Weetabix biscuit. I then got my spoon with the foam insert, and slowly fed myself in silence. The yogurt carton stared at me every morning, longing to be peeled open. Day after day it was either left alone or opened by a nurse. Eventually I used my teeth, until finally one day, after almost ten minutes of detailed pinching, I got enough purchase to pull it ajar. *Ah, finally*, I thought, and went about rewarding myself by eating it. My father came into the ward within the hour. He saw the opened yogurt, queried how I had opened it and had what I can only describe as a mini heart attack. 'That's absolutely amazing, Billy. Honestly, this is unbelievable,' he chirped. I was quick to dismiss the feat. He began telling me off. 'I don't care if you think it's not a big deal … it is a big deal, a *very* big deal.'

It was early March. I was in an all-out war with my SCI. Every hour was consumed by it. Every morning I was getting up and going to *work*. I even started shaving myself, which had been part of the nurse's morning grind. Holding the razor and manipulating it around my face and around the halo was quite the encounter. Roger would watch on from across the room, wincing at the mad man at the sink fumbling around with a Mach 3. I could just about hold it in either hand with a closed fist. So I shaved the left side with my left hand and the right side with my right hand. I would rotate the blade around to do my neck and chin and, before I knew it, I was clean-shaven and ready for my day.

My daily timings for physio and OT were placed on the whiteboard outside the room. I would then plan my other meetings, supplementary training or visits in between. My physio sessions became more advanced. I was walking around the gym, albeit assisted. I was 'training'. Arm day today. I'd get my physio, Tiffany, to leave me at the wall with various coloured bands as I would conduct everything from curls and raises to presses. Our one-on-one sessions mostly centred on core stability. I just wanted to walk around, but without a strong core my posture would never be right. My hip flexors in particular were very tight and painful, which would occasionally lead to a slight leg drag. I conducted endless exercises on all fours or on the Swiss ball, thereby 'engaging the pelvic floor'.

Exercises such as 'bridging' and 'planking' became my new best friends. I couldn't get enough of it. I would be quite fatigued but I regularly either stayed on to do more work, or went back later to do my own workout. I applied my understanding about physical fitness to my acquired knowledge on paralysis and devised exercises to assist. I tried squatting and lunging. I tied weights to my hands to build resistance. I attended extra physio circuit classes, even with the halo still on.

Tiffany was an excellent physio. I had originally worked with another physio called Hayleigh and she was also first-rate. Hayleigh was quiet and reserved but let me push myself through the first few weeks and assisted in my first stands before handing me over to Tiffany. I really enjoyed working with Tiff. I got the impression she was somewhat nervous handling me, as she quickly realised that motivating me wasn't going to be the issue but that slowing me down would be her bigger challenge. Her greatest fear was that

I would push too much and fall or injure myself. Our work was methodical but she knew that she could leave me in the gym with exercises to complete while she attended to other patients and that I wouldn't rest or take it easy.

While physio work was more tangible and required large-scale muscle movements, OT was not as visual in terms of improvement and much more tedious. Besides daily OT I also attended weekly writing classes, which became very frustrating. My highly experienced occupational therapist, Glenda, moulded a wrapping into a figure of eight around my thumb and forefinger, and then she'd slot a pen through the centre. The first day I attempted to write my name I could barely even muster the downward pressure to produce a mark on the page. A week later I could make some marks and write my name like a four-year-old. A week after that I started writing lines – similar to the punishments we received in school. We soon got rid of the cast and ended up wedging the pen between my thumb web and the space between my forefinger and middle finger. For all my improvements, though, I have never returned to writing the way I could prior to the injury.

Other mind-numbing tasks included sensation tests, where I would fish for coins in a bowl of rice. Or sometimes I would work on strength by conducting various finger movements working against a playdough-like substance. We would also work on reactions by throwing a ball, or my pincer movement by pinching and moving pegs on a line. We tied weights on my hand and dangled it from a table as I attempted to raise and lower it as often as possible. I would attempt to twist nuts onto various bolts or play cards with my visitors.

There was an enormous array of tasks, chores and activities for patients to enable any kind of return to everyday living. A group of patients undertook a morning breakfast session, in which the kitchen in the back of OT was taken over by predominantly upper-body-deficient patients as we attempted to make a breakfast of some sort for each other. I had the task of buttering bread. *How hard could that be?* Well, when you can't hold a knife properly, can't hold a tub of butter or a slice of bread steady, and all the items are just at the lower limit of your field of vision, it can be slightly challenging. They gave me an adapted knife with a ninety-degree bend, shaped into an L. I lifted the butter onto my table-top using my palms, then I locked it in using other items around the table. I took a slice of bread and managed to pin it down while I molested it with the buttery knife. My lumpy, holey bread was greatly appreciated by the others.

Although the OT staff could occasionally be slightly patronising without realising it, they were still incredibly kind and caring people with an excellent eye for adaptation. They would make a big deal if you completed any task, but all the while I would smile through gritted teeth as it was immensely frustrating to be celebrating something as simple as writing your name or picking up food with a fork. It is very difficult to articulate how it feels. Naturally I was elated as I became more mobile and could do things that I could not do before, but overall it still frustrated me as I used to be able to do these simple tasks so easily. This was the way I felt about pretty much every ability I regained.

Think about it. Think of the number of things we do every day through the movement of our hands and legs. Name anything. Any task. Change the TV channel. Scratch your nose. Make a cup of tea. Read the paper. Check your phone. Scratch *that* itch. *Oh, I'm thirsty.* Pick up the bottle. Twist the cap. Lift the bottle to the mouth. Control the flow. Return the bottle upright. Put the bottle down. Place the cap back on. And yet for months this was one of a thousand massive daily challenges for me. It still is, and will continue to be, for many less fortunate than I.

On entry to the spinal unit in mid-January, I was briefed that I would have goal-setting meetings once a month with the entire spinal team allotted to me. This included the lead consultant, physio, occupational therapist, social worker, psychologist and senior nurse dedicated to my case, along with Rita, my family and me. I imagine the intent was for the staff to align and manage expectations for patients, while enabling the patients to feel part of the process. My first meeting had occurred in mid-February. My case nurse sat with my dad, Rita and me as we discussed my goals. He told me that the patients run the meeting, not the staff, so, during the first and all subsequent meetings, that's exactly what I did. I could tell they were not used to *these* kinds of meetings. They asked what my short-, medium- and long-term goals were. In the short-term I wanted to travel to and stand for Joe and Sarah's wedding on 4 April. There were also a number of simple goals like the ability to wash myself, independent bowel movement and the ability to drive again.

Then I got on to what I really wanted. I gave a little speech about who I was and what I had done previously. I said that my goal was that by July 2016, eighteen months from then, I would conduct an infantry Physical Employment Standard Assessment (PESA) in the army. This includes walking with 45kgs for 15km in 155 minutes, followed directly by various arduous activities such as a 1km run in patrol order in under eight minutes, carrying two 22kg water jerry cans over 25m eleven times to cadence, a stretcher drag for 10m, a leopard crawl of 18m in thirty-five seconds, and a box of 35kg lift to 1.5m. This is the Australian standard required for infantry soldiers and, even for fully fit soldiers, it is challenging.

The staff looked dumbfounded when I showed them the printout of the test (my army mates had kindly brought in copies for me). I was still mostly immobile, in a wheelchair with a halo brace on. I was a diagnosed CCS quadriplegic, for God's sake! The head consultant was quick to slow me down and try to bring me back to the real world. But I was clear.

I remembered a very short conversation I had had with the consultant on my first time meeting him, while I was in acute care. I told him I was going to work like no one he'd ever seen and that I was going to get better. I felt that he dismissed me then. And he was still trying to bring me back to 'reality'. Of course, he was correct not to give any false hope, but I needed him, and everyone else in the room, to know that this was what I was chasing. *I'm not going to celebrate being able to zip up my pants or to walk to the shop. I want to do what I did before. I want to do things like skydive again.* Although these steps were numbers 100+ and I was still at step five, this was what I wanted. Everyone needed to know what I was aiming for because ultimately, with or without their help, I was going to chase this down. They needed to get on-board this crazy train!

Directly after this first meeting, I had been shattered. My father told me he had never been as proud of me as he was that day. He said he had never seen someone in such a dire situation take control and ownership like he had just witnessed. Both he and Rita raved about my little speech for days afterwards.

Every meeting throughout my time in the spinal unit was then set. The staff knew they would be questioned at the meeting and would need to have answers. 'Is there any reason why I can't attend this wedding? When can I stop my blood thinners? Why is the halo still on?' By March, army medical representatives were attending the meetings, stating that I was essentially theirs and that they would look after me as soon as I was discharged. I could see the medical staff had very little previous exposure to military meetings.

I had hoped to get the halo off by Rita's birthday on 4 March, but they wanted to do some more scans and X-rays before they could be sure. We waited an extra few days, but to tell the truth, I was done with it. I knew it was a case of short-term pain and long-term gain, but I had slept stationary on my back for long enough. I had not had a full-body wash since the accident. My hair was falling out. I was under 60kgs but still couldn't look down to see myself. The halo had served its purpose and I needed it off.

Finally, late on Friday 6 March they removed the halo. My old torturer, John, came down to my bed and briefed me on the process. When he released one pin, I would feel immense pain momentarily until he eased the opposing pin. He said not to be alarmed by the large pop I would most likely hear. 'Great, that'll just be my skull cracking, John?!'

I grimaced my way through the quick process, but the immediate relief was amazing. I thought my head might just fall off for the first few minutes, as my neck was so weak. Very slowly, I tilted my head towards my toes for the first time in 2015. I turned slightly to my left and right. The room seemed different. I had developed sores on the corners of my shoulder blades from the friction of the vest. My chest had sunken inwards and I looked skeletal.

Although they told me not to wash my hair straight away as it would cause further damage, I got undressed and went straight into the shower, where I could finally wash myself alone. It felt *awesome*. I got into some real clothes for the first time since the accident. I felt human again and not like a freak with a satellite screwed into his head. Roger and some nurses kept smiling at me. They said I was unrecognisable. I was delighted that my mother was still in Australia to see me without the halo, and I was allowed to go home for the weekend soon after. Rita was also delighted to see me without the halo. I think I looked a little like her husband again. Just skinny, clumsy and walking like the *Star Wars* character C-3PO on low batteries.

Getting the halo off took the shackles off my rehab. I returned on Sunday evening and people barely recognised me. First thing Monday morning, I was in the gym asking Tiff what she wanted me to do. As they said in *Reservoir Dogs*, 'Let's go to work.' From then until I was released from hospital on 10 April, I worked my ass off. I did extra sessions in the gym regularly. One day I got on the stationary bike and just went for it. I stayed on the bike for an hour, sweating away. The staff hadn't seen paralysed patients doing this. I did extra circuit classes with staff. The guys would push me harder than the others and challenge me to do things that I hadn't before. We did rounds of boxing, weighted-ball slams and weighted-bar exercises. I even did sessions of throwing, catching and kicking with family when I could. Have you ever attempted to catch a ball after sitting on frozen hands for an hour? If so then you have a slight understanding of how challenging it was.

Work began on my walking, posture and endurance. A six-minute walking test turned into a mini personal-best challenge every week or so. On a number of occasions, I took my iPod, plugged in my earphones (after five minutes spent attempting to insert them at my bedside mirror) and walked past the sneaky smokers in the grass courtyard, around the side of the mental-health building adjacent to the SIU and arrived out on the grass front of the hospital grounds. (I had accidentally found this quiet area several weeks previously when my father and I explored the hospital grounds in my wheelchair. Suffice it to say, the cross-country path was a little uncomfortable.) I listened to music while conducting my own sessions of lunging, knee raises, stretching and walking up the slope. I even made some vague attempts at taking a few rushed steps. I basked in the beautiful Brisbane sunshine barely noticing the busy hospital entrance footpath nearby as I even managed to sweat a little. It was my little escape from the unit. If I fell over, or looked silly, no one would see. No judgement. No 'Well done, Billy.' Just me and my thoughts. Each occasion I walked back towards the unit, an enormous sense of gratitude came over me. I was so lucky to be able to experience the sun on that grassy knoll, standing on my own two feet.

Without the restricted view from the halo, my world of functionality opened incrementally. It was fantastic to experience immediate improvements. I was able to raise and lower my shorts. I could mostly dress myself. Shoes were still an issue. I slipped my runners on and off to begin with but it felt like cheating. I would never learn if I continued to take shortcuts. So I started practising tying my shoelaces. I first did it as an exercise in OT, then on my own in the morning. It took time and patience. I kept practising my writing too. We worked on a lot of finger-dexterity exercises and blindfolded sensation tests. At first I couldn't tell the difference between an apple and orange. I had to see things to attempt to manipulate them. Carrying a glass of water was very difficult. My grip was weak so a large glass may have been too heavy to hold. Without sensation feedback, I had little idea if it was slipping or if I was relaxing my grip without noticing. Also, moving with a glass was treacherous as my arms and hands were unsteady and I would have to focus directly on the glass to attempt to react according to the water's movement. Obviously, this meant that carrying any hot drink was dangerous.

Although without the halo I could see much more, and therefore do much more, there were still certain tasks I found difficult to complete. Anything I couldn't see was fiddly. Taking something out of my pocket for instance, or fixing my shorts around the back required great skill. More intricate things like zips and buttons were initially a bridge too far. It was shorts and T-shirts every day to start with. As for a top button on a shirt ... closing that bad boy was my unicorn. I brought my army uniform to an OT session one day in early April. Glenda helped me get dressed as we worked out the various problem areas. Boot laces were getting easier but the shirt buttons were a pain. Once completed, I stood up and looked in the mirror as she commented on how smart I looked. I gazed at myself, recalling my previous fears that I'd never wear this again. *Guess who's back!*

Nick was discharged in late March as he had also had an amazing recovery. His family wanted him to stay longer but his doctor discharged him anyway. I understood why they wanted him to stay; I also wanted to get the most out of the facility while I could, but not at the expense of holding a bed from someone in more need than I. I knew I would be discharged from hospital soon. I was looking forward to leaving and getting on with my life outside the ward. I had visited the medical facilities on the army base in Enoggera with the hospital staff to ensure they were suitable for me prior to discharging. I really appreciated that dedication from the hospital social worker. They showed great care, even in my transition.

At the beginning of April I got a weekend pass from the hospital to go to Stanthorpe for Joe and Sarah's wedding. In actual fact, I went to Joe's stag party on the previous Thursday. It was a strange experience; showering and getting dressed by my bed space in the SIU, then stepping outside to grab a taxi and head out with all of Joe's mates from the UK into Fortitude Valley, with none of them any the wiser. We finished in a terrible bar in the Valley where I even briefly joined the guys on the dancefloor; they were most likely unaware that I was reporting back to the SIU the following Monday. I felt like I had finally made an assimilation back into the big bad world when a tipsy girl asked me to kiss her. I was extremely flattered. I might have been her 'bottom of the barrel' but it felt good! I'm not sure she realised that the skinny guy she was hitting on was recovering from quadriplegia.

I was delighted to be present for the wedding, standing in the marquee watching it all happen. I had picked it as a clear goal, and here I was, standing in my own wedding suit alongside my wife, thrilled for our friends. We had made it. I was also delighted for Joe and Sarah, as they are such great people, and their families had been so kind to us. The Abbotts had been so welcoming and warm, it really felt comforting to stay at their ranch. They showed a level of compassion and friendship that we will never forget. It was funny to return to hospital the following week after feeling so normal again for a while.

The final day in hospital was filled with thanks and praise. I wrote notes and left small gifts for my physio Tiff, my occupational therapist Glenda, the nursing staff (Maureen in particular) and also to Jenny, one of the patients who had a heart of pure gold. I said goodbye to Mitch, my nineteen-year-old roommate, who had not been as fortunate with his return of function. As we both were incomplete quadriplegics with broken C3/4s, we easily could have been in opposite positions. He nodded from his powered wheelchair as I walked from the room out to the car. Mitch's mother whispered to my father, 'You must be overjoyed to see your son walk out of here.' She said it with genuine happiness but my father had no response for a parent in that position. I made a note to come back and visit Mitch as often as I could. We walked down the ramp towards the car. I broke out into the most un-coordinated and ugly attempt at a jog known to man. 'Not many ran out of this place!' I said jokingly to my dad.

After discharge on 10 April, I reported back to the military base in

Enoggera. I was enrolled in the day programme at the physiotherapy centre on base. I was also taking part in a transitional rehab programme run by the PA hospital and had organised an external occupational therapist, Genevieve Lee, to do home visits. This was all coordinated through the ADF. They did everything they could to assist me throughout the entire process. Granted, I had to do a lot of the bookings or organising myself, but anything I asked for, I got. Any assistance I wanted I was given, and the facilities on base far outweighed those anywhere else I had been. The only concern was that the physios on base were not SCI specialists and mostly worked with guys post-operation with ankle, knee or shoulder injuries, so I was a relatively unique case for them.

I was looking forward to getting into a new phase of recovery. I knew I still had a chance to recover more. I needed to stay on task and push even harder now that I was away from the hospital setting. No holding back.

The day programme on base had a panel of less than ten and mostly consisted of guys post-knee or shoulder operations. One other guy had sustained a serious injury from a military accident. To begin with I didn't feel comfortable in the programme. In hospital I was top of the class but here I was most definitely bottom of the heap of broken soldiers. I couldn't even hold a press-up position. I guessed the other guys in the programme couldn't really work out what my injury consisted of, but they knew I was busted badly as I couldn't do many of the exercises. It felt lonely at times during the programme. There was a real sense of solidarity and togetherness in the SIU, as we all had been paralysed in some way, but here it felt as though there was a general lack of appreciation of what a spinal injury actually meant. I felt as though none of the physio staff understood the level I had come from and the huge amount of work I had done to get to this point. Others in the programme would describe me as the guy that broke his neck. If it were as simple as that I would have been very thankful.

My routine was hectic. My body was not used to it at all and I found it draining almost immediately. I was driven into the rehab clinic on base by Rita every morning before 8 a.m. The physio centre had fantastic facilities. We had daily access to a specific 12m heated hydrotherapy pool and a full physio gym with all types of adaptive equipment, balance boards and resistance bands and a dedicated physio staff, each with a working table. The centre even had a zero-gravity treadmill. The user wore a pair of tight shorts, lifted a large plastic bubble around them and zipped themselves in. A user could then programme how much of their body weight they wanted to run or walk on the treadmill with. The bubble would then fill with air and lift the user off the treadmill from the waist down – hence zero gravity. What an amazing recovery tool. Years of dealing with injuries from Afghanistan and Iraq had ensured the ADF had these advanced facilities.

The day programme had a number of hour-long sessions throughout the day: hydrotherapy circuits, injury-specific sessions with our head physio and a number of individual sessions, including cardio, resistance and sessions such as health information, meditation and small games. The physio in charge of the day programme was a very nice guy but on occasion he contradicted the advice I was receiving from the spinal injury specialist physio from the hospital team, who continued to visit once a week. He didn't seem to have much of a structure to some of the sessions and just handed me an exercise print-out for our strength classes. Although some of the other guys seemed to find it difficult to motivate themselves under such open conditions, it allowed me to work really hard. In the hospital someone watched every rep, each set and kept my exercises simple. Here, I was given a handout from the head physio with three workouts with 'recovery from back injury' written on it. *Okay ... I'll try these.* I did every rep of every set of every exercise of every workout. No shortcuts.

Coordinating some of my prescribed exercises, even with no weight, was initially too advanced for me. I tripped over a few times while conducting them. The exercise therapist would regularly approach to query my activities. I showed her my workout sheet and she assisted as best as possible. I adapted certain activities. It was lonely, doing hour after hour mostly by myself with no feedback specific to a spinal injury. But I tried not to feel sorry for myself. I told myself I had been spoiled in hospital. Now it was up to me.

Each afternoon when I was driven home, Rita cooked for me, as I wanted to put on weight and build strength. I drafted a weekly schedule divided into one-hour slots, including visits once a week from the hospital transition team of a physio, an occupational therapist and, on a number of occasions, a social worker. I also had a private occupational therapist initially doing four sessions a week with me, and I was given homework. Oh, and I started writing this book. So whether I was building a Meccano car, writing letters of thanks to friends, downstairs throwing a tennis ball at the wall or extending my fingers through a 'hand-web', I didn't stop until close to bedtime every night. Even watching a show on Netflix I might bring my stationary bike into the room, or grab my hurley and start slowly rotating the shortened grip from side to side to strengthen my wrist. It was all-encompassing. Finally sleep, then repeat the process the next day.

I was shattered and a bit glum. But I worked and worked and worked. I met with my social worker in mid-April. I went into great detail about my training plans. She listened carefully before giving me some excellent advice: she told me it was okay to miss some sessions or do less because I

was actually in danger of neglecting to spend time with Rita. She was right.
Rita had developed serious pain in her lower back, probably as a release of
the stress she had been attempting to control since the accident. She also
had a recovering quadriplegic for a husband. So I needed to look after her
more. I needed to start pulling my weight around the house and spending
some quality time with her. That was an important part of rehab that I hadn't
considered. It wasn't just about me. So I started to make more of an effort
even in small things, such as stacking a dishwasher, something that I found
treacherous. We started to get out a bit more and do some nice things with
friends, including going into the city or to a park during the weekend, or
even just calling over to Joe and Sarah's house. We attempted to relax a bit
by doing something as simple as having a few cold drinks on a beautiful
Saturday afternoon at Eagle Street Pier. While I knew I had to strike swiftly
in terms of getting maximum recovery in the limited time I had, I also had to
be mindful every so often, and be grateful for the improving circumstances
and for the other components in my life.

13

LUCK?

Throughout my recollections of my injury and recovery, as you will have seen, the theme of resilience and self-confidence recurs. However, this is only part of the story. Although mental fitness was my 'X-factor', it accounted for only a part of why I could eventually walk again. I would put the reasons why I can walk again in the following order of importance:

1) Luck;

2) Support;

3) Self-confidence and resilience.

I could have had all the self-confidence in the world but had my accident severed my spinal cord and led me to be a complete quadriplegic, then I would obviously not be walking today. That is a fact, so there is no doubt that first and foremost, I got lucky. Very lucky.

Throughout my life I've been fortunate to be successful in many things, but I've had some bad luck too. My sister thinks it's some sort of proper pay-off in providence; I get lucky in the big things but really unfortunate in the smaller things:

- At age ten I broke my arm while going downhill on a bike and trying to pat my dog. I then broke it again on the first day of summer holidays from school while saving a shot in a soccer game in our back garden.

- During my teenage rugby-playing days I was knocked unconscious on two separate occasions.

- While I was attending college in 2006, my house was burgled. My laptop containing all of my assignments was stolen.

- In September 2009 I broke my leg while playing rugby and missed the chance to go on a reconnaissance commanders course. During the removal of the plaster cast, staff somehow managed to cut into my leg.

- The night before my first day in the ARW I had loaded my car up with all my belongings about to leave my Cork city apartment for the Curragh Camp. However, with the snowy and icy conditions the slope was too steep for me to move it, so I grabbed one bag and shuffled down the hill to the train station. After I got onto the train, the conductor stated that it was a non-stop to Dublin, even though the ticket seller had told me otherwise. I had to beg them to stop in Kildare. The following day (my very first day) the 2IC told me to head down to Cork again to collect the remainder of my stuff. As I drove back up on the Tuesday night, I (along with five other cars) struck a massive pothole outside Durrow, puncturing both left tyres and deploying the passenger curtain airbag. I waited for three hours for a recovery vehicle to tow my car back to Cork. I had to hire another car the following morning.

• Less than three weeks later, a sheet of ice flew from the top of a truck on the motorway and struck the front of my car, severely damaging it and almost smacking me into the concrete motorway partition.

• In 2012 my Toyota Hilux Crew Cab was mistaken for a gang member's vehicle and smashed and keyed to pieces.

• Also in 2012 I returned from a two-week exercise, only to walk into my room in the officer's accommodation in the Curragh Camp and find it completely flooded and smelly. A guy on the first floor had left a tap on in his room and it had been flooding through the ceiling for almost two weeks. I was flying out on a holiday in under twenty-four hours. All my kit, clothing and my personal bed were destroyed.

• A convicted criminal lived in the semi-detached house next to mine from 2010 to 2013, and made our lives in Limerick very unpleasant.

Somehow, though, when it comes to large life decisions or events, lady luck has kindly been on my side. Joining the army is a perfect example of this.

**

In 2001, after serious cramming, I sat my Leaving Certificate exams and quickly got out of Cork. Cape Clear was calling me. From the first time my father took us over at a young age, I fell in love with this Irish-speaking island 9 miles from the mainland of southern Ireland. I made some lifelong friends there too. I first stayed there when I was fourteen and kept going back every summer thereafter, first as a student, then as a supervisor on the Irish-language summer-school courses. I was lucky enough to meet a genuinely great friend, Stiofan, there. Sometimes you just know you'll be good friends with someone. I loved the people and the atmosphere, and the genuine 'craic' that you can only get in truly Irish areas. I started working in one of the three bars on the island too, and worked a little on the campsite. I fished off the rocks when I got a chance and drank any night I wasn't working.

The summer of 2001 was the first time ever that I fully left sport behind as I travelled once more to Cape Clear, this time to stay for the entire season. I had been unsuccessful with Cork minor football trials and had done some interviews for an army officer cadetship but otherwise I was content to be island-living for the summer until school results and college offers – or lack thereof – came calling. I wanted to be a PE teacher, but I had seen the army cadetship leaflet in a career-guidance school lesson and filled it out (with assistance from my mother). I got called for two interviews, one in Cork and one in Dublin, but thought little of it.

When I eventually got my exam results I wasn't too happy. I had just got the points I needed, 485, for PE in UL. But when the first round of offers came out I received no offer from UL. Simultaneously, a letter from the army arrived saying hard luck, you're fifth on a waiting list. I was really disappointed. *How had I not received an offer from UL?*

I suddenly had one of those terrible moments that you get when you realise that you've forgotten something really important. I had totally overlooked the movement and ability test required for PE, which was why the offers for the course didn't come out until round two. 'Okay, okay when is this test?' I asked my parents over the phone to check the paperwork from the CAO and UL. 'Eh, Bill ... it was yesterday,' my mother quietly said.

I spoke to my dad, my trusted advisor on pretty much all matters. 'Right I was on to UL, they can do a test for you personally but it's gotta be tomorrow. This is extremely kind of them, d'you think you can get back and we'll drive up in the morning?'

The race was on. Firstly, I had to get off the island. No ferries were running as the sea was too rough! 'Anyone going to the mainland?' The *fear an tí* (owner) of Tír na nÓg (the accommodation where the summer-camp students stayed) was a man by the name of Micky O'Driscoll. I was friendly with all his family, particularly his wife, Noreen, who was really kind to myself and Stiofan as supervisors on the Irish summer camp. Micky said, in his thick West Cork accent, that he was heading to Baltimore but that it would be very choppy.

Cheers Micky, let's go! The two of us rammed into the cabin which was a few feet higher than the deck of Micky's boat. We rolled out of the harbour and it immediately struck me as being wild. Throughout the entire ninety-minute trip, Micky was super calm. I, on the other hand, was clinging on to an inside rail for what I thought was my dear life. The many songs I had learned over the years of Irish tales of the sea hadn't helped a blind bit. At one stage the front of the cabin ploughed so hard into the open Atlantic sea that I felt like I could see underwater through the glass. Once we rounded Sherkin Island and towards the harbour in Baltimore the sea settled to more of a tired roll. Micky slowly leaned towards me and spoke in Gaelic with his difficult drawl, 'That was hairy enough, Billy, ha.' Ha!

But I had no time to reflect on near-death experiences. I ran straight off the pier and up the narrow road to get the bus back to Cork. I must have stood at the bus stop for no more than five minutes before the Bus Éireann coach with its grumpy, overweight driver pulled alongside. Some three hours later I finally made it to Parnell Place in Cork city, where my father collected me.

Off up to Limerick the following day, where I did a movement and ability test under the supervision of Dave Weldrick, the famed PE tutor from UL. He spoke to me a little afterwards and said not to worry, that I would be getting an offer for PE. We thanked Mary Smith, the department secretary, on our way out, as she had been so kind to accommodate me. I could hardly believe how lucky we were: first to have managed to get a movement and ability test, and then to have made it to the test at all.

The day of the second round offers arrived. My offer for PE came in the post with another letter. The army said that a few people had turned down the cadetship and offered it to me. (I subsequently found out that a total of five people had turned down army cadetships that year, which was unheard of.)

From getting neither to getting both. *What the hell!* I had seven days to make up my mind.

I spoke again with my *consiglieri* and we ordered flowers to be delivered to Mary Smith in UL. I accepted the army cadetship and asked UL if I could defer for a year, just in case I got injured or – more likely – that I hated the military.

On reflection, it seems there was a certain element of luck bringing me to and through a pivotal point in my young life. Had UL not organised a movement test for me, I would have accepted the next best course. Had I not made it to Limerick for that test, I never would have been offered a place. Most importantly, had five people not turned down the offer of an army officer cadetship in 2001, then I would never have joined the military. No experience of military command, no enhanced resilience through a career in the infantry and certainly no exposure to the world of SF. My life-changing moment came at the behest of the choice made by five complete strangers.

***

This sets the tone for luck throughout all aspects of my life: my successful military career; my successful completion of a bachelor's degree; my personal life; my damn outrageous fortune in terms of my accident. Many have broken the C3/4 vertebrae and immediately severed the spinal cord. In fact, those with a high-level incomplete spinal injury (i.e. a higher point of injury on the spine) tend to have less recovery. Many people incapacitated in water ultimately drown. Even those who are reached prior to drowning usually take on so much water that it leads to terrible complications. And yet, none of these things happened to me. Moreover, the first people to come to my assistance in the Kings Beach surf included an emergency nurse and a sports medicine student.

How is it that I have had such good fortune? Law of attraction? Fate? God's will? I have no idea. Maybe it's just my own perception of success, or a positive outlook that I process as being lucky. Some people believe that I was protected through prayer and faith in God. Others are adamant I was watched over by my friends and family members in heaven. Some people even thought I was some sort of miracle. I do not have as strong a faith as some, nor do I believe in destiny, though the thought of a higher entity looking out for me has crossed my mind, as how else can I rationalise this level of fluke? Maybe my ego just likes the thought of such an occurrence. In reality, all I can rely on in this case is the factual information of the accident and injury. The fact is, statistically, I should not be where I am today. Mathematical probability proves it. Before anything else, I am a very lucky person. Why, I don't know. But dwelling on an attempt to find answers to luck is a waste of time in my opinion. Maybe there is some truth to the quote 'the harder I work, the luckier I get', but, either way, if I get the luck of the bouncing ball, I'm still going to smash it into the net.

14

LEAVING TO START AGAIN

LIMERICK, IRELAND TO BRISBANE, AUSTRALIA – OCTOBER 2014

I am so proud to call myself Irish. Here in Australia, I love being able to stand next to people and represent Ireland in the best way I can. Although Rita and I had made the decision to go, when the time came we found it difficult to leave. Rita was particularly upset leaving her friends and family. I was also quietly saddened, not only in terms of friends and family, but because my pride kept whispering into my ear that I was turning my back on my country and that I was somehow a traitor. When the going got tough, I was leaving.

Resigning my commission as an officer was difficult. Throughout my thirteen years in the Irish Army, I was extremely proud to be wearing the tricolour on my shoulder. I loved seeing the garrison flag flying high above Cork city when I was based there. To me, it represented the national pride that Irish people sometimes take for granted. By 2014, however, I knew that I wanted to try something different, yet I still hated the idea of resigning. My commission was signed by the President of Ireland, and the Taoiseach and Minister for Defence had, in essence, given me the right to be a commissioned officer in the Irish Defence Forces. So serving Ireland was something that I took seriously.

I am from a country that had to fight for its freedom. I am honoured to be part of a republic, free from any other nation's will. How could I not be? I grew up in an area where everyone played hurling and Gaelic football, and I frequently travelled to Munster championship games to watch the Cork senior team battle. My teenage summers were spent on an Irish-speaking island, dancing to Irish folk songs and learning Irish ballads. I had been immersed in Irish music and Irish songs, Irish language, Irish sports and Irish traditions from birth.

I was lucky enough to be a Munster rugby supporter from a young age thanks to my uncle and mother. One of the first Munster games I was ball-boy for was in Musgrave Park on the day Munster beat Australia in 1993. I remember running onto the pitch afterwards, dreaming of how I would be asked to move to Australia on a scholarship and play rugby over there. I visualised playing for Munster and Ireland during the winter and for the Cork Gaelic football team during the summer. Dreams of representation confirmed my love for my local area, county, province and country. From as far back as I can remember it had always been a strong but subtle theme in our household. Be proud of where you came from. Be proud of who you are.

On the flipside, modern Ireland was in a bad way. In 2009 a moratorium was placed on all public-sector jobs due to the economic downturn. That meant that three months from my becoming a substantive captain, my promotion was postponed. Taxes rose. Inflation rose. The building sector collapsed. The government made some disastrous decisions, particularly in the banking sector, bailing out Anglo-Irish Bank by taking loans from foreign agencies which we, as taxpayers, essentially had to pay back. Other than the very fortunate, we all had to struggle through, and because everyone was having such a good time only a few years earlier, it was a bitter pill to swallow.

Rita also felt the squeeze as a teacher. She was making less money than her predecessors and, due to increased taxes and levies, her wages were incrementally decreasing. People started to leave the country, including couples and families younger than us. We heard stories of friends who couldn't pay mortgages and were handing back house keys. It was apparent that the country was not recovering well from the global recession. In terms of quality of life, it made no sense to stay. Along with a large proportion of the country, we were under pressure to maintain any level of a comfortable lifestyle, particularly as two public servants.

I had started looking at the option of an overseas lateral transfer to the ADF as early as 2012. I had heard in passing that they were recruiting from other militaries. I was also disheartened with the lack of use of Ireland's premier DF unit, the ARW. I had worked my way to the pinnacle only to realise that the country didn't seem to have any appetite to use us. It would be fair to say that I was a bit disillusioned. So why not investigate other opportunities? While on an overseas deployment to Bosnia in 2013, I submitted my expression of interest to the ADF. We hadn't fully committed to the thought of leaving yet, but Rita had reluctantly agreed to apply to the ADF lateral transfer scheme to see what might come from the application.

It is a common joke that lieutenants are always very fresh, keen and interested, but that the positivity slowly gets stamped on over the years and one can always pick out a senior captain in the mess as they are not smiling and are usually moaning about something. I didn't want to be, but I had ended up being one of those 'cranky captains'. There were issues within the Irish Defence Forces that frustrated me: positive discrimination towards females, a general acceptance of malingerers, and poor morale most likely due to a lack of satisfying tasks. The most irritating issue for me was the complete absence of career management. I required documentation on my personal appraisals to be submitted to the ADF. This was kept under lock and key in the officers' management office in Dublin. These are the guys who are meant to assist in an officer's career management in everything from overseas selection to promotions and postings. However, I was cautious about requesting this information, as they would realise I was looking at options elsewhere and I could potentially get screwed over if I stayed. That's the type of business we were in. It is without doubt the most disheartening part of the life of an army officer. So many times I had seen excellent officers blatantly overlooked in order to accommodate others. Maybe I was a fool, or naive, but I always thought we would be judged on merit, not on who we knew or how we 'played the game'.

No one from the career management office ever sat down with me and spoke about my goals or the army's plans for me. The majority of us had never been spoken to about a career path or provided with any type of formal guidance. There is no such thing as a posting cycle (a planned time frame within a unit) in the Irish Army, which my Australian Army friends are dumbfounded by. There is no structure or guideline pathway projected by the career management office or your chain of command, so you just plan your own path and attempt to make moves as clever as possible to ensure you get ahead of your cohort.

In the Australian Army, officers are posted to a job for, usually, a two-year cycle. They remain with that unit until, in consultation with their supervisor and a career manager, they work out their next posting approximately six months prior to moving. They are appraised for the type of roles they should seek out and what future promotion opportunities they might aim for. The needs of the ADF come first, then the career goals of the individual along with their performance. This sounds simple and obvious and yet, in the Irish Defence Forces, there is no such process, no active career manager, and officers have no idea as to when they may or may not get posted.

My posting on return from Bosnia, to which I alluded in an earlier chapter, was a perfect example of this: I had no consultation with my superiors or the career management office: *'Here's the job, now on your bike, off you go.'* There was clearly no consideration of family living arrangements, no fuel entitlements. Just 'See you Monday'.

I had been told that I would be 'looked after' on my return from Bosnia. I had been in the military for twelve years, including three in the SF. It had been an informal view that post-SF officers were accommodated where possible as a reward for their service. I wanted to live out of my own house in Limerick for a while. Rita had a permanent teaching job in Laurel Hill Secondary School in the city and it just happened that there was an infantry battalion in Limerick with a captain vacancy. Not a massive ask, I thought. Anyone with a little sense would see that it was an obvious management choice to post me to Limerick, inputting some SF information and knowledge into an infantry unit. But things did not go as expected.

I spoke to the assistant Brigade Adjutant of 1 Brigade in Cork in early June, as it was confirmed I would be posted to 1 Brigade. He assured me I would be posted to Limerick as requested and said he would confirm it with the Brigade Commander that afternoon. But for two days I received no return call. Then I got a text message from my buddy Mo from Watergrasshill, who was working in the Brigade Training Centre in Cork. He said he was looking forward to us working together. In Cork.

It turned out that the Brigade had another officer returning from an overseas deployment around the same period. He was a cavalry officer, and there was only one cavalry unit in the Brigade, based in Cork. This captain was very capable, was married with a child and lived in Cork. Yet our postings were somehow switched. While the posting of an infantry officer to work within the Brigade Training Centre is commonplace, posting a cavalry officer to an infantry battalion is unheard of. It equates to a French teacher being sent to work in a German college. I was not given any reason as to why this occurred. In fact, I was never told anything formally. I found it very strange to have a posting altered at the last minute, particularly when the Brigade Commander (the approving authority) had never met me. However, the cavalry officer was well known to Brigade staff. Eighteen months previously, a compulsory random drugs test of his returned a positive result. He outlined almost immediately that he was training heavily as a national-level triathalete and had consumed poppy-seed bread, which may have altered the results. He was immediately placed on administrative duties only, even after a report by an investigating officer and by a senior Brigade medical officer confirmed his innocence in returning a 'false positive'. The cavalry officer pursued the matter with external legal support and scientific evidence, before the administrative duties restriction was finally lifted, and he was then allowed to deploy overseas, handle weapons and perform operational duties once more. Upon his return to the Brigade, the Cork-based cavalry officer was posted at short notice to the infantry unit in Limerick, while I was told to report to Collins Barracks, Cork. To say that this type of behaviour assisted in my decision-making process in applying to join the ADF would be an understatement.

I owned a Toyota Hilux that both Rita and I were very fond of, but due to the fuel costs associated with the daily drive from Limerick to Cork, I had to change it for a Honda Jazz, not the coolest car on the planet. I was not entitled to any fuel allowance as *technically* Cork was closer to home than my previous posting. On a few occasions, due to work commitments, I trained in the afternoon in Cork rather than in the morning. By coincidence, I met the cavalry captain a number of times in the gym. He would have just driven down from Limerick and I would be getting ready to drive up after an afternoon gym session.

Shortly upon my return from Bosnia, in mid-2013, Rita and I travelled to Oxford for my interview with the Australian Army. By the time a contract was sent from the ADF in November 2013, the seeds of my resignation had been well-sown. It was an uncomfortable thought, but I just didn't love the Irish military any more. We weren't sold on 'the Australian idea' just yet, but I still felt I was done with the Irish Army.

It was after Alan's death that we talked seriously about taking up the Australian offer. The whole *you never know when it's your time* thing, I suppose. I had thought about getting into PE teaching, but the money and conditions for new teachers had been cut so badly that it would have been financial suicide for us. I thought about starting a business, but it was too risky in the economic climate of the time. In the end it seemed that the idea to emigrate slowly crept up on us until one night we transferred a lot of money to the Australian Department of Immigration to apply for visas and I accepted the contract. That was it. Off up to bed, as I had to get up at 5 a.m. to get on the road to Cork.

When our visas arrived in February 2014, I submitted my resignation papers. One would think that an ex-SF officer with twelve-and-a-half years' service in the army would get some sort of exit interviews from management. But that never happened. I spoke to my direct boss as I handed in the letter and that was it. The Brigade staff regularly saw me in the officers' mess for morning tea but never once did I receive any form of query as to why I was leaving. The Commissioned Officers Management Office contacted me to discuss how much money was left outstanding on my return of service from my university degree, which I was required to pay back before I left. They never discussed retention with me. I asked a senior member of the Representative Association of Commissioned Officers (RACO) to assist me in ensuring I received my correct entitlements before leaving, but he said that RACO looked after officers who were staying in, not those who were leaving. I quickly realised that no one gave a shit. I was actually quite hurt by all of this, if not surprised. My boss told me that the Brigade Adjutant only commented once on my resignation, and that was to say I was foolish. A few weeks later, out of nowhere, I got a posting to Limerick. How strange! I saw out the rest of my time there, more concerned with planning our new life than anything to do with the Irish Army.

The Irish Defence Forces seemed to be out of touch with what is now the common business practice of good human-resource management. Each army officer (and senior NCO) is an asset that has been heavily invested in. If I were to estimate the amount of money that was spent on my training and qualifications from the day I joined, I would confidently say it was well into seven figures. The state-sponsored investment that has gone into an ARW operator for fifteen years or a Specialist Service officer, such as an explosive ordnance disposal officer, is substantial. These assets should be viewed as such and harnessed in order to get maximum return for investment. Abuse that asset and it will leave or become ineffective.

I wasn't the only one leaving. Many of my cohort, mid-level captains and commandants, were also fed up with the mismanagement and being posted at exceptionally short notice to bases anywhere around the country. The business industry was taking note of this. The head of Aldi Ireland began an active recruitment campaign of army officers with great success. More money, better conditions, performance promotions and clear prospects.

It wasn't like they were taking poor performers either. They recruited some excellent officers from the military, full of functional management and leadership experience, and I'm sure they will be successful. One would assume that DFHQ would have attempted to do something about this mass exodus of officers but, to do so, they would have had to acknowledge there was an issue. No one bothered to renegotiate or manage those who were leaving. No one asked, 'Why are all these guys with over ten years' experience leaving?' In combat first-aid training, the first thing to do is to treat the catastrophic bleed, and the Irish Defence Forces were bleeding badly.

Recent talk of recruitment drives to 'fix' retention rates is nonsense. Almost 50 per cent of my officer cadet class have resigned their commission. Taking in a large number of cadets today doesn't fill the void of captains and commandants who departed yesterday. It will take close to ten years for those cadets to fill the vacancies. The personal knowledge and exposure of those departed officers has been lost forever. The specialist qualifications that they held will have to be regrown, resourced and budgeted for accordingly. It is a terrible business model. The most disappointing aspect of this retention issue is the absolute denial from the Minister of State, the Department of

Defence and the senior management of the DF that any problem exists. 'It's all under control, there's nothing to see here.' It's almost laughable, but in truth the only organisation laughing now is the ADF, who saved a lot of time and money in transferring my qualifications. I believe that I was the first Irish Army officer to transfer directly into the ADF. I doubt I will be the last.

I understand if this appears bitter or ill-tempered. I can see how anyone reading it might think I was simply tired, disillusioned and potentially disloyal. But let me make one thing clear: I loved serving my country. I could have stayed in. I could still be sitting in an office, nowhere near my home, doing a job I didn't believe in and moaning to everyone who would listen. But I disagree with this type of attitude. If it bothered me that much, then I needed to go somewhere else.

So that's what I did.

I got the impression that the feeling was, if you wanted to leave, then *fine, get lost, we don't need you.* It's like a bad break-up. You say to your partner that you're not happy with something and they dump you saying they never loved you anyway. It hurts because I loved the military, and during my time in the ARW I pretty much handed over my life to it. I worked it, lived it and believed in it. Then, one sunny August afternoon, after giving away the last of my kit, I hopped into my car and drove out the front gate of the base in Limerick city, past the unsuspecting soldiers, never to return. The complete anti-climax of leaving an Irish Army base for the last time summed up the disappointment for me.

***

Our dads took us to the airport on 30 September. They were both pretty emotional, which was strange to see. I was taken aback by my father's emotion. Usually a calm man, he seemed quite upset. But we walked through the departure gates and that was it. No turning back.

It took a while to settle in. The weather was beautiful and our rent was paid in half by the ADF. I was quite nervous going onto the base on the first day. It didn't matter how much of a 'legend' I thought I was. No one here knew who I was. I was just some random, funny-sounding guy, I guessed. I didn't know what the soldiering standard would be like. Anything I had seen or learned appeared really professional. But how would I be viewed here, in an infantry battalion that had numerous battlefield honours and had recent combat casualties in Afghanistan?

I was greeted at the front gate by a warrant officer who took me into the base and began processing my paperwork, organising initial online courses, issuing uniforms and giving general briefs and tips. I walked down through Long Tan Lines, the home of the 6th Battalion, The Royal Australian Regiment (6 RAR), for the first time. The actual buildings seemed dated and a little underwhelming, but I immediately noticed each company had its own building in a perfect line down one side of the street, while the Bn HQ maintained central over-watch from the other side. Each company's only discriminator was the change in footpath rim colour. Administration Company was brown, Alpha Company was mustard yellow, Bravo Company was blue, Charlie Company was green, Delta Company was red and Support Company was purple/black. Each company had their young fit soldiers in their respective colour-coded T-shirts standing in formation outside the grass square ready for physical training at 7.25 a.m. It made for a very positive first impression.

I picked up on some apparent differences almost immediately. My initial thoughts were that the ADF looked after its own much better. I still hold that opinion. We had financial assistance for our housing, we had a number of external support agencies available to us, such as a Defence Community Organisation, and I was even allowed to use the CO's vehicle and take some local leave to assist in the initial transition items, such as buying a car or getting a phone. Even during my first few days' exposure, it appeared as if everyone in the battalion took their job seriously. I also realised that I had much to learn as there were so many different processes, terminology and meanings.

After a week or so, I began to pick up that most things were similar, but not the same by any means. I understood the concept of a lot of simple things without full exposure and actual knowledge. The training staff ran a number of basic lessons for me to help in my transition but mostly it was osmosis. I just had to get in there and work it out as best I could. I also picked up on some less positive differences. Maybe it was a different environment, but I felt that field-ranked officers treated junior officers with an inherent abruptness, probably forgetting that they too were junior officers once. On my second day in my new company, my OC bluntly ordered me back to my office to conduct an unimportant online course at 7 p.m., as I was heading out the door. We were the only two in the entire building, and I was his 2IC. Although I knew that he was just setting the tone and making an initial stand, it felt apparent that I was bottom of the food chain again. In Ireland I was well-known and well-respected, and decisions I made were listened to, with superiors willing to heed my advice. In the ADF, I felt like I was a 'nobody', another washed up 'Lat' (lateral transfer from another military – usually the UK) thinking he knew more than he actually did.

The working atmosphere reminded me of old-school male environments, yet the language used was much more affluent and business-like. '*We set the conditions for successful completion of ATLS 1 by enabling actions,*' which meant '*we let sections train themselves*'. I struggled to compete with this kind of language. My military writing skills have always been average, so I felt foolish at times. But I was in the Australian military now, so I needed to adapt to it, not the other way around. I was reinventing myself. I deliberately kept my office free from any army pictures and presentations.

People will judge me only on what I deliver now, not anything I did before.

This was my self-talk reminder, so in fact, it became just another challenge for me to overcome. It was very frustrating to start at the bottom again but as long as I tried to keep my ego in check, I felt I would do myself justice and people would see me for who I believe I am.

***

I often think back to my time in Australia prior to my injury. I sometimes envy that man, not knowing how good he had it. He was fit, keen to start his new life and full of hope. I was already setting my sights at SF selection the following year. I had run through the various entry tests by December and passed them all. I didn't know much about the Australian processes or procedures, but I was really happy that Rita and I had shown the courage to move. I was thrilled that we were standing on Australian soil and I was in an ADF uniform. Sometimes, when you visualise something, it startles you on the day that it actually turns into a reality – like you had somehow seen this previously.

Prior to my injury in December 2014, it had already been a massive change for us; the biggest of our lives. We had left our comfort zone. We had left our normality behind us. We had to accept all the hundreds of tiny differences between Ireland and Australia. We weren't completely happy in Ireland but we could have continued to moan our way through life by giving out about our earnings, our government, our lack of career progression and everything else we could think of. Instead we did something about it. If you are not happy, then do something about it. Don't wait for it to happen, make it happen.

Coming to Australia changed my life forever in a way I could never have foreseen, but do I regret it? Not for a second. The 'ifs, buts or maybes' are irrelevant. We got out into the world and we took chances. I would regret still being in Ireland, hating my job and wondering what could have been elsewhere.

As part of my army contract, we became Australian citizens in May 2015. I was – and am – very happy to be an Australian. It is a multicultural country full of immigrants, and I have no problem calling myself Australian. I feel that by wearing the uniform I somehow represent all the Irish in Australia, both past and present, and my voice is theirs. I am a proud Irishman and will never forget who I am or where I am from, but I am also now proud to represent Australia. I owe the Australian health system and ADF so much for assisting me in my greatest hour of need. I am proud to serve a country that has helped me so much and I hope my service does all the (Irish-) Australians proud.

15

THE MASTER
OF MY FATE

BRISBANE, AUSTRALIA – POST-MAY 2015

I was invited by my boss to attend the 6 RAR ANZAC day commemorative service with Rita on 25 April 2015. This would be my first time meeting most of my work colleagues post-injury. I was weak, tired and very underweight. My once tight-fitting wedding suit was now loose and I required Rita's assistance to close buttons.

The welcome I received was very pleasant. People came up and shook my ice-cold, floppy hand, noting how amazing it was to see me. I vowed to myself that I would not use this as an opportunity to give myself a rest but instead I would to continue to work hard. As Thin Lizzy's Phil Lynott would say, 'Fighting my way back'.

By the end of May I returned to work part-time. Slowly, I resumed basic activities within work. I attended meetings, getting various statistic returns and reports to my superiors. It was continuously challenging. I was consistently under self-induced pressure to adapt and overcome.

It was the only way to grow.

I also began trying to run in May. It sounds crazy. It seems nearly impossible. Paralysed in January but jogging by May. By 'running' I really mean that I would shuffle along for 50m, scuffing my feet off the ground. It was very clumsy, fatiguing and awkward. Physically it felt terrible, but to 'run' felt amazing. I used the zero-gravity treadmill in the rehab centre almost daily, starting with only 20 per cent of my body weight, then the next day dropping to 30 per cent and so on. I then took myself out to the running track where 50m quickly became 200m, then 1km, all within two weeks.

On Thursday 18 July 2015, after running 2.4km on the Gallipoli Barracks running track, I cried.

A little more than twelve minutes previously, I'd stood at the start line, taken a deep breath, leaned back onto my heels, then pushed off the red hardened track. For years I used to love stepping off on a run. I would bounce off the ground, stamping my authority on the clock against me. I loved pumping my legs like pistons, feeling the heavy burn deep in the centre of my chest. A sense of peace came through the power and strength I found in my running. I did everything from intervals, sprints and plyometrics to distance running, road racing and adventure racing. Without ever solely focusing on it, I had come to love running.

Not this time. I scuffed my foot across the start line and began my waddle. My arms swayed and shook violently across my body. My legs felt like lead. There was no rearward leg extension, with minimal lift over the ground, and my toe strike was inconsistent. As I passed the 400m mark I felt like I was moving backwards. I hated how slowly I was moving. I was already hurting. Concentration had to be maintained, as a slight lapse would almost certainly lead to me scuffing my sole, stubbing my toes, jarring my back or falling over. My lower back was incredibly tight and my neck ached. My upper back was completely rigid. My legs felt like jelly. My nervous system was making life exceptionally difficult for my muscles. I knew what I wanted my body to do; it just wouldn't obey. My entire body felt like it was in shock, while simultaneously feeling like I was wading through knee-high mud. At the 1,200m mark I attempted reading my stopwatch but couldn't steady my wrist enough to check if I was within the six-minute bracket. My forearms seemed to have electricity blasting through to my fingertips. I was fading fast.

A quick series of emotions ran through my head. The massive frustration of my awkward and painful running wrestled against the elation of the thought that I may actually complete a 2.4km fitness-test run in under twelve minutes eighteen seconds – the required pass time for the Australian Army. The activity I had learned to love, and which had once come so naturally, was now an endured motion. But the fact that I could even tolerate this action was such a relief, a delight that couldn't be ignored. I was thrilled but frustrated. Overjoyed but disappointed. Grateful but not satisfied.

At 1,600m I knew I would be close. Only I knew what I had endured. Only I knew the agony I pushed through to get to this point. Only I knew how to dig deeper and push through the intense pain, the stiffness and the frustration. I wanted my body to move faster. I forced as much as I could. I longed to break free from these paralysing shackles just once so that I could feel that beautiful fluid motion that I had taken for granted for years. If I just forced it harder maybe I could burst into life, like in the scene in *Forrest Gump* when he breaks from his steel leg braces and into a magnificent stride. *Give it your all, Billy, and smash free from this malaise. Keep pushing. Keep working. Lift those legs, Billy.*

The finish was closing in. I attempted to speed up with 200m to go but

I just seemed to be working even harder to maintain the same slow plod. Come on, get there. Throw those legs forward with everything you have.

I crossed the finish line, taking a few clumsy strides to break my rhythm. I looked at my watch, and just about made out the time as my arms were still unstable from the effort. I started walking down the track with my face scrunched up, trying hard not to, but, there I was, a thirty-one-year-old infantry captain in the Australian Regular Army with tears falling down my face.

There were no clapping party or Facebook updates, no support team or medical specialists, just potentially a few bewildered morning runners on the track querying the emotional stability of a skinny weirdo. I had never understood how people cried when happy until that very moment. I just couldn't hold in my emotion. I was beyond ecstatic. As I broke down walking away from the finish line, I wanted to bounce off the ground and leap into the air. I wanted to scream my voice hoarse. After everything that I had withstood, this was my physical proof. I could do it. Somehow, I had made it happen. Life had beat me down hard but I prevailed.

> Under the bludgeonings of chance,
> my head is bloodied, but unbowed.

***

After I started running again in May, I had signed up for a 10km run in Redcliffe, running past the beautiful Woody Point, which was to be held on 19 July, just a few days after the fitness test at Gallipoli Barracks. A couple of days before the race I ran 4km. That was the furthest I had attempted up until that point but I thought I'd give it a go. Rita was nervous. I asked her if it was because she thought I wouldn't finish it. She said she was 100 per cent sure I'd finish, but just asked me to promise not to fall or hurt myself.

I lined up towards the very back of the field. I looked forward at all the guys and girls in front limbering up with such ease. On the gun they all bounded off. I so wanted to bounce off with the flow and ease of a runner. I was so jealous of their smooth strides. But I shuffled awkwardly along, at a pace barely quicker than that of a brisk walk, my legs not extending or bending fully, with my forearms flopping and shaking across my sides and chest. I wore a GPS watch but I couldn't hold my arm nearly steady enough to read it. I wore gloves too as the lack of dexterity and the frost-nip from my previous life as an SF soldier made my hands very cold. I waddled round the course, scuffing my soles, jarring my back and eventually finished in a little over fifty-seven minutes.

Crossing the line, I smiled broadly. I thought about everyone else finishing around me and how unbelievable it would have sounded if I told them my story. How less than seven months previously I was paralysed from the neck down. How I was classified as a quadriplegic. How I could have used the wheelchair car space prior to the run. But it didn't matter that they didn't know. It mattered that I did it.

I don't know why I had to do a 10km run, but I felt that maybe it was another milestone in returning as close as possible to my pre-accident body. Maybe it was because it was the distance I always challenged myself to compete at. Either way it vindicated my efforts to that point. It reaffirmed my belief that *yes – I can do these things*. Although I didn't enjoy the mechanics of running any more, I now knew I could do it.

***

After my return to work in May 2015, my weaknesses were well hidden. In particular, my upper body and hand difficulties were not well known, and I liked it that way. Guys noticed I wore gloves, even sometimes in the office, but they were unaware that not only were my hands very susceptible to the cold, they also had very poor grip and sensation.

I had adapted my handwriting, but was quite slow at transcribing when I returned to work. I tried not to write in front of superiors where possible. I was even more concerned about my basic military skills. Closing a helmet chinstrap was near impossible – I required assistance with that for some time. Although passing my basic fitness test was key to justifying my employability in the infantry, I also needed to pass my weapons assessment.

The first time I fired a weapon was in 2001. I was eighteen years old. Still a teenager, lying on a range, firing an assault rifle. It was incredibly exciting. The thrill of shooting a gun, wow! Everyone wants to be good at it. Everyone pictures themselves as that natural-born marksman. It's the reason why shooter games are so popular. However, I was not a natural. In fact, no one is a natural. Shooting is a skill. Over time, and with good coaching, you can get better at it. But like almost all skills, it requires practice. The more consistent and high quality the practice, the better the skill becomes. Although I managed to place in some army shooting competitions, it was only during my reinforcement cycle in SF training that I became much more skilled at shooting from various assault weapons and pistols, and that was mostly due to the enormous amount of time I spent on the range. Hours of practice, building up eventually to a high level of complex 'combat' shooting skills. As with my drumming in a former life, I found it to be a personal challenge that through practice and persistence became quite enjoyable.

The weapons assessment in 2015, post-injury, required personnel to pass a range shoot, getting twenty rounds within a prescribed grouped radius. This would mean I would first have to pass a test on my elementary weapon skills. Every day after lunch I called into the quartermaster's vault and withdrew my Steyr F88 personal assault rifle. I then would take it down to my office and close the door. The first time I tried lifting the weapon up to a firing stance from the standing position, I could hold it for about two seconds. I didn't want anyone to see how terrible I was. I couldn't pull the cocking handle rearward without lowering the weapon to my hip. I couldn't open my webbing to extract a magazine and put it onto the weapon (a practice drill tested). I couldn't even disengage the locking lug to take off the barrel. It was pathetic. Any NCO training a recruit would have taken the weapon away for safekeeping.

I started small. I sat on my chair (even standing for a period while holding the weapon was tiring) and flicked the safety catch from safe to fire and back to safe again. This vital finger movement was so challenging that I had to turn my elbow inward to generate the required power with my right thumb to push the safety catch through to the right side of the trigger mechanism. I sat there on the first day for over thirty minutes just listening to the distinct 'click' from side to side as I began to retrain my hand in a movement that had been an instinctive action for years. 'Click … click … click.' I then took my hand off the weapon, closed my eyes and attempted to find my way back to disengage, then re-engage the safety catch. Again. Again. Again.

The following day I would practice disengaging, holding a firing position, then re-engaging. Over and over. The next day I practised taking the magazine off and putting it on again. I made it a point to practice the application of the safety catch every day. I looked at it from a safety point of view. Would

I be satisfied with allowing someone that can barely hold a weapon upright to fire one? I have run enough live-fire ranges to know what looks dangerous. Nothing can go wrong with the F88 once the safety catch is applied, so if I was in any doubt as to whether I could hold the weapon correctly, or handle it safely during any drill, all I had to do was apply the safety catch. Everything else I could refine through continued practice, but I had to be able to keep the weapon safe. I practised my basic drills every day until I was happy they would pass the standard.

I asked one specific officer to test me as I knew he would be objective. I would not sign off anyone unable to achieve the basic standards, for any reason. Although I was slow and awkward in my drills, I did not breach any safety or skill aspects and was cleared to conduct the weapons shoot.

The following day I travelled up to the other end of the base to the weapons simulation centre to conduct my shoot with a number of soldiers from the unit. Basic weapon shoots are allowed to be conducted in the simulation centre as required. The centre is extremely advanced, even down to accurate weapon recoil. Adopting the lying position with the rifle was so difficult that I was sweating heavily and I had to work hard to hold the front of the weapon up with my left arm. On my first attempt at firing twenty rounds I was all over the screen. I failed the shoot.

The other soldiers in the room didn't bat an eyelid. 'You wanna give it another go there, sir?' said the junior NCO running the activity. 'Yeah, apologies fellas,' I sheepishly replied as the other soldiers stood back from the firing line and took their webbing off, having successfully completed the shoot. I could feel their eyes on my back as I lay down again.

My main issue was that I was still too weak and rigid through my upper body. On my first attempt I was too deliberate, concentrating deeply on the correct application of the marksmanship principles. I was tiring so quickly that it was rapidly affecting my shot. So, I adapted. For the second go, I fired four quick groups of five single shots, not overthinking it. I passed! The range manager printed off my sheet and handed it to this gleeful, sweaty captain. As the group casually walked out of the facility, I couldn't help pinching myself. Another great day in becoming a soldier again. I could bloody well fire my personal weapon once more.

***

In September I drove to a military exercise area north of the Sunshine Coast (by now I had passed my driving retest) in order to get myself requalified on commanding live-fire ranges. No one ordered me to requalify, but what an amazing feat it would be for me to run a live-fire range as a recovered quadriplegic.

As part of one of the ranges, I had to act as a thrower of a live grenade, before then swapping positions and being the supervisor. I felt sorry for the young private acting as the supervisor, as he watched this skinny, foreign guy with dodgy hands walk robotically into the firing bay. I thought back to a grenade incident in Ireland and laughed. How long ago that seemed.

In October 2003, as a quite junior 2nd lieutenant, I had been charged with running a live grenade practice in the Curragh grenade range. All was going well until about halfway through the practice when an old corporal came into the throwing bay. He was one of the mechanics in the barracks and I didn't know him very well. I gave him a safety brief, including the actions that would be required of him on my orders of commands and the actions he'd need to undertake should anything go wrong in the bay.

He lined up opposite me and we faced towards each other slightly pivoting out over the wall to my right, his left.

'Pick up grenade,' I ordered and he took it from his pouch.

'Prepare to throw.'

He twisted and then pulled on the pin with his left hand, extended it towards the front wall, and held the grenade back behind him, with the fly-off lever pinned against the grenade body.

'Throw grenade.'

'GRENADE,' he shouted as he swung his arm across, as opposed to over, his body, which is an incorrect drill. It was like someone throwing a skimming stone. The fly-off lever sprang away as the grenade bounced off the front wall and back down onto the ground behind us. He looked up at me with rabbit-in-headlight eyes.

'TAKE COVER,' I shouted as loud as I could as I grabbed the corporal and guided him out through the four-foot offset wall to our rear left, ensuring we went out the opposite direction to the location of the grenade in case we kicked it ahead of us. We moved right, then quickly left, then I got him down and bent over him. We actually had about a second to spare.

BOOM.

The air around us tightened slightly and a lot of debris flew over the wall. Anyone who deals with demolitions or has fired anti-armour weapons knows this feeling. (Actually it's pretty awesome!)

I gave the corporal a few minutes to relax, then brought him in to throw his second grenade. It was important to do that, for him and me I think. I was nervous on the second one, but he got it away this time, just.

So on a similar range in Australia, some twelve years later, I reminded myself of that corporal. I really didn't want to be him. Off to the side of the range, I picked up small rocks and practised releasing at the right time. I think the privates on the course watching me were looking around for the crew of *Punk'd* to jump out.

In I walked, with my skinny weak frame and awkward grip. Grenades are designed to be thrown by right-handers so, as a left-hander, one must turn their wrist completely inward to enable the right-hand access to twist and extract the pin. I attempted to nod at the supervisor under assessment to let him know that I was not nervous, just taking my time to get it right. I didn't win the prize for furthest throw for sure, but I successfully got the grenade away and over the wall. Afterwards, I smiled, thinking that maybe I should recommend grenade throwing to my previous occupational therapists to improve hand dexterity. No better motivation than a live grenade!

After I completed a number of supervising roles during various live-fire activities, the staff were satisfied that I could safely run ranges. I was thrilled. I'm not sure why I should have been, as most officers try to stay away from running live-fire ranges. My family and friends wouldn't understand the relevance of this requalification, but from a purely personal perspective it felt great. I was worth something; I was bringing something to the table again. The level of self-satisfaction was immense.

Late September, after successfully getting my range qualification and visiting some other training courses in Wide Bay, I drove back down the Sunshine Coast to Brisbane. I decided to take a small detour. I took the turn off to Caloundra. I bought a pair of board shorts in a local surf shop while staring at the body boards on sale. I parked up on the road behind the beach. I got changed and walked over the grass knoll. I stopped exactly at the spot where Rita and I had been lying on New Year's Eve.

I began to feel nervous as I traced my steps down to the water. I passed the Kings Beach warning signs. The water rushed over my feet as I eyed the very spot where I almost drowned, the spot that had altered my life. I turned to my left and right to ensure that I wasn't alone before I faced into the ocean and waded in.

I was quite tense, as the waves were more powerful than I remembered and I was much weaker than before. I rushed to get out beyond the cresting waves before they knocked me over. A few hit me on my way. *Relax, Bill.*

After ten minutes, I decided I had had enough of reminiscing and started my move ashore. I was cautious of turning my back on the strong waves as I trudged towards safety. Sure enough, I saw a big wave coming towards me, just as I hovered in the dangerously open depth. Although I braced myself, it struck me hard, knocking me onto my hands and knees.

I hurriedly stood up and shuffled out onto the beach. It was pretty innocuous, to be fair. At first, I was angry at myself for foolishly getting knocked down, but then I realised that falling over was the best thing for me, knowing I was brave enough to go back in.

I kept my visit to myself as it wasn't a big deal for me. I felt that it had to be done in order to get over any fear I may have had about the water, but I didn't want it to be a massive ordeal tracked by Snapchat followers or Facebook friends. It was, like everything else, just part of the process. It wasn't the end, not even near it.

***

In January 2016 I drove to the skydiving drop zone in Toogoolawah, alone. For so long, I had thought that I would never again feel the incredible rush of air zipping past me as I ploughed through the atmosphere at terminal velocity. My brother had picked up my logbook a year previously and said how sad it would be to never fill in another line. But here I was with my logbook on the back seat of our Toyota Yaris, Foo Fighters turned up loud, as I drove towards the drop zone. (The song 'Learning to Walk Again' made the hair on my neck stand on end!) I wasn't sure if they would allow me to jump. I wasn't too concerned about exiting the aircraft but I was anxious about the reaction of my body to the chute opening and the landing.

I arrived at reception and spoke with the same lady I had signed up with in December 2014 when I did a few jumps there. She didn't remember me. I tried explaining as best and as simply as I could, but she seemed unfazed. She called an instructor over. He took a look at my licences and ratings, shrugged and said, 'Go for it, mate!'

I was thrilled.

I requested an instructor to jump with me to monitor me. They thought I was overkilling it, as my previous coach rating held some sway. While I didn't want to talk myself out of a jump, I wasn't going to be foolhardy. This was not the time for bravado. I told the staff in no uncertain terms that I needed an instructor to watch me at the very least! So they sent the youngest instructor known to man to liaise with me. He barely had time to ask what was going on before I told him exactly what I was going to do and what I required him to watch.

I needed to know my that body position would be stable. To stabilise the body in freefall, the easiest position is belly to earth, arching the back with arms and legs loose and slightly away from the body. The better the arch, the more stable the skydiver. My arch would clearly be horrendous as my back was as stiff as an ironing board, but I still had to maintain stability somehow. Also, I needed to be able to feel, grab and pull my pilot chute handle, which, with limited hand dexterity and sensation, may be tricky. An instructor jumping with me could observe my body position, critique it with hand signals and, if I was not stable, he could grab an arm or a leg to stabilise me.

I revised my emergency procedures and up we went. I couldn't believe it. No one else in the Cesna Caravan was any the wiser that there was a recovering quadriplegic in this load about to jump solo from 14,000 feet.

I was a little nervous. Had I bitten off too much here? I like pushing myself but I also needed to be aware of my limits.

A few weeks previously I got a big fright when I attempted to dive headfirst into a swimming pool and jarred my neck. I went too far too soon with that one. Was I doing the same here? If I got a hard opening my body would snap from horizontal to vertical very rapidly and jar my neck. If the ground wind speed died down too much I would have a fast landing and probably be unable to run quickly enough to remain standing, flattening myself in the process.

Relax, Billy, come on, you know self-doubt gets you nowhere. Coach yourself. Step by step. Visualise the jump in your head. Repeat the jump over and over. See your body position. Then focus only on the first step, the exit. Set up and exit the door correctly, then worry about your next task. The door slid back. It was very difficult for me to find the clip for my helmet under my chin. I set up at the door. The prevailing wind almost blew me back into the aircraft. *God, I'm still weak. This is it. Ready, set, goooooo.*

Needless to say, it wasn't pretty. But it was safe and I felt comfortable in freefall. Stable. I reached for my pilot chute and found it easily. At the required height, I pulled it out and my canopy followed above my head. After my initial checks, I pulled my goggles down and gazed across the skyline at 2,000ft. I let out a massive roar. I was so happy. It was just so surreal to think of where I was a year before, how utterly destroyed my body was and how, from the absolute brink of death, I was just after freefalling through the air.

I appreciate how some may see this as reckless, or selfish, or unfair to my loved ones. You are probably correct. I got lucky, after all, so why would I actively seek opportunities to conduct activities where I increase the risk of serious injury? *Many others didn't get as lucky as you did. Why are you putting those that love you through this worry and concern again? Why return to clumsy running with a high chance of falling? Why go back to the army and run complex live-fire activities? Why jump out of planes and plummet to earth at over 150mph? Haven't you learned your lesson? Haven't you had enough?*

No, I haven't had enough. I do all of this because it is who I am. I do it all because without the hunger to attempt these things, I would lose myself. Some days I do go down that dark road. I think about all the things that I know I just cannot do. SF selection and service, competitive sports and running freely. These are things that made up a lot of who I was. It hurts to think that I can't do these things. So, while I accept my current limits, I must strive to attain all that I can. That's key to the mentality required. I'll adapt, I'll improvise and I will overcome. It's the intrinsic motivation that will never leave me. I will become the best me possible.

I hope to continue to work as close as possible to the tip of the spear in the ADF. It's not the same as passing selection and serving in an SF unit. I know this more than most. If you're in, you're in, but if not it doesn't matter what the circumstances are. But I'll get stuck in. I'll work in whatever capacity the ADF want and hopefully I'll be of assistance. If it doesn't work out, then so what? I've a PE degree, haven't I? A recovered quadriplegic as your PE teacher, there's a first! Maybe I'll look at management or leadership roles outside of the military. Maybe I'll study human psychology and deliver talks or lectures. Maybe I'll run some adventure races, or marathons again. Or maybe none of the above. But it is nice to have the choice.

I choose to believe in myself and those close to me. I cannot control gravity when I freefall, but I can control how I shape my body to react to the resistance. I cannot control everything, but I control me.

I am the master of my fate:
I am the captain of my soul.

Epilogue

BELIEF AND BELIEVE – HOW I HOPE TO HELP YOU

How My Belief Helped Me

Growing up I was ferociously competitive. I loved to compete against anyone, doing anything. From table tennis to table quizzes. As a teenager, I was uncomfortably competitive, finding it difficult to stomach being beaten at a computer game or even a game of chess. And I couldn't hide it. I had been relatively unsuccessful in sport; however, instead of losing confidence, I seemed to gain resolve through my various disappointments. Not being selected for representative teams in Gaelic football or rugby, losing another final, or forgetting lines during a play were all events that could have made me crawl under a rock and give up. But I didn't sulk or moan about my failures. I started using them as motivation to increase my effort.

After joining the army, I began to enjoy running as an activity, as we had to do plenty of it. I had never run long distances before, but I had always thought I had good endurance. I had no real proof of this, but I felt that

I had good stamina because I knew that I wouldn't stop easily. Because I thought it was easy, I signed up for the Dublin Marathon during my officer cadet training in 2002. Not only did I not do any training for it, I also went out on the Friday and Saturday nights prior to the Monday race and got quite drunk. On Sunday, after signing in for the run, Mac and I visited the infamous nightclub, Copperface Jacks. Although I stayed off alcohol that night, we didn't bed down until close to 4 a.m. We awoke in Bayside, running late, and had to change in a taxi en route to the city. We were late across the start line and spent the first 3 miles dodging walkers. It hurt like hell, but we finished almost five hours later. There had been no talk of giving up. Never. Although I had grossly underestimated the difficulty of a marathon, we got it done, for no reason other than pure stubbornness.

As I progressed through my twenties, my feelings towards running began to change. It probably mirrored my personal motivation towards many things. It wasn't about trying to win, it was more about besting my best. My mind was maturing and my motivating factors became much more inwardly focused. Instead of beating others, I was beating myself. I chased times such as 10km in under forty minutes, or marathons in under three hours and thirty minutes, which were only achieved through a lot of hard work and determination.

During my time in the ARW, I developed a further hobby: I competed in trail- and hill-running races, then eventually full-distance adventure races. I loved the challenge. While something like a 10km road race led to a quick run, I had started to find long-distance road running somewhat boring. But during an adventure race or trail run there was so much to see; even when working hard I always managed to admire the scenery. I really hurt after my first attempt at a Wicklow adventure race, as the change from a mountain-run leg to a racing-bicycle leg over mountain roads absolutely blew my muscles apart. After a few more attempts, however, I started to get quicker, became more effective on changeover and grew stronger on the bike.

By 2014 I had completed a number of adventure races around Ireland. I competed in the St Paddy's Day Killarney adventure race, where I finished eighth overall, coming first in my wave. I was really chuffed, not so much with my finishing position but more so with the progress I had made from my initial attempts, where I had walked up parts of the mountain with my hands on my knees. Now I was pounding the trails, tearing up mountain roads through some of the most beautiful scenery in Ireland. I learned to love running, cycling and, probably most importantly, I enjoyed enduring. I loved doing something hard but always fighting through it. I didn't like the pain – no one does – but I did like the elation of completing something difficult. And the more I challenged myself, the more confident I became in my ability to endure. After completing one tough challenge, I had less doubt in myself for the next one. I backed myself to go faster, longer or harder. Each time I did something tough, it made me believe that I was a tough guy, a 'never give up' guy. I just wouldn't stop, ever. For each new challenge I could reflect on previous difficult occasions and on how I had overcome them.

I have been put through resistance to interrogation exercises on four occasions during my time in the military. The first time was undoubtedly the most stressful. I had never before experienced such a level of discomfort and lack of control. It's not so much the painful positions your body is placed in for extended periods of time that bother you, nor is it your senses being stripped away as you are blindfolded, ear-muffed and bound, while hateful noises are looped through your brain. It's not even the administering of force on painful pressure points or the aggressive handling, or dogs barking, or cold water being flung over your shivering body. The most difficult part of the entire process is the mind's ability to 'let go'. I was not in control. I had to be okay with that.

One of the most effective techniques for interviewing is waterboarding. Whatever creative way it is administered, the end result is simple: your captor has control over when you take your next breath, not you. I have been 'lucky' enough to be exposed to this type of treatment and it is a truly horrible feeling. I flinched, wriggled and fought to break free until it suddenly stopped, giving me the respite I needed to regain any form of thought process. I would be asked a question knowing that should I decline to answer I would be submitting myself to further treatment. But even at this crazy and unbelievable point I was happy not to give in. I wasn't projecting a defiant and aggressive mindset; in fact, it was more of a Zen-like focus. Being comfortable at being uncomfortable. After I experienced interrogation techniques such as sensory deprivation, subsequent exposures became less traumatic – not easy, by any means, but certainly easier. By the time I was 'put into the bag' (put through an interrogation activity) during my survival instructor's course in 2011, I not only maintained my calm but had also developed strategies to make the 'softening up' process less stressful, keeping my mind occupied while making my body appear frailer than it actually was. Whatever the torture, whatever the stress position given, whatever the deprivation applied, it just didn't get to me. Of course it hurts. Of course it's insanely distressing, but I remember thinking, *Do you honestly think I'm ever going to crack and give you the information you require?*

The tightening of the halo brace felt like a 'softening up' activity. Being paralysed reminded me of interrogation. I lost control of everything other than my mind. I compartmentalised certain aspects of my paralysis and equated them to parts of these activities. *Go on, tighten it harder, I'll never give in*, I thought. *Go on, pull out that catheter, you won't break me.*

Even early on, when I was told I was paralysed from the neck down, I knew that whatever the outcome, I would take it and move on. It was crazy. It was insane. One minute you are a normal able person with no appreciation of how lucky you are to be able to move. The next minute you are unable to move and lucky to be alive. Sometimes I think back to the accident and I get a little freaked out by it. I start to think about all the 'what ifs'. *Where would I be now if I hadn't been injured? What if that boy hadn't seen me face down in the water? How far away was I from drowning, from dying?*

But in the immediate aftermath of the accident I wasn't scared. Although I could – and still can – think, see and feel negative thoughts, nothing will ever change what occurred. So, instead of dwelling on what was already done, I focused on each immediate issue. I chased it down like every race I ever ran, every game I ever played, knowing I was strong enough to push through the pain, the setbacks and the lack of control. At the time of the accident, I was as fit as I had ever been. What a fall, in every sense of the word. But true strength is about how we rise from the bottom.

Rehabilitation is a difficult process for anyone to undertake. It's the forgotten child of medical care. No one likes rehab. It drains the soul, as all you want to do is get better quickly. If surgery is the sprint, then rehab is the ultra-adventure race, sometimes with no finish line. *The challenge of a lifetime.*

The toughest part of rehab is not the tedious, repetitive physical exercises, or the chirpy physiotherapist constantly fault-correcting. It is the personal drive needed to continue to strive towards your end goal. Remaining motivated is without doubt the biggest challenge. When improvements are virtually non-existent, and exercises seem so frustrating, is it any wonder that people have a tendency to fade away from rehabilitation? They have stayed afloat for a long time but eventually they get tired of treading water and stop swimming. They sink. This is completely understandable, as anyone who has gone through prolonged rehabilitation will attest.

But I couldn't let myself drown. No way. I had been furiously determined in hospital and there was no reason to slow down now just because the gains were less apparent and it was getting tougher. If I didn't keep chasing for full recovery, then what hope had I of reaching my maximum potential? I worked my ass off. I constantly challenged the medical staff working with me. *I'm not just another SCI patient. I'm different. I'm off the bell curve, and you won't find me in any research paper. I am the exception to the rule.*

Almost twelve months after the accident, my military medical doctor in Brisbane made a comment about my mentality. After a long discussion of what my next goals and plans were, he stated that he had never seen someone as motivated as me this far into rehabilitation. He said that I was still at full throttle, at a point when most others fade away, usually through broken will and spirit. But it's a mind game. If I gave up, I'd never get another ounce of recovery; on the other hand, if I worked hard I might get something, even if it was just a fraction. *Even the thought of a fraction more is better than the acceptance of nothing.*

I have been told to 'manage my expectations' in terms of recovery many times. I like challenging that phrase. Had I managed my expectations and not attempted to reclaim my pre-accident body, then I firmly believe that I would not be as advanced as I am today. Medical professionals may know and understand the condition, but they don't know me. Phrases such as 'managing expectations' to me sound like 'you can't' or 'I don't think so'. It feels like a covert way of saying 'you are getting ahead of yourself and you expect too much'. I call bullshit on that. I expect the best from myself. Even to this day, I argue with military medical professionals over my medical employment categorisation. They don't understand why I want to continue to gain further upgrades and wish to receive parachuting medical clearance. They attempt to tell me that, due to the serious nature of the injury, I should not be upgraded any further. I challenge that premise. *Tell me why I cannot and I will prove you wrong if I can.* I don't think the medical staff fully appreciate the frustration or the motivation behind chasing these medical clearances. It is much more than just a physical issue. In my head, I need to know that I am back to normal. That I am fully functional. That other people won't hold me back by telling me I cannot do something.

My Mental Fitness Theories

In this section I will describe some of my favourite theories related to resilience. *But hold on, does this really matter? Why should we worry about being mentally strong? Why don't I go about living my life and not concern myself with stupid 'mind tricks'?*

My college lecturer once outlined to his fresh-faced students the four principles of games:

1) Physical fitness;

2) Skills;

3) Tactical Awareness;

4) Mental Fitness.

He stated that in order for a person or a group to defeat another, they must be superior in the sum of the four principles. I can recall almost nothing from this lecturer other than this simple yet amazingly accurate assessment. Although a team might be physically fitter and more skilful, for example, they may lose to a team applying better tactics with extra motivation to win.

A simple point to be taken from this is that mental fitness is a multiplier for success in competition. If all else is equal, it is mental fitness which becomes the determining factor. 'They weren't hungry out there today', or 'I just wasn't feeling it', or maybe 'I was absolutely spent after she overtook me'. Physical fitness as a differentiator is easy to quantify. We have any number of scientists who can tell us who is fitter. We can use strategy and analysis to determine tactical awareness, both at individual and group level. We can provide rough estimates of skill levels for individuals and groups through reflection on previous performance and the amount of time spent on quality skill-specific practice. But how do we quantify mental fitness? How can we tell how motivated someone *really* is for a race/game? Mental fitness is an unquantifiable 'X-factor', so although we know that it is important, we don't know how much of an effect it has on success. The following theories outline how we might build this 'X-factor' in order to succeed, even when the odds are against us.

Theory 1: The Hurt Locker

Matt Fitzgerald details the concept of how a race is like a firewalk in his book *How Bad Do You Want It?* (Aurum Press, 2016). The analogy relates to our *true* physical limit versus what we achieve on any given occasion. Ahead of you is a wall. The wall represents your absolute true physical limit. You can never reach the wall as to do so would kill you. (For instance, the human body at its peak should be able to run 100m in six seconds – however, this is impossible as the body would essentially be committing suicide and the mind would not allow that to occur.) Between you and the wall is a firewalk of hot coals. Clearly it is uncomfortable to walk on hot coals but the longer you can endure stepping towards the wall, the closer you will get to your true limit until you have to jump off. That point represents your achievement today. Everyone else you are competing with also has their own wall. The distance to their walls is different (depending on other factors, such as their physical fitness). However, although your wall may be close while the others' walls are far away, they may jump off the hot coals quickly, while you have stepped further down the coals and jump off ahead of them. Therefore, you succeed. The message being that those who can better endure 'the hurt locker' – or, in this case, the 'firewalk' – are more likely to succeed. Those willing to push themselves further on SF selection, for example, are more likely to pass. Those who are more tolerant of pain during interrogation are less likely to break. Those that push limits relentlessly during rehabilitation, despite the 'hot coals' underfoot, are more likely to recover.

Theory 2: Perceived Rate of Exertion

All the experiences illustrated throughout this book are descriptions of how I saw something, not actually how it happened. They are my perception of events. The exact same applies to effort. We work to what we believe is a particular percentage of our maximum. This theory is called the perceived rate of exertion (PRE). After an activity, we rate the difficulty on a scale of 1 to 10, 10 being our maximum and 0 being no effort. After a timed run, for instance, as we cross the finish line we rate how hard that was out of 10. Our maximum of 10 is not our *true* limit, however, but our *perceived* limit and our effort rated is only rated against this perception. For instance, why is it that regardless of the distance we travel in a maximum-effort run, it is always towards the very end that we push hardest and feel the most effort, and when crossing the line feel as if we could go no further? Why is it that our pace for a 400m maximum-effort race and 3.2km race would be so vastly different? Even though I can run much faster than my pace while running my 3.2km, my mind says, *this pace is the fastest speed/maximum effort your body can work at for this distance.* This pace is, therefore, a guess. Remember that technically the body's true limit cannot be reached but our closeness to this limit can be altered. The point in all this is that our mind will make us stop before our body does. We run as fast as possible for 5km at maximum effort, and grade our PRE at 9 as we finish. But what if we tell ourselves that what we actually feel is more like a 7? That our body has the capacity to do more than we feel it does. A lot of US Navy SEALs speak of the 40 per cent rule, a concept I love. It is the belief that when you think you have reached your maximum capacity, you have in fact only reached 40 per cent of it.

This brings us to the second part of perception: our inclination towards effort. When something is difficult we rate how difficult it is. But if perception is how I feel, then it is brought about by 'how I feel about how I feel'. If I feel physically under pressure during an activity, then I can either feel positive about this feeling, i.e. I have more to give, or I can feel negative towards it, i.e. I can't maintain this and I need to slow down. My perception is affected by how I am inclined to react. If, like the SEALs, I programme my mind to believe that I have more to give, then my perception of my effort decreases and I am therefore more likely to produce a higher effort.

Pushing through barriers is how people succeed; for example, it is how one athlete with almost identical capacity to their opponent will defeat them. They are more willing to put themselves into the hurt locker and allow their perception of the effort they are giving to shift. They are, therefore, bringing themselves closer to their real limit. I like to think of it as 'heart', but the bottom line is that we have to believe that we always have more to give.

Theory 3: Self-Efficacy

In 1986 renowned psychologist Albert Bandura published his theory, named the Social Cognitive Theory. It described how people learn through observing others. An essential tenet of his theory was the term 'self-efficacy', subsequently further developed in his book *Self-Efficacy: The Exercise of Control* (1997). The term is defined as being the confidence in one's own ability to achieve intended results. It is closely linked with perception, motivation and one's prior exposure. For instance, if I have never bench-pressed 100kg before, and I'm feeling weak today, I will not feel confident in achieving this goal. If I don't think I can do it, I am more likely to fail or, worse still, I won't even try.

Let's relate this to SF selection. Candidates know the failure rates. They know, looking around on the first night, that most will fail. But those who assess that they are going to pass, and therefore show higher self-efficacy, will have higher confidence, are more likely to produce higher effort levels and, through a positive mindset, are more likely to succeed. Conversely, others who believe that they are too unfit to attempt selection – even if they have an interest in SF service – make the choice to never attempt the course.

I use self-efficacy to fortify my resilience. My interrogations are a simple example of this: prior experience increased my judgement of how I was going to perform and therefore I was less stressed. Most importantly, when I was told I was paralysed, I looked back on all of my challenging life experiences to judge that I was extremely resilient and that I could and would prevail. I *knew* I was the type of person who could cope with this injury and I *knew* I could rehabilitate from the injury if there was a chance because I *knew* I wouldn't give up. Why? Because a life of not quitting said so.

Theory 4: Goal Setting

James A. Eison, John G. Nicolls, and subsequently Carol S. Dweck were the first to develop what is commonly known as Goal Orientation Theory. The theory suggests that one's goal can be either task- or ego-orientated. This means that someone is focused either on mastering the actual *task* of achieving the goal for extrinsic reasons (e.g. learning a language for no specific reason), or solely on an ego-orientated goal (e.g. winning an Olympic medal).

It is suggested that task-orientated goals are more likely to be successful when someone is intrinsically motivated (by internal factors, such as self-achievement), whereas ego-orientated goals are mostly successful when someone is extrinsically motivated (by external factors, such as recognition from others). What does this mean? It means that someone who is motivated to beat someone else is ideally placed to succeed in competition. When we say a team was 'really hungry' for the win, it means that they were highly motivated to win, not to play a perfect game. The Vince Lombardi adage 'Winning isn't everything, it's the only thing' comes to mind. In fact, being extrinsically motivated is ideal to achieving great success in ego-orientated goals, for example, winning the league, getting that high-profile job, or any perceived success to the rest of society. Ego orientation seems to be what mostly motivates us today.

What has any of this got to do with mental fitness? Studies have shown that people who have ego-orientated goals and are extrinsically motivated give up on the goal sooner than someone who is intrinsically motivated. How many times have we tried a diet or training regime and 'fallen off the wagon'? The main reason for this is that we are motivated by *external* reasons and are not truly *internally* motivated to succeed.

For instance, I was initially extrinsically motivated to pass SF selection, as I wanted to show people that I was good enough. But as the course progressed my mindset changed, so by the end of the course I wanted to serve in the unit and passing the course was merely the by-product.

My post-quadriplegia goals, such as running a 10km road race or sky-diving again, were for me. I wanted to be as close to the 'pre-accident me' as possible. *Why didn't you post your fantastic progress on Facebook, or Instagram, Billy?* Well, each to their own, and I would not judge others, but personally I didn't need extra motivation or yearn for compliments and 'well-done' sentiments. I craved the satisfaction of achieving another goal. It's what worked for me.

Remember the infantry PESA I outlined as a long-term goal in my paralysed, halo-wearing state during my first patient goal-setting meeting in the SIU in January 2015? The medical staff were quick to bring me back to reality, it seemed. However, I successfully completed the infantry PESA on 8 September 2017, over two and a half years later, a feat that the vast majority of the army would struggle to do. I didn't need to do it for any reason other than I had said that I was going to do it.

Theory 5: Being a Leader

If strong mental fitness requires us to take ownership, have high levels of self-efficacy and the ability to lower our perceptions of effort, then a key to achieving these is the concept of leadership. What is leadership? I personally define it as 'the art of using influence in order to achieve a desired outcome'. This is not limited to others, however; we can also influence ourselves into positive future behaviours.

The key to leadership is leading by example. If I lead by example in whatever I want to achieve, then I set the tone. I should expect high standards of myself and hold myself to task. I need to set the example for others and for myself. As a result, I become more responsible, more accountable and more resilient.

I led in the SIU by forcing myself to make my bed. No one else made their bed. But when I said to myself that I was making my bed every day, I was setting an example. Then, by being *that* person, I had to make my bed every day. I had to work my ass off in physio. I had to, because I wanted to prove that hard work paid off. *I'm going to work really hard, and so can you.*

Practical Applications: 'So What?'

What is my purpose in writing this book? I have shared my story and my theories not for personal gratification, not to preach from the pulpit or for financial gain. The purpose of recounting all the details of my injury, or life events, is only to give weight to the advice I give now. A common military rhetorical phrase used during briefing or orders is 'so what?' This essentially questions 'what is the relevance of this to me?' So what does it matter to anyone else that Billy Hedderman managed to regain an astounding level of function from diagnosed quadriplegia? 'How should this affect my life in any way?' My hope in this section is to outline some practical applications for my mental fitness theories, which I have used during my life, so that they may be of use to anyone, whether injured/sick or not, and assist them in getting the most out of themselves.

Sometimes I ask myself how much of my recovery was down to luck – in terms of the initial damage done – and how much movement was recovered because it was 'me'. That may sound ridiculous, and may insult or offend others who have suffered similar fates with lesser outcomes. It may sound like I'm some cocky guy who thinks that his state of mind brought him back from paralysis. But I know there are people out there who, no matter how tough their mental strength, will not overcome certain obstacles. I do not suggest for a second that self-belief is a cure for incomplete quadriplegia. All I know is that, in my individual circumstances, it helped immeasurably. I knew I would do everything and more, and it would never break me. Things aren't easy. But if you believe in your toughness, it helps. It doesn't make that backpack any lighter, or that race any shorter, but it helps. It's the ultimate mind trick. Mind over matter.

Why did Nelson Mandela inscribe Henley's poem 'Invictus' on his prison wall? I suspect it was because he needed reminding of the phrase 'mind over matter'. As I do. When I'm hurting, I say to myself that I am stronger than the hurt, that I am tougher than the pain and that I can deal with it. That I will get through it, whatever the situation. As anyone can.

For some, pushing to and through a perceived limit is too physically painful or stressful. Maybe they just like being comfortable. Not everyone is a natural firewalker, after all. But if we are disinclined to push ourselves, then it will be difficult to actually achieve our goals, and this will create feelings of low confidence and disappointment, causing us to spin around in a state of underachievement. Alternatively, if we set our goals low in order for us to achieve them with minimum effort, we then immediately decrease self-efficacy and stay on a continuous loop of low-to-average satisfaction. We continue to lift the same weight or run the same speed because we don't think we can do better. My practical application to break this cycle is doing one simple thing: *refusing to give up easily*.

This is difficult to achieve. It's easy to say you'll never quit when you're comfortable. But it's so tempting to give in when you're hurting. You want something to stop because you don't like discomfort or pain. And the option to stop is always close by. 'Never give up' is a nice meme, but not quitting is against our nature, which is why those who don't give up are more likely to achieve. Psychologists describe methods to improve our mental fitness as 'coping skills'. These are ways that we 'trick' our mind into becoming more resilient. I suggest we should practically apply the following coping skills or strategies: 1) Internal locus of control; 2) Reflection; 3) Angry resolve; and 4) Self-talk to help us not to give up. I may not have fully understood these terms before some research but, without realising it, I have been using them for most of my life.

1)   *Internal locus of control* is a fancy psychology term that I like to simplify as 'ownership'. It is the key to helping you not to quit. If I take ownership of my situation, one of two things can happen: I can either feel trapped and panicked about my decisions and actions, or experience massive relief knowing that my fate is in my hands. If I remind myself that how I feel *about* how I feel is important,

then I can choose the latter. For example, I chose how to react to my paralysis. I chose how to react to the physical hardship of the SF selection course. I chose how to react to the death of my friends. Being accountable for yourself is not a hindrance, but a freedom to embrace. *I* decide where my life is going to take me, and I am not a victim of circumstance. 'Shit happens', as the bumper sticker says, but it's what we do afterwards that makes the difference. We don't hide behind pity or stronger personalities or shame or doubt. We become responsible for everything we can. It empowers us to make things happen. We are the drivers of our lives, not just passengers. I firmly believe that, should we abide by this principle, then we would be far less likely to give up, and by consequence much more likely to succeed.

2) *Reflection* is key to our mental fitness. Using prior experiences as an indication of future performance can assist us greatly in our self-efficacy or judgement on how we will perform. For example, 'the last time we played this team they beat us heavily, so we'll be lucky to win today', is a simple thought process that sets us up for a sub-optimal performance. But we can use past experience to assist us, too. My belief is that a negative past occurrence equates to a positive result on future self-efficacy. Essentially, if I have done something hard, or been unsuccessful, or had to cope with bad news, I can 'bank' this and then withdraw it at a future time when I need affirmation that I have experienced tough times before but came through them. This can sometimes be called the power of failure. Michael Jordan was once quoted as saying, 'I have missed

more than 9,000 shots in my career. I've lost almost 300 games. 26 times I was trusted to take the game-winning shot and missed. I've failed over and over and over again in my life. And that is why I succeed.'

The old saying 'what doesn't kill you makes you stronger' comes to mind. Recent studies also make interesting comments on past difficulties. In a paper published in the September 2012 edition of *Sports Medicine*, David Collins and Áine MacNamara argued on the subject 'why talent needs trauma', outlining that athletes with exposure to a certain level of trauma were more likely to display higher levels of resilience.

The practical application of reflection could be done prior to attempting a difficult task, by reminding yourself of challenges you have faced in the past that will improve your confidence in your ability to achieve the current task. For instance, I know I can now use the fact that I prevailed though quadriplegia to greatly assist my mental capacity for any future challenges; indeed, it makes me feel mentally unbreakable. Thus, using the coping skill of reflecting on a previous challenge will ensure you are less likely to give up.

3)   We can develop this further and use these previous negatives to increase our ability to produce '*angry resolve*'. This is where we use anger as a coping skill to push our perceived limit in specific instances. Get angry with yourself for your previous performance. Hate your body/mind for being so slow or weak. *Stand those stupid weak legs up straight, Billy. Get them up, GET THEM UP*. But be careful not to overstep the mark into negative thinking. Remember,

this is only a short-term tool to assist in a performance, not a self-loathing scenario where you end up despising yourself.

4) Use *self-talk*. I use it constantly. I use keywords, phrases or images to work as a trigger for focus. If I'm lifting something, for instance, I'll say the word 'strength' loudly in my head just before I lift. When I'm running, I'll visualise a smooth running motion, and say the word 'flow' in my head to focus on the feeling, not the biomechanics of the movement. But even more than just imagery and 'keying' words, self-talk is mostly about being inwardly positive. It serves as a reminder to stay on track. It does not need to be during or just prior to the activity either. During a quiet time in any given hospital day I would drift off into my own thoughts, reminding myself to 'push on, work hard', and 'never to feel sorry for myself'. Positive self-talk promotes higher self-awareness. *You are one tough dude, Billy* I would say to myself. Yes, it drives egotism and potential arrogance, but it creates an environment where the self-talker believes it before they do it. If belief of being in control of our own destiny and using past experience to improve resilience are the strategies (the 'what'), then self-talk is one of the main skills (the 'how') in achieving your goals.

For me, resilience is the key tenet of mental fitness. My personal examples are only stories. There is no requirement to pat me on the back or tell me how well I did. Reflect instead on the instances I have outlined and then the reasons why you may believe I have prevailed. Take note of those reasons. I implore you to use them. Pick apart my theories and test my practical applications. My absolute intent for this entire book is that, through reading it, you will take some of the aspects of 'how' I succeeded in overcoming my paralysis and apply these newly acquired mental-strengthening skills to whatever situation you wish. If one person tells me that my story or advice has assisted them, then all of the work that went into writing this book will have been worth it.

ACKNOWLEDGEMENTS

I wish to acknowledge all the love and support I received from so many people from 1 January 2015 to this very day. I still have a folder at home filled with cards, letters, photos and printed emails from people from all walks of life. From those I am very close to, to people I have never met. From my local village of Watergrasshill, to locations around the world. The good wishes I received from everyone were incredibly humbling, and I thank all those who in any way supported us from the time of my accident. It would be near impossible to list everyone; however, I would like to give specific thanks to the following:

To my immediate family for all their unwavering support, now and always. They are stone mad, but without them Rita and I would be lost. We 'gotta be happy with that'.

To all my extended family, both Heddermans and Maddens, as their letters, messages and kind words really helped in keeping me going, and I greatly appreciated their time, effort and care.

To Rita's family and wide group of friends, who went beyond anything I could imagine. Their thoughtfulness and kindness were deeply appreciated.

Regards to my college crew in UL, for all those amazing times, and all the wonderful messages of support and offers of help: Allan Mulrooney, Donal Mealey, Ross Lynch, Aidan Lonergan, Aoife Kelly, Claire Fannin, Ger Ryan, Diarmuid Carr and many more. A very special thanks to the very handsome Conor Daly for his visits and wit.

A great big thanks to all of my old friends from school and Cork, for their messages and their weak efforts to keep spirits high through terrible jokes – Bucks, Dave, Gregs, Markie, Stiofan and Brian Condon. Thanks guys. I'd like to single out my oldest friend in the world, Barry, for his fantastic support, multiple trips to visit me, and his ability to vanish when I began to bleed heavily through my penis! Really appreciated everything, Bar … I believe it's your round.

To all of the ASE committee/Annacotty crew: Catriona, Ailish, Mark and Grainne, I cannot put into words how much you helped us during a very tough time. To Liam, Louise, Donal, Dave, Tom, Tara, Shane, Seanie Fitz and everyone involved in the Sports Extravaganza, the Rubber Duckies or Annacotty crew, thank you all.

A big thanks to the Connollys and Feeleys for their kind words and support throughout my time in hospital and beyond.

To Zenith; cheers guys. At least now I have an excuse for being out of time.

To the staff of the PA: your level of care was like nothing I have ever seen and I believe that my recovery was in no small way enabled by you all. A special thanks to Tiff, Glenda and Maureen.

I received many messages from the Irish Army, from privates to brigadier generals while dormant on a hospital bed. The military seems to evoke a sense of family, togetherness and support that very few workplaces can emulate. By the amount of good wishes I received from military members in Ireland, I couldn't help but feel proud. Thank you all, particularly Mike, Mac, Gorey, Mo, J Bag and all others in the 78th Arena for keeping morale high when standards were low!

I received a picture card of my SF selection course signed by the guys in the ARW. I had it pinned up alongside my bed and made sure to look at it each morning as they hoisted me into my wheelchair. This picture increased my drive to work hard, and to maintain an honesty of effort, as these people would expect. Cheers fellas.

Believe it or not, we actually know a few Australians out here, including the entire Abbot clan and Annette, Glenn, Shannon and Siobhan. Thanks Wendy and Terry for your open arms, and cheers Netty and co. for the very punny jokes.

During my time in hospital, ADF uniforms became a regular occurrence on the ward. 'Mateship' at its finest. Few people had any real exposure to me during my first number of weeks in the ADF, so they didn't really know me. But it didn't seem to matter much. I was one of theirs. The unit Padre's enthusiasm and infectious positivity regularly kept me striving to stay gracious, yet hungry to get better for everyone's sake, not just my own. Leo, God bless you, and thank you.

I was visited by army mates from the base in Brisbane regularly. To Simon White and his wife, Priscilla, to Joe and Sarah, Andy McClean and his wife, Jen, and some of the guys from work, including Michael Jack, Pat Carmody, Harry Christenson, Grant Young, Doug Thornton and Sandi, I will never forget your kindness. Your visits made me feel like I wasn't forgotten and that I was part of the team. Thank you all so much.

One morning, while I was lying motionless on my bed, the unit Padre mentioned to me that the guys from my unit had organised a visit to my house and spent the day cutting the grass and tidying the outside areas. I was absolutely blown away. Months later, I spoke with privates and corporals who were involved. I was struck by the genuine satisfaction they showed in being able to help and how happy they appeared to see me back in uniform.

It shocked me because they barely knew me. I hadn't even built much rapport with them at this stage and yet they were willing to volunteer for one of their own in need. To feel that type of genuine support and care is extremely gratifying and also motivating. I never felt like I was not part of the Australian military. To all in 6 RAR, and particularly those who assisted us during our darkest times, thank you very much.

As previously outlined, I started this project as a hand-therapy activity. I didn't know where it was going to end up but certain people along the way assisted, prodded and guided me through the long process to one day actually publishing a book with my name on it.

I'd like to thank Sarah O'Donovan for her selflessness, huge effort and belief in my ability to get this from a rambling mess of a Word document to a coherent story and for ensuring that I 'stayed the course'.

I'd like to thank all of those I asked to read and provide feedback on various chapters, as I really appreciated their honesty and understanding. I hope I didn't offend any of them, as they also just so happened to be characters in some of my stories. A massive thanks to Darragh Groeger and Mike Norwood for reviewing the manuscript entirely and providing honest feedback, excellent points for consideration and detailed spelling and grammar critiques, and the title of the book!

I must also thank Patrick O'Donoghue from Mercier Press for believing in me and seeing something that others did not, working tirelessly with me for almost two years and always projecting a positive outlook during our many WhatsApp calls. I'd also like to thank Mary Feehan, Deirdre Roberts, Noel O'Regan, Wendy Logue and all the rest of the staff at Mercier for their professionalism, assistance and good-natured support throughout this entire process. I haven't a clue how a book actually ends up on a shelf, but Mercier have made it extremely easy for me, even from the other side of the world.

***

I met Rita on 26 September 2003. I remember it well as it was the same night that my father's mother, Chris Hedderman, died. Nan was a larger-than-life character and was an influence on all of us growing up. She had single-handedly raised my father's family following the premature death of my grandfather, Bill Hedderman. It seems as one major influence left on that night, another entered.

Rita and I had a challenging relationship at times, as everyone does. We broke up. We got back together. We broke up. We got back together. We endured many difficulties together. We matured together and, God knows, I had plenty of maturing to do. We are different people. In fact, we are quite different. Most things that interest me don't interest her. Sport, military and adventure activities do not appeal to her. As much as fashion and languages don't wow me! But, so what? It works for us, so we are happy with that. Rita is a reserved and private person in general and expressly told me not to put too much about her into this book, but I will outline some aspects of our trials during this period.

I have always had a relatively calm and focused outlook during times of crisis. Whether it be a broken-down vehicle, a tragic event or just a stressful situation, I usually keep my cool. I was concerned in this particular instance that Rita may not. It must have been exceptionally difficult to see her partner in a paralysed state. Imagine your own partner in such a situation. How would you react? It would be natural to feel despair, worry and even guilt. *'We've now got no chance of the life plans we had, and I'll probably be this person's carer for life. This wasn't my plan. I didn't want that. I wanted to have kids someday. Or at least the choice. I didn't want to push a chair around. How will I ever find this person physically attractive again?'*

These are acceptable – and logical – thought processes as one might struggle to come to grips with the gravity of the situation. But not once did I see Rita's commitment waver. Not once did she become overwhelmed by what I had turned into. Her actions and attitude over those first few weeks were nothing short of incredible. She took the lead in caring for me physically, helping me make decisions and keeping me company. She never appeared to feel sorry for herself, constantly projecting positive effort towards me. As the weeks progressed, she grew strained, physically tired and, eventually, once the initial shock subsided, she began to find space for her personal 'processing'. She started feeling severe pain in her lower back, which medical professionals couldn't identify. It became apparent that it was most likely a release-point from the built-up and bottled-up worry, fear and anxiety that she never outwardly expressed. It must have been exceptionally challenging for her. She told me how nervous she was every time I shuffled around a room, as I looked so fragile and so weak. She had never seen me like this before. She cared for me so much that she 'just wanted to wrap me up and never let anything happen to me again'. The emotional worry must have been almost overwhelming. Still, even with the burden of a potentially complete change of life and enormous level of concern and worry, she made it her absolute priority to enable me to focus on my recovery. She was always propping me up when I needed it. Some may wallow or run away, but although she was fighting her own demons, she threw everything to one side to help me first.

This has also been the case on previous occasions in our relationship.

ACKNOWLEDGEMENTS

When in my greatest hour of need, when the self-believer needed help, someone to lean on, she was always there for me. She flew from Sydney to be with me after Aidan's death. She consoled me after Alan's death. She supported me during my most challenging times. My biggest fear was the burden I would be for Rita should I remain paralysed. I couldn't let that happen if there was a chance I could move again. But either way, whatever the outcome, she was alongside me. She was all-in, no matter what. There was never a question about it. Some would retreat, hiding in their own sorrow, or look to find condolence in family or friends, but not Rita. I'm usually the more assertive one, but when I was in this very unusual position of vulnerability she took on that role. She looked after me and continues to. My self-belief, my recovery and my life are due to Rita enabling me. She sacrificed her own well-being for me. I love her dearly and my respect for her knows no bounds.

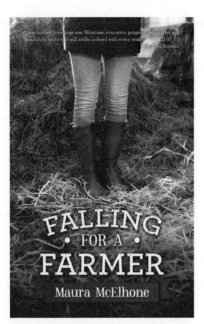

978 1 78117 604 7

'I was hooked from page one. Hilarious, evocative, poignant, perceptive and beautifully written, it will strike a chord with every reader. I LOVED it!'
Patricia Scanlan

After living in California for close to a decade, Maura McElhone returns home to Ireland looking to put down roots. But when she meets a handsome farmer she soon finds herself in at the deep end of a whole new way of life, from helping a sheep give birth to witnessing a slaughter, and being left in the lurch when it's time to make the silage. *Falling for a Farmer* chronicles the often humorous and sometimes sobering experiences that arise when town and country collide. This is one woman's true-life story of her journey from wide-eyed townie to full-blown farmer's girlfriend.

www.mercierpress.ie

MERCIER PRESS

We hope you enjoyed this book.

Since 1944, Mercier Press has published books that have been critically important to Irish life and culture. Books that dealt with subjects that informed readers about Irish scholars, Irish writers, Irish history and Ireland's rich heritage.

We believe in the importance of providing accessible histories and cultural books for all readers and all who are interested in Irish cultural life.

Our website is the best place to find out more information about Mercier, our books, authors, news and the best deals on a wide variety of books. Mercier tracks the best prices for our books online and we seek to offer the best value to our customers.

Sign up on our website to receive updates and special offers.

www.mercierpress.ie
www.facebook.com/mercier.press
www.twitter.com/irishpublisher

Mercier Press, Unit 3b, Oak House, Bessboro Rd, Blackrock, Cork, Ireland